JOURNEY TO THE Ph.D.

JOURNEY TO THE Ph.D.

How to Navigate the Process as African Americans

Edited by *Anna L. Green &*
LeKita V. Scott

FOREWORD BY
Brenda Jarmon

Sty/us

STERLING, VIRGINIA

Published in 2003 by

Stylus Publishing, LLC
22883 Quicksilver Drive
Sterling, Virginia 20166

Library of Congress
Cataloging-in-Publication Data
    Journey to the Ph.D. : how to navigate the
        process as African Americans / edited by
        Anna L. Green and LeKita V. Scott;
        foreword by Brenda Jarmon.--1st ed/
            p. cm.
    Includes bibliographical references
        and index.
    ISBN 1-57922-078-9 (alk. paper) —
    ISBN 1-57922-079-7 (pbk. : alk. paper)
    1. African Americans—Education (Graduate)
    2. African American graduate students—
    Social conditions. 3. Doctor of philosophy
    degree—United States.
    I. Green, Anna L. (Anna Lucille), 1970–
    II. Scott, LeKita V. (LeKita Vaney), 1971–

LC2781.J69 2003
378.2'4—dc12
                                2003009343

First edition, 2003
ISBN: hardcover 1-57922-078-9
ISBN: paperback 1-57922-079-7

Printed in the United States of America

All first editions printed on acid free paper

It is my saddest and happiest heartfelt wish to dedicate this book to my mother, Jacquelyn C. Green who is deceased. She was my first teacher and never stopped expressing the importance of education. This is instilled in my being and I am a better educator, scholar, and person because of her. Thank you momma. I love and miss you.

—Anna

I would like to dedicate this, my first edited work, to my parents— Don L. and Barbara D. Scott. I am who I am because of your patience, guidance, and unwavering support. Know that I love you both with all that I am.

—LeKita

CONTENTS

PART III: SURVIVING THE ACADEMY

FOREWORD
Lift Every Voice:
African American Students
Surviving in Higher Education

As painful as it is to confront the fact
that we are still not free, it is doubly
painful to acknowledge what began
it all. And yet, we can never understand America, nor can we ever
understand Black America until we
confront slavery . . . Least we forget
whence we have come.
—*Cole, 1993*

Thus, I begin this foreword with from whence we have come. As I read
the captivating "voices" of these young scholars who have "survived"
their treks through higher education *in spite of*, I am compelled to pay
homage to our African ancestors so "least we forget whence we have
come." I also offer Dr. Johnnetta Cole's passage because it highlights
that we stand on the backs of those who paved the way just so we could
have the opportunity to pursue higher education, and it highlights the
importance of mentoring, which is a major theme throughout this very
timely publication.

Mentoring is a task that can be dated back to Africa and our early
ancestral days. Imagine being taken from your country, your family, and
everything that you are familiar with and forced to adopt another culture
and in particular, a culture that does not have your best interest at heart.
Essentially, this is what happens when an African American student or
any other minority student enters a Predominately White Institution
(PWI). As I think back to the millions of Africans who died in the Middle
Passage and those who threw themselves into the ocean and took

a stance to die rather than be subjected to an "unknown" lifestyle, my heart pounds. But it pounds even more when I think of those who made it over the Middle Passage—those who mentored, cared for, and supported each other in a way that allowed them to be able to survive many years of inhuman, barbaric, and subhuman treatment. Those who survived the "torture" are those whose blood, sweat, tears, and shoulders we stand on today. For had it not been for those Africans, then we would not be enjoying the fruits of their labor in the academy or otherwise.

When we examine the days of slavery, we find many of our ancestors who mentored others along the way—for example, Harriet Ross Tubman, W. E. B. Du Bois, Sojourner Truth, Frederick Douglas, Ida B. Wells Barnett, Marcus Garvey, Mary McLeod Bethune, Garrett Morgan, Charles Drew, Bishop Richard Allen, and Madame C. J. Walker. Yes, it was typical for people of African descent to mentor one another, and now it is our time to honor the past by never giving up and by continuing this historical legacy. Even in the hallowed halls of the academy we must continue to mentor each other. However, it is equally as important, if not *more* important, for the academy to have in place a mentoring system, particularly for students of color, because all students new or matriculated need encouragement and support. However, African American students in particular tend to be more isolated, more burdened with the service activities, and subject to recurrent discrimination and resentment as the voices in these chapters tell us. Therefore, it is imperative that we support each other and that we help faculty and staff at PWIs and Historically Black Colleges Universities (HBCU) understand how important it is that our research interest be respected; that appropriate mentors and advisors are provided; that the isolation and exclusiveness that African American doctoral students and African American students in general feel at a PWI be addressed with *action rather than ignored;* and that social networks at PWIs be provided to deal with the social isolation often felt by African American students as addressed by the authors and the voices herein. Until these issues are addressed, our voices must seek and demand equal treatment, justice, and respect within the hallowed halls of the PWI. The Academy is decorated with brothers and sisters who have done just that or are currently doing just that. For example and to name a few—sister scholars such as Johnnetta Cole, Barbara White, Barbara Haile, Mary McLeod

Bethune (deceased), Penny Ralston, Joyce Dickerson, Lorraine Black-man, Camille Cosby, Michele Chappell, and brother scholars such as Asa Hilliard, Na'im Akbar, W. E. B. Du Bois (deceased), John Chambers, Israel Tribble, John Hendrik Clark (deceased), Bernard Watson, Irving McPhail, Lee Jones, John Hope Franklin, and Billy Close—all have mentored their students at PWIs and HBCUs.

We have a legacy to uphold—in spite of the institutionalized racism, sexism, and sometimes inhuman treatment that makes us "want to holler," and we do! Through it all, we have managed to stand steadfast as scholars, mentors, and "sisters" and "brothers" who have made significant impacts in the field of higher education. But, we must not rest on our laurels as there is *still* much to be done, and it becomes more apparent after reading these survival stories.

As African Americans in the academy, and particularly at PWIs, we must be careful that we don't find ourselves called upon to be the "spokesperson" for every Black issue. Interestingly, even in this new millennium, some folks have not figured out that sisters or brothers in the academy, for that matter, are not the spokespersons for every Black issue or for every Black person in America. We, too, come from various within-group cultural and ethnic backgrounds. Regardless of and in spite of these issues, the academy should be held responsible for instituting a very good mentoring system for new students; if one is not in place, one must be created. Otherwise, our students will continue to find themselves so overloaded, overburdened, and isolated that they may decide to drop out.

As a "sister" who survived a PWI (Florida State University), when I first began my doctoral work at FSU, I was not formally mentored. As a matter of fact, we had no formal mentoring system in place. Often, African American graduate students, especially those who are just beginning their careers, find it very hard to navigate the system, unless a senior faculty person becomes a very good mentor to them. In my case, I went three years without a senior faculty person taking me under their wing. I certainly made myself known and developed good relationships within the department and in particular with the departmental secretary. I introduced myself to the services staff, organized my time effectively, used productive active hours for research and writing, and I attended all the social functions in my department. Still, as the voices herein describe, I, too, felt the isolation.

As I observed other students studying together, and cheering each other on, I wondered how I would ever become a part of their world as many of the voices herein describe. As you read these survival stories, you will find that they, too, had to stop feeling sorry for themselves and get busy producing. I, and these voices, developed a significant motto in our lives and that is to *never give up*. Allow these voices to share with you from whence they have come so that you can be very clear of the authors' mission, and my mission, which is to utilize this publication to offer a source of support and mentorship, particularly to African American students at PWIs who face stereotypes, discrimination, prejudice perceptions, and who are struggling to find the "best fit," often in hostile territory.

It has been demonstrated that effective mentoring is essential to career development. No doubt mentoring during my college years assisted me in achieving my goals. These voices herein speak of allowing your determination, your drive, and your will to succeed overpower any obstacle in your way! Further I, and they, believe that adopting an "I can" attitude is one way to propel you to the next level in the academy or in life in general. However, let's be clear that adopting an "I can" attitude is *not* the only thing you need to do to be successful during your journey through the academy or life.

As these voices have persevered, persisted, and coped with some extraordinary situations in life, we must remember, it is not so much a question as to "how" they survived, because I believe that the Lord is able and that the Lord has not brought any of us this far to leave us. Our ancestors often sought the Lord through song, prayers, and spirituality to survive. It is not any different for most African Americans today. We are taught to lean on the Lord. We know that what God has for us is for us. Further, in my opinion, and I believe the opinion of the voices herein, it is more a question of *will the PWI's academic environment be supportive of and adjust its motivational, environmental, and institutional factors to embrace the African and African American experience in this country and begin to judge African American students in doctoral programs at PWIs on the content of their character and not their race?*

The stories and voices of this publication speak to the fact that effective mentoring was essential to their journey in the academy. These mentoring relationships have served as an invaluable channel of information and other intangibles for their success, for we know that unfortunately,

African Americans often lack access to important mentor relationships in the PWI academy—a phenomenon that can handicap them throughout their professional lives. Without mentors, women as well as men can miss opportunities that would help bring them into leadership positions.

Most African Americans know that mentoring has been a cornerstone to our survival. Therefore, it is not unusual for us to mentor each other. How then do we get the PWI academy to provide realistic, holistic, and prolific mentors? How can we help the PWI academy admit that the "isms" do exist and that minority women, and specifically Black women, are often at the brunt of oppression and discrimination in the academy's hallowed halls? Brothers and sisters, we have a difficult task, because until the academy is willing to *admit* to its own flaws, we may be begging this question twenty years from now. But, because my ancestors did not give up in their quest for freedom, we must not give up in our quest for equal and just treatment as academicians. After all, an American institution of higher education should not be so much a set of buildings and grounds, or a hierarchy of administrators, or even a body of students as it is a community of individual scholars engaged in instruction, investigation, and interpretation in areas of their own expertise. In my opinion, and I believe in the opinion of the authors and the voices herein, it is the perpetual task of such a community to recruit and nurture a steady flow of new members and in doing so, assure that the new members are given every opportunity to survive *in spite of.*

As "gatekeepers" in and to the academy, it behooves each of us to take charge of the situation; to be sure *not* to sit back and wait for a mentor to come to us—the voices herein didn't wait. Often we know in our heart of hearts that "something just isn't right." Therefore, we must *stand up* and *be heard!* We are researchers, scholars, teachers, mentors, and human beings who deserve the utmost respect. It's important to stand up for what we know is right or we may fall for anything.

By no means am I trying to trivialize discrimination, oppression, unjustness, sexism, or racism. However, I am asking that we keep a positive attitude in the face of such setbacks. Our foremothers and forefathers withstood the throngs of racism, sexism, and oppression. In the words of the old Negro hymn, I say, we *should be no ways tired!* As an African American sister in America, I refuse to let the bowels of years of mistreatment and discrimination make me a victim in or out of the academy. I'm going to continue to make a difference for those who are sure to come after us—just as these voices herein have done! In the academy, we can build a bridge for each other as mentors. We can motivate, inspire, empower, and encourage each other to build bridges that connect in sturdy ways the lives of those of us who have been blessed with skills, with education, and most of all with compassion for those among us stricken with poverty and despair.

In closing, I offer to African American graduate students wherever they may be on this planet, the following survival strategies—many of which are echoed by the voices in this book. The strategies are:

- Choose a good, interested mentor and begin to build a strong working relationship with him or her. Reach out to your mentors; we all were new at one time and would have loved some guidance and a sounding board.

- You may want to choose several different mentors for guidance in research activities or grant writing, for teaching advice, and for advice on juggling your personal life and career. Try to find a mentor within your department.

- Interact with your colleagues; get familiar with their work and inform them of yours. If they appear disinterested, don't give up—there is someone out there who will be willing to help you—press on!

- Don't rely on the department to give you important information (e.g., writing examinations, examination policy, and tenure procedure); find out for yourself from outside sources and clarify, if you can, with the department head.

- You will be a more balanced person, and a better scholar, if you remember the importance of your family and a life outside academe!

- Don't forget to take the time to enjoy yourself. Maintain perspective on your life as a university teacher and researcher. Take regular breaks from your work, share time with family or friends, engage in some form of physical exercise, go for a walk, listen to music, and so forth.

- Above all else maintain your sense of humor!

- Keep your words sweet; you never know when you'll have to eat them!

- Put God first! Develop your spiritual self. Trust in Him and acknowledge Him in all that you do. The Spirit will never let you down—trust in that "gut" instinct that the Spirit gives all of us!

- Remember: Prayer changes things!

Through it all, rest if you must, but don't quit. Avoid taking on more than you can handle; avoid trying to change the world or your department in one day; avoid getting too depressed if things do not work out. Pray about it, then seek out your mentor and talk with him or her; avoid criticizing publicly or privately. Practice diplomacy when conflicts arise, and try not to get overwhelmed. Keep smiling; other students as well as these voices have managed to navigate the hallowed halls of academe, and so can you.

I know that it's difficult. I've been there; I'm still there; and, I'm surviving! Let me assure you that my strong faith in God, my dogged determination, and my commitment to "not ever give up" have given me the fortitude to survive the hallowed halls of academe. Simply remove the word "I can't" from your vocabulary and replace it with a more positive statement, "I'm not able to at this time." This statement alone will propel you to the next level. By staying positive with "I'm not able to at this time," you allow yourself the opportunity to come back at a later time to complete your task. At the very minimum, don't we have an obligation to mentor our own selves in this way? After all, *attitude determines altitude and how far you will go in life.* Keep a positive attitude! I often remind myself of a statement that someone else coined—that is, life is like an elevator. When you get up in the morning, you can *choose* to press the *up* button or the *down* button. It makes more sense to me to press the up button. Don't you think so?

Quitting early is quitting too soon! When the seeds of doubt come, jump-start yourself from the historical legacy of our foremothers and forefathers. Keep the faith and know that God loves you and so do I!

BRENDA JARMON, Ph.D.

Reference

Cole, Johnnetta B. (1993). *Conversations: Straight talk with America's sister president.* New York: Bantam Doubleday Dell Publishing Group.

Hope. Confusion. Fear. Joy. Uncertainty. Excitement. These are all terms that describe, for many, the process of deciding whether to obtain a Ph.D. Is this degree absolutely necessary in my field of study? How will I find the time to complete this degree, continue to work full-time, and support my family? Where do I begin?

As I reorganized and filed paperwork in preparation for the fall semester, I found a statement that I had written in the spring semester of 1991 as I sought membership in a campus organization. I had written that upon graduation from my undergraduate institution, I would pursue graduate work in either Texas or Florida. In December 1993, I received my master's degree from Texas A&M University; in December 2000, I received my doctorate from Florida State University.

While I always knew that this was something that I had to accomplish because I was in the field of education, there were certainly times when I felt hope, excitement, confusion, fear, joy, uncertainty, and peace. Having experienced all of these things personally, the notion of sharing this information with those who are considering walking the same path was a must for me. Hence, the need for *Journey to the Ph.D.: How to Navigate the Process as African Americans*.

There are disturbing trends in the continuing underrepresentation of African Americans in higher education. According to a report published by Higher Education and National Affairs American Council on Education (Black Issues, 2002), 27,622 doctoral degrees were granted in 1999. Of this number, 1,596 (5.9 percent) were awarded to African Americans. These statistics are extremely disturbing when twenty years prior, 1,058 (4.4 percent) of all doctoral degrees granted were awarded to African Americans. This is a difference of only 536 people over a twenty-year period.

While many studies maintain that record numbers of Blacks are receiving Ph.D.'s, this number remains disproportionate to the number of African Americans graduating from high school and attending college. Malveaux (1996) makes a strong argument for the need to challenge anti-educational theories regarding race, IQ, affirmative action, and the notion of "receiving too much education." This confrontation must occur so that we are better represented within the academy. Research and publications must be written for us and by us. We must regularly come into contact with more African American deans, tenured faculty, department chairs, and doctoral students in the academy.

Access and entry of African American women and men to higher education is an important factor, but even more critical is the quality of the educational and professional experiences that these women and men encounter during their matriculation at Predominately White Institutions (PWIs) and Historically Black Colleges and Universities (HBCUs). What is striking about African American doctoral students are the common experiences that resonate among men and women scholars across different geographical and cultural divides. These experiences directly influence the success and retention of African American women and men seeking degrees in higher education. Hence, the need for *Journey to the Ph.D.: How to Navigate the Process as African Americans.*

The chapters of this book are divided into three parts: Entrance into the Academy; Adapting to the Academy; and Surviving the Academy. In Entrance into the Academy, Kamau Siwatu begins with an excellent discussion and in-depth time line for understanding and applying to graduate school. Tim Wilson, Nelson Soto, and Jami Joyner ask and answer the question: Why pursue a doctoral degree? They discuss issues such as attending school full- versus part-time, meeting family obligations, and relocation. Additionally, they outline the application process and tasks to be completed within each month leading up to the application deadline. KaaVonia Hinton-Johnson discusses the motivational, environmental and institutional obstacles of entering and remaining in higher education as an African American student. And finally, Randal Pinkett shares the various decisions that he had to make while deciding which academic program to pursue.

The second part, Adapting to the Academy, begins with a reflective work from Stephen Hancock. He writes from a personal battle with managing family and graduate school responsibilities. He talks about understanding himself as an African American male while attending a PWI. Catherine Cushinberry adapts to her classroom environment as both a student and student teacher. The attribute of being an African American female is used greatly throughout her teaching and learning experiences. Along similar lines, Felicia Moore writes about her trials and tribulations as an undergraduate science major at a PWI. Anthony Graham chronicles the factors that have worked for and against him in his pursuit of his educational dream. And Terrolyn Carter tries to understand her place at a PWI after being an undergraduate student at an HBCU. To conclude this part, Jonda McNair highlights her research interests in children's literature and her experiences as a graduate student at a PWI.

The final part of this publication, Surviving the Academy, focuses on those things that are imperative in successfully completing the process. First, Courtney Johnson explains her survival mode while pursuing a Ph.D. in science at a PWI. She utilizes her survival mechanisms in the classroom, academic department, and in personal situations with peers and faculty. Lisa Watts then makes a strong connection with the Sankofa Bird of Ghana by using its appearance as an analogy for her experiences in a doctoral program at a PWI. After this, April Peters takes a look back in trying to go forward as an African American female attending a PWI. She measures the history of African Americans in general and African American women in particular. Tamara Duckworth-Warner does an excellent job of spelling out what a mentor within the academy should and should not do for an African American graduate student. She points out specific things that might aid students in the process of selecting a mentor and maintaining a professional relationship with him or her. Along the same lines, Tarcha Rentz speaks of her experiences as an African American female at a PWI and the role that mentoring plays in her academic and professional life. In the next chapter, James Minor likens the relationship that a student has with a mentor to a marriage because a commitment toward a common goal—graduation—should exist between the two individuals. The next set of authors, Carolyn Hopp, Vincent Mumford, and Franklyn Williams, do an outstanding job of explaining what it means to be a mentor and have a mentor. They discuss their progression through academic programs at PWIs and the purpose of reaching back to guide other individuals along the academic journey. These individuals also discuss their reasons for choosing to be mentors and the satisfaction that they derive from serving in such a capacity. Each person provides examples of the things that have contributed to their individual and collective success. As a conclusion to the entire book, Dr. Anna L. Green highlights her experiences as a graduate student and offers additional tips for success for African American students pursuing a Ph.D.

Hope. Confusion. Fear. Joy. Uncertainty. Excitement. Whether you have begun your doctoral program or not, these are all feelings that you may experience while reading this book. However, in the end it is our sincerest hope that you will take with you the idea that, as we share our challenges with you, we also share our successes. Hence, the need for *Journey to the Ph.D.: How to Navigate the Process as African Americans.*

References

Black Issues in Higher Education. Jan. 3, 2002, v. 18, 23, 32(2).

Malveaux, Julianne (1996). Wanted: More black graduate students. *Black Issues in Higher Education.* July 11, 1996, v. 13, p. 44.

ACKNOWLEDGMENTS

Anna L. Green, Ph.D.   I would like to acknowledge my God who sees and knows all that I do, as I try to do it to please Him. I acknowledge the unconditional love and support that my family gives me continuously. My siblings are my rock and I turn to them for strength and courage and they are always there for me. I thank them and love them tremendously.

LeKita V. Scott, Ph.D.   I would also like to acknowledge the Creator for making me, my family for continuously sustaining me, and the village for raising me. I am extremely proud and eternally grateful to be standing on the shoulders of my ancestors. Thank you!

We are both eternally grateful to Stephen Hancock and Jonda McNair, both contributors to this book, because the idea to write about the "journey to the Ph.D." was their brainchild. Our sincerest thanks go to you both because you planted the seed. Additionally, we acknowledge Stylus Publishing for giving us the opportunity to express our voices and the voices of many graduate students at a time when the educational arena is in need of diversity and enhancement. We are also very appreciative of our professors and colleagues, who have unselfishly assisted in our transitions from graduate students to academic instructors. We will certainly continue in the effort of assisting others who follow and make it our mission to become leaders in academia.

PART I
ENTRANCE INTO THE ACADEMY

Kamau Oginga Siwatu

Hometown: Orange County, California
Current Institution: University of Nebraska–Lincoln
Department: Educational Psychology
Personal Philosophy: I am because we are, and because we are, therefore I am.

I

THE PATHS AND OPPORTUNITIES TO GAINING ADMISSION TO THE GRADUATE SCHOOL OF YOUR CHOICE

Education is our passport to the future,
for tomorrow belongs to the people
who prepare for it today.
—*Malcolm X*

We must be ever mindful that engaging in a discussion with Afrikan/Afrikan American[1] women and men regarding their experiences as doctoral students while in pursuit of their respective degrees is a testament to the diligence of our ancestors whose survival and resistance makes it possible for us to be here (academe) today. While a discussion of this magnitude has historical significance, increasing the pool of Afrikan/Afrikan American Ph.D.'s, showing prospective graduate students the paths, and highlighting the possibilities of gaining admission into the "house of education" is of equal importance. I am humbled by the opportunity to assist in the preparation of future scholars, thinkers, and intellectuals who will inherit the title Brothers and Sisters of the Academy.

The main thrust of this chapter is to introduce to some and remind others of the steps required for admission into a graduate program. The chapter begins by addressing the questions "why graduate school" and "why the pursuit of a graduate education is necessary." In order to assist students in gaining admission to a program that will be both academically and professionally enriching, the chapter highlights key factors that should be considered when choosing which schools and programs to apply to. The remainder of the chapter provides tips to prospective students on how to obtain successful letters of recommendation, how to write a thorough statement of purpose, and how to finance graduate school.

Summer Before Graduation

Is Graduate School Right for You?

There are many answers to the question "Why should I pursue a graduate education?" Some of the key reasons people make this choice are for career and salary advancement, career change, professional licensing, and to pursue careers in teaching and research. Within the last ten to fifteen years there has been a gradual shift regarding the requirement needed to obtain an "entry-level" employment position. The once hailed bachelor's degree has lost its door-opening capability and is now replaced by the advanced degree and the marketability that accompanies it. When determining if graduate school is right for them, people often consult statistical abstracts to learn more about how much their degree will be worth. Several research studies have found that on average, a graduate education will be worth 35 to 50 percent more than just having a bachelor's degree. According to the United States Census Bureau, a person with a master's degree earns up to 24 percent more than those with bachelor's degrees, whereas those with Ph.D.'s earn 35 percent more than individuals with master's degrees (cited in Peterson's (2001) *Graduate schools in the U.S.: A compact easy to use guide to graduate and professional programs in the United States*).

After residing in the workplace for a number of years, professional interests and career aspirations have the tendency to change. Professionals who outgrow their current occupation find that obtaining a graduate degree is the best way to receive training for the new field. Professionals in the helping fields such as psychologists and social workers often need to meet licensing requirements in order to be employed and therefore must also work toward a graduate degree. It is a good idea to know your goals and career aspirations when contemplating whether graduate school is right for you. Due to the intense nature of graduate study, an assessment of your goals and aspirations beforehand will assist you in succeeding in graduate school.

August

Choose the Graduate School (Program) That Is Right for You

With approximately 1,300 institutions that offer graduate degree programs, it is never too early to begin the search for a graduate program that fits your academic and professional needs. With the increased availability of the Internet, finding comprehensive lists of institutions that offer degrees in your area of interest is now easier than ever. Table 1.1 lists the names of a few websites that offer program searches. These search engines often return the names of a large number of institutions. Faced with a large number of programs to choose from, the question arises, "How do I choose the graduate school (program) that's right for me?" Unlike the initial process of finding where your program is being offered, the process of strategically selecting the program is a long and tedious task. However, it is important that you make the decision wisely. To assist you in this endeavor it may be helpful to consider these factors: (1) the reputation of the faculty, (2) the quality and reputation of the program, (3) the university environment, and (4) the cost of living and the availability of financial assistance.

The Academic and Professional Background of the Faculty

Knowledge of the professors' research interests and current projects is a good way to assess the academic fit of the department compared to your interests. Article and journal databases provided by university libraries can be resources for obtaining faculty research interests. After conducting an author search, depending on the type of database you use, the results will show you what that person has published and/or presented at professional conferences.

The Quality and Reputation of the Program

The quality and reputation of the program (department) is measured by several factors. These factors include the percentage of faculty research and publications; the total number of faculty disaggregated by full, assistant, and associate professors; and the number of doctoral degrees

Table 1.1   Websites That Offer Graduate Program Search Engines

Name	Site	Description
GradSchool.Com	http://www.gradschool.com	Contains the listings of over 53,600 programs Search by school or subject
Grad School Matchmaker	http://www.embark.com/ grad/grad_research	Based on your preferences on a scale of . . . you can search for programs by type of program, location, cost and aid, selectivity (i.e., acceptance rate), and study of body characteristics (i.e., percent of minority enrollment)
GradView.Com	http://gradview.com/search	Search by concentration, location, degree type, and student body size
Petersons: The Grad Channel	http://iiswin/ prd01.etersons.com/ gradchanel/search	Use the search wizard to locate multiple programs with one search

awarded within the department. The U.S. News and World Report (2002) conducts rankings of the popularity of graduate schools. The results of their findings are published in the magazine's annual edition of *Best Graduate Schools.* Many graduate students often depend on the

Table 1.2   Websites That Offer Graduate School Rankings

Name	Site	Description
Business Week Online	http://businessweek.com/bschools/	Contains the profiles to over 225 MBA programs Rankings are based on the results of surveys administered to recruiters and students
National Association of Graduate and Professional Students	http://survey.nagps.org	Provides the rankings of education, engineering, humanities, life science, physical science, social science, and professional programs
Ph.Ds.Org	www.phds.org/rankings	Provided by National Research Council, the rating for programs offering degrees in arts and humanities, biological sciences, engineering, physical sciences, mathematics, and social and behavioral sciences
The Social Psychology Network	http://socialpsychology.org/rankings	Provides the rankings to doctoral programs in psychology, by concentration and location

results to identify highly reputable and quality programs (see Table 1.2). Recognition can be attributed to the amount of criticism that has accompanied these rankings (The Washington Monthly Online, 2002). Words of caution: Many of the results are based on departmental rankings rather than the programs that are nested inside the department.

Some programs and departments have student advisory councils (SAC). Current students often make their names and contact information available through SACs, so that the council can refer prospective students with questions about the department to students in the program. Some questions you may want to ask the students include the following:

- What are your thoughts and feelings about this institution, department, and program?

- How do you like your professors?

- Are there sufficient funding, research, and teaching opportunities for the graduate students in the program?

- What is your advisor like?

- What do you think of your fellow classmates?

The University Environment

As a prospective graduate student, the university environment and all that it possesses should be considered in some detail since this is the place that you will be matriculating and living for the next two to seven years. If the opportunity for an on campus visit presents itself, schedule a visit to the library, student union, and other places of importance to you. The goal here is to pretend to be a student for a day or two to see if you would be comfortable during your tenure at the institution. If a university visit is not possible, current graduate students can also shed some light regarding the university environment.

For many students who graduate from undergraduate programs at Historically Black Colleges and Universities, the lack of minority representation can cause some concern when choosing which graduate school to attend. "Anxiety Over Demographics," published in *Black Issues in Higher Education* (Hurd, 2002), discusses the topic of diversity in America's colleges and universities. A discussion regarding the trends in higher education revealed that Afrikan American enrollment was high although the number of Afrikan American tenured faculty did not reflect this trend. For many students in search of support networks, this may be discouraging and a factor in a final decision.

September

Send Away for Applications That You Do Not Have

Once you have sized up the program using the suggested requirements, it is necessary to begin to narrow down and finalize your options. After you have chosen which school to apply to, if you have not done so already, request applications at this time. The rule of thumb is to apply to five or six schools in order to increase your chances of acceptance. The cost associated with applying to multiple schools can become quite expensive. Many schools provide fee waivers to students who are financially unable. Table 1.3 illustrates the costs associated with applying to five graduate schools.

October

Begin Writing the Statement of Purpose

In early October, begin composing a rough draft of your statement of purpose. Writing your statement of purpose requires an extended amount of time and a thorough reflection of your goals and aspirations. The statement of purpose allows you, the applicant, an opportunity to describe in detail the following:

- What area/field you want to specialize in
- Why you want to pursue a degree in this area
- The value and meaning of your experiences in your field and the impact these experiences play in your decision to pursue a degree in this area
- Your intended use of your degree
- How you will be an asset to the institution
- The professors' work in the department that is most relevant to your interests while highlighting your research interests

The admission committee typically uses the statement of purpose as a way to gain a better understanding of the applicant's intent and whether the prospective student's interests are congruent with the mission and research objectives of the program. A well-written statement

Table 1.3   The Cost Associated with Applying to Five Graduate
Programs in Education (for Illustration Purposes Only)

The cost associated with applying to five degree programs	
Application Fees	
Stanford University	$75
University of Nebraska–Lincoln	$35
Temple University	$40
University of Florida	$20
University of Illinois–Urbana–Champaign	$40
Subtotal	**$210**
Transcripts (the above schools require two copies of transcripts from each school that you attended)	
University of California Los Angeles (Master's Degree) $6.00 × 10 copies	$60
Florida State University (Bachelor's Degree) $5.00 × 10 copies	$50
Tallahassee Community College (Associates Degree) $5.00 × 10 copies	$50
Subtotal	**$160**
Standardized Admissions Tests	
Graduate Record Examination[1]	$105
Graduate Record Examination Subject Test	N/A
Additional Score Reports	N/A
Subtotal	**$105**
Miscellaneous Fees	
Mailing supplies	
Stamps (application packet and letters of recommendations)	
Phone calls to school	
Etc.	
Subtotal	**$30**
Grand Total	**$535**

[1]Domestic Registration Fee.

of purpose is tailored to each program that the applicant is applying to, and it provides a well-defined research objective.

Common mistakes made by prospective graduate students when writing their statement of purpose include the following:

- Listing nonprofessional interests
- Plaguing the statement with negative comments and experiences
- Using big words, unnecessary vocabulary, and academic jargon with the intent of trying to impress the committee members
- Providing a comprehensive list of achievements instead of relative accomplishments to the degree seeking program
- Failing to grab the attention of the committee and opening the introductory paragraph with sentences such as, "My name is" and "I was born in"

Before submission, the draft should undergo several revisions. It may be helpful to have a few of your professors and others read it. They may be able to give you valuable feedback on how you can improve your statement of purpose.

Request Letters of Recommendation

Virtually all graduate degree programs require applicants to furnish three or four letters of recommendation from their professors. The admission committee will place a strong emphasis on the letter of recommendation. For this reason it is imperative that you do everything in your power to receive a highly favorable and impressive recommendation from your current and former instructors. Follow the appropriate protocol for requesting a letter of recommendation when seeking strong recommendations from the referee. It may be in your best interest to set up an appointment with the referee well in advance of the application deadlines. On the day of the scheduled meeting, bring with you a portfolio consisting of: (1) a resume, (2) a copy of transcripts, (3) a draft of the statement of purpose, (4) classes taken from the referee and grades received in each, and (5) relevant research experience. During the meeting, be prepared to articulate your academic and professional goals. All of this information will assist the professor in writing an effective letter of recommendation on your behalf.

During your meeting, should he/she agree to write a letter of recommendation, it is good to have information notifying the referee when the letters need to be mailed, mailing addresses to where the letters should be sent, and the purpose for which the letter should be written (i.e., type of degree being sought, scholarship, fellowships). Out of courtesy, you should also supply the referee with stamped mailing envelopes.

Look into How You Can Finance Graduate School

Most graduate students need some type of assistance in meeting the high costs of financing a graduate education. There are two forms of financial assistance available to graduate students. These two forms of assistance are commonly referred to as funds and financial aid. Funds are a source of financial assistance that is based on merit. These funds mainly come in the form of fellowships and assistantships. Along with a monthly stipend, fellowships cover the cost of living expenses and tuition. Many doctoral programs offer graduate fellowships to Afrikan American and other underrepresented students in various Ph.D. programs. In addition to university funded fellowships, there are also a wide range of national fellowships, including the Fulbright, Mellon, National Science Foundation, and National Research Foundation.

Other types of funding opportunities include teaching and/or research assistantships. These assistantships also come with a stipend (ranging from $8,000 to $15,000 per year) and tuition waiver. Teaching assistantships are part-time jobs that involve teaching undergraduate classes in one's major (i.e., Psychology 101, Introduction to Geography, World History). These undergraduate classes range in size from 30 to 200 students.

Research assistantships are also part-time jobs (ten to twenty hours per week) given to students who assist a professor with their current research projects. Some professors have their students go to the library to retrieve journal articles and books, conduct literature reviews, collect data, and/or analyze data for their research interests. Professors in search of research assistants often require that the student have some type of research experience.

At this juncture in your education, you have probably become quite acclimated with the financial aid process, which is the second type of financial assistance available to graduate students. As a graduate student, you are entitled to borrow up to $18,500 each academic year.

However, only $8,500 of this yearly total can be in the form of subsidized student loans. Each graduate student should be cognizant that the maximum amount that can be borrowed is $138,500 (United States Department of Education, 2002).

Take Entrance Examinations[2]

One of the requirements for admission into graduate school is taking and scoring relatively high on the mandatory admissions tests. The results from these standardized tests will play a major role in the decisions that are made regarding your acceptance into the program. Table 1.4 contains a brief description and overview of the popular entrance examinations along with the average scores for Afrikan American and White American test takers for each of the tests in 1995.[3]

As you may notice, several of the exams are no longer administered in the traditional pencil and paper format. With the increased availability of computers and higher technological abilities, the testing industry has gradually made a shift toward the use of Computer Adaptive Testing (CAT). As the name implies, the test adapts to each examinee's ability level. That is, each examinee's ability level is estimated constantly throughout the duration of the test. During the test, the difficulty of the items fluctuates depending on the ability level of the test taker. The ability level changes each time an item is answered correctly or incorrectly (Meijer & Nering, 1999; Straetmans & Eggen, 1998).

For those unfamiliar with how computer adaptive testing works, it can become a threatening experience the day of the test. Therefore it is recommended that you acclimate yourself with the rationale and process of adaptive testing. Like everything else, there are certainly pros and cons related to this type of testing. Consult your nearest test preparation agency or company, such as Kaplan and The Princeton Review, for more information regarding this topic. The Educational Testing Service has free downloadable demonstrations on their website, www.ets.org.

Begin a Rough Draft of the Application

It probably goes without saying, but all applications that you submit should be neatly typed or word processed. The process of typing out an application has become an easier task as more departments and schools

Table 1.4 Summary of Entrance Examinations

	Graduate record examination[1]	Law school admissions test[2]	Graduate management admissions test[3]	Medical college admissions test[4]
Skills and Knowledge Assessed	Verbal, quantitative, and analytical reasoning	Strategic thinking, critical reading, and analytical reasoning	Verbal, quantitative, and analytical reasoning	Verbal reasoning, competency in the physical and biological sciences
Registration Fees[5]	$105	$96	$200	$180
Length of Examination	2 hours and 15 minutes	2 hours and 55 minutes	3 hours and 30 minutes	5 hours and 45 minutes
Testing Format	Computer Adaptive Testing	Paper and Pencil	Computer Adaptive Testing	Paper and Pencil
Scoring Scale (points)	200–800 per section	120–800	200–800	1–15 per section
Average Score[6] Black	411—Math 393—Verbal	142.6	411	Physical Science—5.79 Verbal—5.72 Biology—5.74
White	535—Math 498—Verbal	153.7	523	Physical Science—8.22 Verbal—8.23 Biology

1. Source: www.gre.org.
2. Source: www.lsat.org.
3. Source: www.gmat.org.
4. Source: www.aamc.org;
5. Registration fees reflect the cost associated with taking the test in United States.
6. Source: *African American Education Data Book. Volume 1: Higher and Adult Education* (Nettles & Perna, 1997).

allow electronically submitted applications. The hidden danger about submitting your application electronically is that, unlike Microsoft Word, you don't have the spell checking capabilities. Therefore proofreading before submission is a must (Cohen, 2002).

November

Complete a Final Draft of the Application

Unlike your monthly rent and bills, you should not wait until the due day to mail in your application. The application and supporting documents (i.e., GRE scores, letters of recommendation, transcripts) should be *on file* by the application deadline. As the deadline approaches do not hesitate to call the department secretary to confirm that your file is complete and ready for review. If there ever was a time that you did not procrastinate, this is the time! If you choose to procrastinate, consciously or unconsciously, it will cost you.

Request Transcripts

The graduate admissions office at the school you are applying to will require that copies of your official transcripts be on file before the application is reviewed. With a record of all your undergraduate and graduate information (if applicable), the admissions committee will use your transcripts to examine how well you performed in your major area with a high emphasis on the upper division classes that you took during your junior and senior years of college.

Retake Entrance Examinations (Optional)

Included in Table 1.4, is a comparison of the performance of White American and Afrikan American test takers on the respective tests. The Black and White test score gap is a phenomenon of Afrikan Americans scoring lower than White Americans on most forms of standardized achievement and intelligence tests (Jencks & Phillips, 1998). This trend is also found on all forms of graduate admissions tests. Students unfamiliar with this trend have the tendency to worry about the relation of their scores compared to the program's entry requirements. Many students choose to retake the exam for a second and perhaps a third time in an attempt to receive a higher score.

Each program's view on taking the entrance exam multiple times varies. Before retaking the exam, it is advisable that you contact the department and ask them about their procedures and thoughts about taking the exam multiple times. It is good to keep in mind that your complete scoring history is made available when you have your results forwarded to each university. In other words, the committee will see the number of times that you took the test along with the results. Some programs take the average of the two (or more) scores, whereas others choose to refer to the latest test scores.

January/February

File for Financial Aid

Beware of approaching financial aid deadlines for the various institutions that you are applying to. Financial aid deadlines may be due before the applications for admission are due. If this is the case, file for financial aid even though you have not been officially admitted. Failure to monitor the financial aid deadlines can result in missed opportunities to become eligible for university fellowships and other sources of financial assistance.

Interviews and Campus Visits

As programs begin the process of narrowing down the candidates, they may request a formal interview. Interviews give you the opportunity to discuss goals, objectives, and interests in detail. You can do several things to stand out from the rest of the applicants. Toward the end of the interview, the faculty member(s) may give you an opportunity to ask questions. Seize this opportunity to give the committee the impression that you, too, are concerned about the academic fit of the department as it relates to your interests. Although you may know the answers, the following provides an example of some questions that you may want to ask the committee during the interview:

- What do you think are the program's strengths and weaknesses?
- How many students are in the program? What are the racial demographics?

- What type of financial assistance is available through the school and department?

- How long does it normally take students to complete the program?

- What are you looking for in the graduates that you accept into the program?

- What should I expect from this program?

On the day of the interview, bring with you several copies of your portfolio that you prepared in the fall. If traveling from out of town, arrange to take a campus tour and talk with other graduate students and faculty members.

March

Getting Accepted and Dealing with Rejection

Once the applications are submitted, the waiting begins. The longer you wait the more you begin to reflect and ponder the possibilities. Perhaps it goes something like this:

> I followed all of the advice given in this chapter and by others, scored reasonably well on the admissions test (i.e., GRE, LSAT), wrote an excellent statement of purpose, and received outstanding letters of recommendation. My file was even complete three weeks prior to the deadline. Will I be one of the top choices for admission into the program?

To the satisfaction of many prospective graduate students, once the application and the supporting documents are reviewed, decisions and notification are made quickly. At the earliest, depending on the initial application deadline, decisions are usually made starting in late February and continue throughout March and early April. As soon as a decision is made, some committees notify the applicant (those who have been accepted) informally by way of a phone call or a message sent via e-mail. Regardless of whether you have been accepted or not, expect an official letter in the mail notifying you of the much anticipated acceptance or the dreaded rejection.

Dealing with Rejection

Graduate programs often receive fifteen to twenty times more applications for admission than they have available space and funding. This means that more than 80 percent of the applicants will be rejected. For this reason alone, in order to increase the chance of acceptance, many advisors recommend applying to multiple schools/programs (five or six). In the event of rejection, it is recommended that you kindly request feedback from the program in order to better the chances next time (assuming that there is a next time). Possible explanations for rejections include the following:

- The lack of research experience
- A poor academic record
- Failure to meet the admission requirements (i.e., adequate admissions test scores)
- A poor letter of recommendation (many professors admit to unintentionally writing poor recommendations as a result of knowing very little about their students)
- Poor fit between the applicant's interests and the department's objectives
- Failure to have a completed application and/or supporting documents on file at the time of review

Acceptance

If the applicant is accepted into multiple programs, there may be a need to reassess the pros and cons before making a final decision. There is no need to make a hasty decision; graduate programs usually do not require a formal letter indicating your intent until April 15. Before making a final decision, there are several factors to consider. Many of these factors have already been discussed earlier in this chapter. If you have already investigated these factors before choosing which graduate school to apply to, now that you have been accepted, the question of "how much?" becomes an issue. In layperson's terms, are they showing you the money? Moreover, are they willing to? Everyone realizes that graduate school is very expensive and therefore the amount of money or the lack thereof must be addressed. The funds that are offered vary greatly from one university and program to the next (Greene & Greene, 2001).

Conclusion

The purpose of this chapter is to inform prospective and current graduate students of the protocol of applying to master's and doctoral programs respectively. Getting into graduate school is indeed a complex task that requires lots of work and advanced planning. Taking advantage of the increased availability of information on the Internet should also make the task of choosing and selecting which graduate schools to apply to and locating funding opportunities easier. The following websites may help you get started.

A Guide to Getting into Grad School
http://www.csus.edu/indiv/t/tumminia/grad.htm

Graduate School Resource Page
http://aug3.augsburg.edu/mcnair/cswlgrad.html

College Comparison Worksheet
http://www.usnews.com/usnews/edu/college/coworks.htm

How to Receive a Less Than Enthusiastic Letter of Recommendation
http://psych.hanover.edu/handbook/peeves2.html

The Guide to Graduate and Professional School Fellowships
http://www.imdiversity.com/employerprofiles/grad_school/gs_fellowcontents.asp

Fellowships and Scholarships of Special Interest to African-American Students
http://www.imdiversity.com/villages/african/Article_Detail.asp?Article_ID=55

By following the guidelines in this chapter and the listed websites, your chances of gaining admission into graduate school will increase compared to a person seeking admission without any sense of direction. This chapter offers only a piece of the solution in attempting to increase the pipeline of Afrikan American doctoral degree recipients. As a current graduate student and future faculty member, I welcome you to the house of education.

Notes

1. The author has made a conscious decision to spell the words Afrikan and Afrikan American with the letter *k* rather than the traditional letter *c*. Since the letter *c* is nonexistent in indigenous Afrikan language systems, the author will spell it the way found in most Afrikan languages, rather than the colonial British way.
2. Preparation for these entrance exams should begin as soon as you know that you are interested in going to graduate school.
3. Source: *The African American Education Data Book, Volume 1: Higher and Adult Education* (Nettles & Perna, 1997).

References

Cohen, K. (2002). *The truth about getting in a top college: An advisor tells you everything you need to know.* New York: Hyperion.

Educational Testing Service (2002). *Computer Based Testing.* Available: [www.ets.org].

GMAT (2002). *Format and content: An overview.* Available: [www.gmat.org].

Graduate Schools in the U.S.: A compact easy to use guide to graduate and professional programs in the United States (2001). Lawrenceville, NJ: Peterson Thomson Learning.

GRE (2002). *Description of the general test.* Available: [www.gre.org].

Greene, H., & Greene, M. (2001). *Making it into a top graduate school.* New York: Cliff Street Books

Hurd, E. (Ed.). (2002). Anxiety over demographics a window into the future. . . . Both welcomed and feared [special issue]. *Black Issues in Higher Education, 18*(16).

Jencks, C., & Phillips, M. (1998). The Black-White test score gap: An introduction. In C. Jencks & M. Phillips (Eds.), *The Black-White test score gap.* Washington, DC: Brookings Institution Press.

LSAT (2002). *Frequently asked questions.* Available: [www.lsat.org].

MCAT *About the MCAT.* Available: [www.aamc.org].

Meijer, R., & Nering, M. (1999). Computer adaptive testing: Overview and introduction. *Applied Psychological Measurement, 23*(3), 187–194.

Nettles, M. T., & Perna, L. W. (1997). *The African American education data book: Volume 1: Higher and adult education.* Fairfax, VA: Frederick D. Patterson Institute of The College Fund/UNCF.

Straetmans, G., & Eggen, T. (1998). Computerized adaptive testing: What it is and how it works. *Educational Technology, 38,* 45–52.

The Washington Monthly Online (2002). *A review of the methodology for the U.S. News and World Report's Rankings of Undergraduate Colleges and Universities.* Available: [http://www.washingtonmonthly.com].

United States Department of Education (2002). *The student guide: Financial aid 2002.* Washington, DC: Author.

U.S. News and World Report (2002). *2003 Graduate School Rankings.* Available: [http://www.usnews.com/usnews/edu/grad/rankings/rankindex.htm].

Tim Wilson

Hometown: Fairfield, California
Current Institution: University of Missouri at Columbia
Department: Education Leadership and Policy Analysis
Personal Philosophy: Seek the truth in that which you oppose and the error in that which you espouse—the truth is somewhere in the middle.
—Robert J. Nash

Nelson Soto

Hometown: Lorain, Ohio
Current Institution: Indiana University
Department: Educational Leadership and Policy Studies
Personal Philosophy: Frederick Douglass taught that literacy is the path from slavery to freedom. There are many kinds of slavery and many kinds of freedom. But reading is still the path.
—Carl Sagan

Jami Joyner

Hometown: Edmond, Oklahoma
Current Institution: University of Missouri at Columbia
Department: Educational Leadership and Policy Analysis
Personal Philosophy: Faith without works is dead.
—James 2:26

2

DECIDING IF AND HOW TO PURSUE DOCTORAL WORK

Introduction

We have heard many people talk about their experiences as doctoral students. These individuals have spoken about the coursework, research and other assistantship experiences, publishing, and the inevitable job search. What we have not heard a lot of is conversation about how to get into a doctoral program. What should prospective students be thinking about? How should one finance graduate school? How do you write those god-awful personal statements?

Because every journey starts with a single step, we have decided to focus on the first one—deciding if and how to pursue doctoral work. The goal of this chapter is to help readers weigh the factors related to deciding whether to pursue a terminal degree, as well as to provide a more comprehensive understanding of the decision-making process as it relates to pursuing doctoral education.

Why Pursue a Doctoral Degree?

As current students, we can attest to the fact that pursuing a doctoral degree is hard work. Grasping the information you are exposed to is not the hard part (although statistic courses can be a challenge). The challenge lies in balancing coursework, assistantship, and other personal responsibilities. With that being said, why would anyone want to pursue a doctoral degree?

There are a few reasons as to why a doctoral degree is beneficial. First, many agencies are increasing in size and complexity. Institutions of higher education are an example of this. These institutions require increased expertise in administrations and governance. The need for greater expertise requires advanced training, which can be obtained by earning a doctoral degree in higher education or college student personnel.

The desire for career advancement is another reason why people pursue doctoral degrees. Using higher education again as an example, Townsend and Weise's 1991 study on national survey of 1,100 randomly selected, senior-level administrators revealed that 47 percent of the respondents hiring a chief student affairs officer preferred candidates with a doctorate in higher education, as opposed to a terminal degree in another academic field. A final reason for pursuing a terminal degree is the desire to conduct research and/or teach. The doctoral degree trains you to be a scholar and researcher in your chosen field (Jerrard & Jerrard, 1998).

Questions to Consider

Before you fill out your first application form, you will need to consider some fundamental questions about pursuing a doctoral degree. These questions are not meant to scare you off—they are designed to get you to consider how your pursuit of a terminal degree will impact other areas of your life.

Why Do I Need a Doctoral Degree?

This is a simple, yet fundamental question. We have already listed three reasons as to why a doctoral degree is beneficial, but you must decide why *you* want a doctoral degree. Is your career advancement dependent on more education? If so, is the doctorate the right degree for you to pursue, or would a master's or specialist's degree accomplish the same objective?

Are you considering a return to school because it is something you want to do, or are you going to school because it is the only thing you know how to do. People who have gone to school nonstop know what we mean; or is someone living vicariously through you? If you are considering a terminal degree because being a student is the only thing you know how to do or because someone else is living vicariously through you, then we strongly urge you to reevaluate your decision to return to school. In many ways, pursuing a terminal degree is a solitary endeavor, requiring a certain degree of selfishness. If your heart is not in it, then do not pursue the terminal degree.

Full-Time versus Part-Time

The authors are all full-time students and therefore, we can take advantage of internship and assistantship opportunities. We can take a full load of classes every semester allowing us to complete degree programs within four years. Our life circumstances have allowed us to be full-time students, so we have decided to take advantage of this.

Not everyone can afford to take a break from work in order to pursue a degree. Some people have student loan debt from their undergraduate and/or master's program to pay off, while others need to pay off the mortgage and/or credit cards. People already working at colleges or universities may want to take advantage of their institution's tuition reimbursement program, where the university pays a certain portion of a full-time employee's tuition. There are also some people who simply do not want to rush through their doctoral programs and prefer the idea of being a part-time student.

While part-time students take longer to finish their degree programs, they do not necessarily have to endure a pay cut, nor do they have to incur as much debt as full-time students. Taking less than a full load of courses may also be less taxing on part-time students (assuming your full-time job is not very hectic).

Whether you decide to pursue doctoral work full-time or part-time, it is important to weigh the pros and cons. The decision you make regarding this basic, yet important, issue will set the tone for many other factors to consider, such as the impact on family members and relocation.

Family Obligations

When Tim was eight years old, his father retired from the Army after nearly thirty years of service and decided to go back to school. When this decision was made, Tim and his older brother were both enrolled in Catholic elementary and high schools, while their oldest brother was attending a state university. Fortunately, Tim's mother was working full-time as a registered nurse and his father had his retirement income, so money was not as big an issue as it could have been.

While the money situation was taken care of, there were other considerations. How would Mr. Wilson's full-time student status impact his children who were still living at home? How would Mr. Wilson's student status impact Mrs. Wilson? Would Mr. Wilson be able to balance being a full-time student with being a husband and a father? These are the types of questions Mr. and Mrs. Wilson had to address. Your questions may not involve a significant other or children. You may have to consider the impact your schooling may have on extended family or parents that you may be responsible for. As was the case with deciding whether to be a full- or part-time student, it is important for you to weigh the pros and cons and conduct yourself accordingly.

Relocation

As a prospective student, you may not be willing or able to commute to the school of your choice. You must then decide whether you are willing to relocate. This decision might be a little easier if your intentions are to be a full-time student. But if you already have a good job, you may be more hesitant.

If you are willing to relocate, it is a good idea to develop a set of criteria that your new community must have in order for you to move there. We strongly caution you not to attend a school without considering the community in which it is located. You will have enough stress related to school and you will need to find positive outlets in order to maintain your sanity. If school is stressing you out *and* you do not like the community, you will have a very difficult time finishing your degree.

When Tim was going through the application process, he made it a point to fly out to each campus and explore its surrounding community. While this can be very expensive and time consuming, Tim found it to be worthwhile—mainly because he had lived in areas that were not always user-friendly for people of color. You must develop your own set of characteristics that a new community must have in order for you to live there—for example, churches, community centers, and barbershops and hair salons. Developing such a list is a worthwhile exercise because it will not only help you evaluate a surrounding community, but it can also help you evaluate the awareness level of various campus personnel.

Our Unsolicited Advice to You

It has been said that hindsight is 20/20. In the spirit of looking in the proverbial rearview mirror, we offer the following (unsolicited) advice.

- *Decide early on, what it will take for an institution to earn the honor of having you enroll as a student.* This is an important step because the criteria you develop will set the tone for your entire search process. Once you come up with a set of criteria, stick to it.

- *Determine how you want to pay for your education.* This idea is connected to the first idea in that one of your criteria for selecting a school may very well be the financial package they offer you. If you know you want to minimize loans as much as possible, then you will probably want to gravitate toward the school offering more grants, fellowships, and tuition waivers.

- *Decide on your dissertation topic early.* This may not always be possible, but it can be an advantage if you know the topic of dissertation research from the start. Knowing your area of research will enable you to better evaluate prospective faculty and also allow you to direct some of your course assignments (e.g., term papers) toward your dissertation. This will make life a lot easier when it is time to write your dissertation.

- *Have an idea of the types of experiences you would like to have as a doctoral student.* This is important because the experiences you have as a doctoral student can prepare you for success once you graduate. Thus, in order to develop ideas about the experiences you want to have, think about what you would ultimately like to do once you have earned your degree, and then think about the experiences you will need to have as a student in order to reach your ultimate objective.

- *Have a clear understanding of why you are pursuing a doctoral degree.* This is important because pursuing a doctoral degree is a serious endeavor. There will be times when the only thing that gets you through the process is knowing why you are in school in the first place and what the ultimate payoff for you will be. If you are not sure about why you want to pursue a doctoral degree, you might be better off waiting until you have a better understanding of why you want to go back to school.

- *Carefully weigh the pros and cons of all factors in your decision-making process.* We know this seems like common sense, but it is worth repeating, especially if your decisions will affect people other than yourself (e.g., significant others, extended family members, children).

- *Stick to your guns, but be willing to be flexible too.* When it comes time for you to make a final decision as to where you will pursue your terminal degree, you may have to make some compromises, such as taking on more debt than you want to or having to lose status because you will be a student as opposed to a full-time employee. As long as you know what you are and are not willing to do, this should not pose much of a problem for you.

- *Talk to currently enrolled students.* As a rule of thumb, currently enrolled students can provide a wealth of information for prospective students. Make sure you speak with currently enrolled students, as they will answer the questions that faculty may not be able (or willing) to answer. However, remember that neither students nor faculty have all of the answers—you will have to base your decision on input from both constituencies.

- *Start the process early.* We cannot stress this enough—if you are working full-time, this becomes even more important as writing drafts of your personal statements, filling out applications, and visiting campuses is a time-consuming venture. The sooner you start, the less stress you will feel as you move through the process.

Conclusion

Doctoral study can be a wonderful experience in regard to personal and professional development. In order to get to this point, you will need to do the preliminary work necessary to lay a foundation for the good experiences that are available to you. Part of the preliminary work lies in investigating prospective graduate programs and evaluating them based upon your needs. We hope this chapter helps you begin the process.

References

Jerrard, R., & Jerrard, M. (1998). *The grad school handbook: An insider's guide to getting in and succeeding.* New York: Perigee Books.

Townsend, B., & Weise, M. D. (1991). The higher education doctorate as a passport to higher education administration. *New Directions for Higher Education, 76,* 5–13. San Francisco: Josey Bass.

KaaVonia Hinton-Johnson, Ph.D.

Hometown: Murfreesboro, North Carolina
Current Institution: The Ohio State University
Department: Education
Personal Philosophy: Give the world the best you have, and the best will come back to you.
—Beatrice Lassiter

3

"DREAMS HANGING IN THE AIR LIKE SMOKE"

A PERSONAL REFLECTION OF FACTORS INFLUENCING ENROLLMENT AND PERSISTENCE IN HIGHER EDUCATION

Introduction

The number of students of color, particularly African Americans, in higher education has been consistently low (Allen, Epps, & Haniff, 1991; King & Chepyator-Thomson, 1996; St. John, 2000; Thomas, 1987; Wilson, 1992). Though African Americans experienced an increase in college enrollment during the 1970s and 1980s, African Americans had high attrition rates and low academic performance (Wilson, 1994). In 1983, 31,190 doctoral degrees were awarded; surprisingly, only 1,000 were awarded to African Americans (Matthews & Jackson, 1991; Slaughter, 1989). However, African American professional degree attainment seems to be increasing. During the 1990s, the number of professional degrees earned by African Americans increased significantly. For example, from 1992 to 1998, there was an 8.6 percent increase in African American earned master's degrees and doctoral degrees (St. John, 2000).

According to St. John (2000), a growing number of African American students who are attending doctoral school are enrolling in Historically Black Colleges and Universities (HBCUs) as well as Predominately White Institutions (PWIs). The purpose of this chapter is to explore and reflect on my experiences in doctoral school at a PWI. I chose to attend a PWI not because it is predominately white or because its college of education is ranked among the best in the country, but because it was the only one accessible to me. My husband is in the military, so my choices of universities to attend were limited. In fact, The Ohio State

University is the only school in the four states my husband was allowed to transfer to with a doctoral program in English education.

Historically, most African Americans earned professional and undergraduate degrees, primarily, at HBCUs. Wilson (1994) argues that this changed in the late 1960s and 1970s because of TRIO programs (college reach-out, upward bound, and regional science and mathematics institute) and several GI bills developed after major wars. Allen, Epps, and Haniff (1991) add that African Americans gained greater access to higher education in PWIs in the 1960s because of the Civil Rights Movement. These initiatives made it possible for more people of color to gain access to higher education at colleges and universities that traditionally serve predominately white populations (Allen, Epps, & Haniff, 1991; Wilson, 1992; Wilson, 1994). To illustrate this point, Wilson (1994) writes that in 1965, "600,000 African Americans were in college and 65 percent of them were in historically black colleges. By 1980, African American enrollment had doubled to 1.2 million but only 20 percent were in historically black colleges" (p. 196).

Nevertheless, the increase in the number of African American students enrolled in higher education programs at PWIs has done little to alter the small number of tenured Black faculty on these campuses, the amount and degree of negative experiences Black students face, or the low achievement and high attrition rates of Black students (King Chepyator-Thomson, 1996; Wilson, 1994). The literature states that students of color have unique needs that often go unmet at PWIs (Allen, Epps, & Haniff, 1991; Brazziel, 1988; King & Chepyator-Thomson, 1996; St. John, 2000). Further, much of the literature on Blacks in higher education uses the deficit model to discuss the experiences of Blacks, particularly males, in higher education (Coaxum & Ingram, 2002). Oftentimes, the Black woman's experience in higher education is ignored, as the larger number of studies about the Black experience in higher education focuses on Black men (Carroll, 1982; Johnson-Bailey, 2001; Matthews & Jackson, 1991). Traditionally, Black women, as Carroll (1982) suggests, "[have] been excluded from institutions of higher education as [they have] been excluded from all other opportunities" (p. 117).

Moreover, the studies on Blacks in higher education often concentrate on the negative experiences of students of color who attend Predominately White Universities and Colleges. There are almost no studies that focus on the successful Black students who earn professional degrees at PWIs yearly. Though many scholars have discussed the alienation Black students feel at PWIs (Allen, Epps, & Haniff, 1991; Beckham, 1988; St. John, 2000) or the need for special programs and Black faculty (Allen, Epps, & Haniff, 1991; Beckham, 1988; Clark & Garza, 1994; Wilson, 1994), there is almost no discussion about what Black students themselves feel contributes to their own academic success at PWIs or what they believe enhanced their experience. Additionally, there is little literature that includes the individual voices of Black students (King & Chepyator-Thomson, 1996; Lewis, Chesler, & Forman, 2001). Moreover, much of the literature neglects to consider students' personal experiences and reflections on their experiences while pursuing graduate degrees at PWIs.

Only a few studies serve as exceptions (Johnson-Bailey, 2001; King & Chepyator-Thomson, 1996; Lewis, Chesler, & Forman, 2001; Ross-Gordon & Brown-Haywood, 2000). In these studies, literature reviews, and discussions with research participants, researchers found several factors that contribute to the success of students of color in higher education:

- Motivational, environmental, and institutional factors (King & Chepyator-Thomson, 1996)
- Internal and external motivation (Ross-Gordon & Brown-Haywood, 2000)
- Relevant academic curriculum and role models (Ross-Gordon & Brown-Haywood, 2000)
- Self-efficacy (Ross-Gordon & Brown-Haywood, 2000)
- Networks of support (Johnson-Bailey, 2001; King & Chepyator-Thomson, 1996; Ross-Gordon & Brown-Haywood, 2000)
- Coping mechanisms (i.e., silence, resistance, and negotiation) (Johnson-Bailey, 2001).

My Approach

This chapter is an attempt to contribute to the growing body of literature that focuses on the experiences of Black students in higher education. King & Chepyator-Thomson (1996) found three factors that affect African American students' decisions to enroll in higher education and their ability to attain professional degrees. As stated earlier, these factors are motivational, environmental, and institutional. Motivational factors pertain to an individual's personal beliefs and desire to achieve. There are two kinds of achievement motivation: intrinsic motivation and extrinsic motivation. *Intrinsic motivation* is motivation that stems from a desire to fulfill an "internal need to be competent and self-determining," and *extrinsic motivation* is motivation based on a need or desire to be rewarded or recognized (King & Chepyator-Thomson, 1996, p. 171). Environmental factors include the campus racial climate and personal networks of support, for instance, family, friends, and advisors. Finally, institutional factors are entities that are specific to the university or college: admission policies, availability of assistantships, and other means of funding and networks of support related to academics. It is difficult to discern which of these factors most influenced my success in doctoral school, especially since I believe each factor has contributed significantly to my overall positive experience as a doctoral student. For this reason, I consider how each factor—motivational, environmental, and institutional—has affected my own enrollment and journey toward degree attainment at a Predominately White University in the Midwest (King & Chepyator-Thomson, 1996).

Coaxum & Ingram (2002) write, "Polite (1999) posits that the voices of African American males are rarely heard in research literature" (p. 2). I would argue that this is true for African Americans in general. As Johnson-Bailey (2001) aptly states, ". . . Black women [also] go unnoticed and unresearched" (p. 98). Black feminist theory suggests that Black women's individual experiences are valuable as well as useful "as a criterion for assessing knowledge" (Johnson-Bailey, 2001). As a result, this self-study focuses on my own successful experience as a doctoral student. The following questions are considered in this paper: (1) Why did I decide to enroll in doctoral school? and (2) What has sustained me on my journey toward earning a doctoral degree? It is my hope that my "schooling story" (Johnson-Bailey, 2001) or "life notes" (Bell-Scott, 1994) will help illustrate the need for rigorous recruitment of students and faculty of color and the implementation of programs designed to meet the unique needs of students of color on predominately White campuses.

Deciding to Enroll

Motivational Factors

I was both intrinsically and extrinsically motivated to enroll in doctoral school. My motivation to obtain a terminal degree is intrinsic because it has been my personal goal for quite some time. However, my motivation is also extrinsic because I believe I will not get tenure as a college professor without a doctoral degree. King & Chepyator-Thomson (1996) explain: "A person who is extrinsically motivated exhibits achievement-oriented behavior based upon external incentives such as social approval, a doctoral degree, a higher paying job, [and] tenure or promotion" (p. 171).

Environmental Factors

Growing up, I knew only one person who had gone to college. I often read books and watched television programs and movies about people who attended college, but I did not think it would be accessible to me. When my eighth grade teacher, Ms. Anderson,[1] presented the idea to our class as if it were something attainable, I started to believe I would go to college. I even began to dream beyond the bachelor's degree. Ms. Anderson became the measuring stick I used to determine my own potential. I wanted to do everything she did, but with a twist. She went to a Predominately White University; I went to a historically black one *and* a predominately White one. She pledged a Black college sorority, Alpha Kappa Alpha (AKA); I pledged Delta Sigma Theta (DST). She taught middle school students; I wanted to teach college students. Because of Ms. Anderson, I began to aim high. Luckily, she was not the last African American teacher to encourage me to pursue my goals.

Before attending a PWI, I attended an HBCU in North Carolina. My experience at an HBCU helped me never to lose sight of my dream of earning a terminal degree. When I was a sophomore, I began to work for the chair of the English department at my college. Teachers and the chair of the department took me under their wings and provided me with the grooming I needed to become a success. Whenever obstacles seemed to cloud my vision or circumstances threatened to hinder me from attending doctoral school (i.e., I got married my junior year of undergraduate study), the chair of the English department would remind me of the low percentage of African Americans who earned the Ph.D. Or he would tell me about his wife who earned her Ph.D. while being both a wife and mother. I also had the luxury of being a member of The Ronald E. McNair Post-Baccalaureate Program, a program designed to help prepare students to pursue graduate degrees by giving them opportunities to engage in research.

The nurturing experiences I received at an HBCU are not unique, for as Dr. William H. Boone, associate provost and interim dean of graduate study at Clark Atlanta University argues, "[Black colleges] differ from . . . other schools. . . . You don't get as much teaching and hands-on care [at other schools] as you do [at HBCUs]. Our professors are involved with a lot more than research and teaching. We do some real close mentoring, for instance, that you don't get other places" (St. John, 2000, p. 38).

Institutional Factors

Earning a Ph.D. has been my long-term goal since I was in the eighth grade. However, throughout my schooling, I lacked the academic confidence I needed to believe that my dream would become reality. After earning a Bachelor of Science degree in English education, I went on to earn a master's degree in English and Afro-American literature at the same university.[2] Nevertheless, even while I maintained a 4.0 GPA upon graduating with my master's, I questioned whether I had what it took to do well at a so-called *elite* university. Some Black people and the larger part of society said I had gone to an inferior college. "Anyone can make straight 'A's at an HBCU," they said, and I started to believe them. Despite this, I applied to a Predominately White University anyway. To my surprise, I was accepted.

Clark & Garza (1994) identified several misconceptions that students of color have about graduate school studies. For example, according to Clark & Garza (1994), students of color believe GRE scores determine graduate school admittance. I too believed that I would not be admitted to graduate school because of my Graduate Record Examination (GRE) scores. Then I thought, if I am accepted, I will not do well. Besides, my GRE scores said I would fail. Nevertheless, my personal experiences confirmed that the GRE does not "assess every discipline-related skill necessary for academic work or all subjective factors important to academic and career success, such as motivation, creativity, and interpersonal skills" (ETS, 1991, qtd. in Clark & Garza, 1994, p. 306).

When I entered the doctoral program, I was worried about whether or not I could prove that I was in school based on my own merit. I constantly doubted my ability. Had grades just been handed to me before, or had I earned them? Did I really know anything after five years in college? I wondered. But after the first grade report went out and I found that I got an "A" in each of my classes, I was able to focus more closely on my studies. I now realize that my anxiety about grades was largely due to images of graduate and professional school students I had seen on television or read about in books.

Journey Toward Degree Attainment

Motivational Factors

Because my dream of earning a doctoral degree has been "hanging in the air like smoke" for nearly fifteen years, giving up has never been an option for me. Nevertheless, there are times when I feel I cannot go on because I am tired or cannot financially afford to do so. It is at these times that I read Lucille Clifton's poem "Dreams Hanging in the Air Like Smoke" and remind myself that I would not feel complete if I did not achieve this goal.

Spirituality is another motivational factor that allows me to be persistent. I believe that earning a Ph.D. is a part of God's plan for my life, and this helps me stay focused and committed to my studies.

Environmental Factors

It is through various networks of support, my academic advisor, and my family that I find the strength to continue to pursue my dream, despite obstacles. Additionally, the positive campus climate at The Ohio State University (OSU) certainly contributes to my ability to persist. Doctoral school would have been very difficult for me had I not had a supportive academic advisor. I believe that had she not encouraged me and answered countless e-mails and phone calls from me,

I would not have been able to persist. My mother and other family members have also been supportive. Often my mother tells me that while she does not fully comprehend what I am doing, she supports me and encourages me to do what I do to the best of my ability. Additionally, my son serves as a powerful motivational force for me. He has been with me every step of the way. His mere presence reminds me daily that I must be persistent in my effort to obtain a terminal degree. I cannot tell him we went through the stress and uncertainty of candidacy exams to give up now. He would never understand why during Christmas break I spent more time shut up in my room trying to type a dissertation proposal than I spent playing with him, only to give up and give in. I want my son to see me and know what perseverance looks and feels like. Most of all, I want him to know that our sacrifices, his and mine, have not been in vain.

According to King & Chepyator-Thomson (1996), "Research indicates that African Americans, once enrolled, have negative college experiences and higher attrition rates as compared to their white counterparts" (p. 170). Further, King & Chepyator-Thomson (1996) report that 46 percent of the respondents in their study of African Americans and their experiences on college campuses "felt they had experienced overt acts of racism at their doctoral institutions" (p. 174). Fortunately, the racial climate at OSU is such that I have not experienced overt racism. However, I am not suggesting that my race has never negatively affected my experiences in doctoral school. By this I mean that I have often felt out of place or as if I did not belong on campus or in classes simply because I am not white. Repeatedly, I have felt surrounded by whiteness to the point of frustration. Countless times I have been in social and educational situations where I have remained silent because the conversation was about matters I could not and did not want to relate to. Carroll (1982) best describes the dilemma I sometimes find myself in when she writes:

> There is no one with whom to share experiences and gain support, no one on whom a Black woman can model herself. It takes a great deal of psychological strength "just to get through a day," the endless lunches [read classes] . . . in which one is always "different." The feeling is much like the exhaustion a foreigner speaking an alien tongue feels at the end of the day. (p. 120)

Lewis, Chesler, & Forman's (2001) recent study clearly reveals that students of color attending PWIs experience "high levels of alienation" and "pressure to assimilate" (pp. 75–79). King & Chepyator-Thomson (1996) aptly describe the environmental factors at Predominately White Universities that can be challenging for African American students: ". . . there are few African-American professors, students, administrators, organizations or activities, and consequently the campus climate offers little with which black students can identify" (p. 171). In another study of African American adult students, researchers surmised that some of the elements related to the academic success of African American students include motivation and relationships with people including faculty, family, and peers (Ross-Gordon & Brown-Haywood, 2000). I agree with these findings, and I believe I have been successful in spite of loneliness and alienation largely due to the closeness of my relationships with family and friends. In fact, the majority of my friends live in the city and are not affiliated in any way with the university setting. This removal from the campus environment helps me to leave academia behind while I interact in an atmosphere that provides me with greater comfort and acceptance.

Institutional Factors

I attend a Tier 1 research university that has repeatedly proven its commitment to recruiting students of color. The university employs several recruitment efforts each year, including Graduate and Professional School Visitation Days, a program that gives students of color an opportunity to observe campus life at the university. According to our website, www.osu.edu, OSU is a national leader in granting doctorates to African Americans. In addition to this, my school is ranked among the top twenty institutions that grant doctoral degrees to American Indians and Alaskan Natives. This information is based on data from the Higher Education and National Affairs American Council on Education. Moreover, OSU has worked in various capacities with Historically Black Colleges and Universities to help increase the enrollment of African American students (www.osu.edu). Over the last decade, my field, education, has consistently attracted the largest number of African American students pursuing the doctorate. This information operates as an impetus for me, and it indirectly helps me to withstand attrition.

The institutional factors that have sustained me on my journey toward earning a Ph.D. are these: (1) the university's ability to provide adequate funding for graduate students, (2) the university's commitment to recruiting and retaining students of color, and (3) the university's devotion to culturally specific programs like PROFS (Providing Research Opportunities for Future Scholars). When I enrolled in doctoral school, I taught high school full-time in order to support my son and myself. After my first year of attending doctoral school part-time, my academic advisor urged me to attend school full-time though she knew I could not afford to do so. To show her support of me, she worked hard to see that I received an assistantship that pays for school fees and provides me with a monthly stipend. Nevertheless, we both knew the stipend would not be enough money for my son and I to survive on, so I also applied for loans.

Each school year, I consider returning to work full-time to avoid loans, but because I want my degree, I continue to rely on borrowing money instead of working full-time. Brazziel (1988) and King & Chepyator-Thomson (1996) suggest that African American students rely heavily on loans to finance graduate school. Moreover, they suggest that other types of aid, for example scholarships, should be made available so students do not have to depend on loans.

One of the greatest factors that influenced my ability to persist at OSU is my participation in PROFS. I was accepted as part of the PROFS Fellow group my second year in the doctoral program. When I became a PROFS Fellow, I had no idea how much the experience would influence my journey toward obtaining a doctoral degree in English education. Before I knew it, the culturally engaged nature of the program had provided me with a home away from home, an atmosphere that nurtured and supported my research interests. PROFS has provided me with many opportunities I am sure I would not have had had I not been in the group. I realize we are fortunate to have such a program. King & Chepyator-Thomson (1996) reveal ". . . the support for social policies and programs that would aid African Americans' pursuit of higher education degrees has dwindled largely due to 'downturns in the U.S. economy'" (p. 170). This is unfortunate because students of color matriculating through PWIs often have unique needs and actually benefit from such programs.

One of the things I am most thankful to the PROFS group for is the relationship I have with peers and faculty. At our monthly meetings we talk about our academic progress, or in some cases setbacks. These discussions motivate me and offer me guidelines to help ensure my own success. Many times I have felt "out of the loop" or "in the dark" about the procedures necessary for earning a Ph.D., but because members in PROFS are at various levels, I am exposed to information most students have to stumble upon accidentally. For example, because there were PROFS members who had gone through the candidacy exam process before I did, I was able to query them about the procedure before my exams. I believe that my discussions with several fellow PROFS members about their experiences helped me succeed when I went through the process. Now there are PROFS members who have secured teaching positions at various universities. As a result, I have had conversations with them about job seeking strategies, and they have shared copies of vitas, cover letters, and other tips that will help me find a position when I go on the job market. The guidance they have given me is priceless.

The same can be said of my relationship with faculty members, particularly faculty and staff of color. King & Chepyator-Thomson (1996) argue, and I concur, "Students of color need examples of success to encourage them . . . to look toward the future as professionals in their field of interest" (p. 171). I feel comfortable going to a number of faculty members of color for information about academics and professional development. I am fortunate, as some doctoral students of color attend universities that, according to King & Chepyator-Thomson (1996), have "no black professors in their doctoral programs or departments" (p. 172). In contrast, I have had opportunities to present and write with faculty members who may not have known me had I not been a part of PROFS.

Faculty and PROFS Fellows have also motivated and encouraged me to excel in academic research endeavors. A few years ago, Brown (1999) revealed that few African Americans had had a chance to conduct scholarly research. I feel fortunate that engaging in serious research is expected of me. It is through listening to and talking with faculty and PROFS Fellows, that I realized that it was OK for me to do culturally specific research. I learned that my identity as a Black woman would not make my research on young adult literature by and about

African Americans any less valid. This was a breakthrough for me because I have always had a love for my people and a willingness to work to see how I can help bring about a positive change in the lives of Black children.

The use of traditional methodological and epistemological approaches to the type of research I engage in would be inadequate, for traditional methods of inquiry are largely informed by European worldviews (Christian, 1994; Dillard, 2000; Joseph, 1995; Scheurich & Young, 1996). Repeatedly, epistemologies derived from the "socio-cultural histories of people of color" are devalued and dismissed as illegitimate (Scheurich & Young, 1996, p. 9). This is especially true for Black feminist theory, which continues to struggle to maintain recognition and validation (Christian, 1994; McDowell, 1994; Scheurich & Young, 1996).

In an important essay, Christian (1994) asserts, "for people of color have always theorized—but in forms quite different from the Western form of abstract logic. And I am inclined to say that our theorizing (and I intentionally use the verb rather than the noun) is often in narrative forms, in the stories we create . . . in the play with language, since dynamic rather than fixed ideas seem more to our liking" (p. 349). Since traditional theory is "reductively defined" (McDowell, 1994, p. 569), and in spite of the fact that Black feminist theory is often unacknowledged as "theory," it still seems to me that one of the most productive and informative ways to approach literary works by African Americans, particularly women, is through the use of Black feminist literary theory. Black feminist literary criticism and its devotion to analyzing how Black female characters negotiate issues of race, class, and gender informs my work. Recently, I studied how two contemporary young adult novels, *I Hadn't Meant to Tell You This* (1994) by Jacqueline Woodson and *Crossing Jordan* (2000) by Adrian Fogelin, negotiate issues of race, class, and gender as they depict interracial friendships between young girls.

My research leans heavily on the work of Black feminists such as Mary Helen Washington, Barbara Smith, and Deborah McDowell. These scholars, among others, have contributed to, and in some cases, largely defined what is often thought of as Black feminist literary criticism. For instance, Mary Helen Washington's work illustrates her preoccupation with establishing an African American female literary tradition while focusing on common themes and intertexuality within the works of Black women. Washington (1990) maintains, "[W]riters speak to other writers. They change, challenge, revise, and borrow from other writers so that the literary tradition might well look like a grid in one of those airline magazines that shows the vast and intricate interweaving patterns of coast-to-coast flight schedules" (p. 7). I believe this statement can also be applied to the African American young adult literary tradition. Presently, I am studying young adult literature written by African American women in order to highlight and define intertexual themes within and across the works of several young adult African American women writers. This research is important because it begins to lay the groundwork for tracing a literary tradition among African American young adult writers.

Under the guidance of my academic advisor, faculty members of color who serve as my mentors, and PROFS Fellows, I have invested in my future. My journey has been a successful one. Nonetheless, it will come to an end (or a beginning) soon, and I will at last see my dream of earning a doctoral degree come to fruition. But what will become of me after I earn my degree? Will I be able to find a place for myself in academia? In 1982, Carroll wrote: "Obviously, no serious efforts have been made until very recently and on a very limited scale to recruit or promote Black women to important staff, faculty, or administrative positions in institutions of higher learning" (p. 121). Similarly, in 1991 Mickelson & Oliver assert: "Despite the almost twenty years of [recruiting faculty of color, particularly African Americans, and women] minority scholars—particularly African Americans—remain significantly underrepresented at practically all levels of faculty employment" (p. 177). Further, historically, African Americans have been excluded from faculty positions in higher education, and only recently has there been "[t]he appearance of noticeable numbers" of them in colleges and universities across the country (Mickelson & Oliver, 1991, p. 178). Based on this information, my future as an assistant professor in the college of education at a college or university seems uncertain.

Conclusion

According to Clark & Garza (1994), Nettles' 1990 study revealed that

> The quality of life for minority students has virtually been ignored by many institutions. . . . [I]nstitutional researchers and administrators tend to concentrate on quantitative rather than qualitative factors in higher education, noting increases in the number of students but ignoring their experiences on campus. (p. 305)

In this chapter I have attempted to give voice to my own experiences as a product of an HBCU who is now a Ph.D. candidate at a PWI. I hope that the information contained here will complement the small but increasing number of studies that describe factors that affect students of color who pursue higher education degrees at PWIs. I believe accounts of personal experiences are valuable and are an asset to studies about students in higher education. Such accounts provide opportunities for individuals to give rise to their own voices while telling their own stories. For as Morrison (1994) argues, ". . . [I]t is no longer acceptable merely to imagine us and imagine for us. We have always been imagining ourselves. . . . We are the subjects of our own narrative, witnesses to and participants in our own experience . . ." (p. 375). Finally, I propose that culturally specific programs, a generous number of faculty of color, and a positive racial climate at PWIs will provide a setting that is conducive to educating all students.

Notes

1. All names of individuals are pseudonyms.
2. Afro-American is the descriptor printed on the actual certificate.

References

Allen, W. R., Epps, E. G., & Haniff, N. Z. (Eds.). (1991). *College in black and white: African American students in predominantly white and historically black public institutions.* Albany, NY: State University of New York Press.

Beckham, B. (1988). Strangers in a strange land: The experience of blacks on white campuses. *Educational Record, 68*(1), 74–78.

Bell Scott, P. (1994). *Life notes: Personal writings by contemporary black women.* New York: W. W. Norton.

Brazziel, W. F. (1988). Roadblocks to graduate school. *Educational Record*, 68(1), 108–115.

Brown, L. M. (1999). Creating opportunities for faculty research. *Black Issues in Higher Education*, 16(20), 34–39.

Carroll, C. M. (1982). Three's a crowd: The dilemma of the black woman in higher education. In G. T. Hull, P. B. Scott, & B. Smith (Eds.), *All the women are white, all the blacks are men, but some of us are brave: Black women's studies* (pp. 115–128). New York: The Feminist Press.

Christian, B. (1994). The race for theory. In A. Mitchell (Ed.), *Within the circle: An anthology of African American literary criticism from the Harlem renaissance to the present* (pp. 348–359). Durham: Duke University Press.

Clark, M., & Garza, H. (1994). Minorities in graduate education: A need to regain lost momentum. In M. J. Justiz, R. Wilson, & L. G. Bjork (Eds.), *Minorities in higher education* (pp. 297–313). Phoenix, AZ: Oryx Press.

Clifton, L. (2000). *Blessing the boats: New and selected poems 1988–2000.* Rochester, NY: Boa Editions.

Coaxum, J., & Ingram, T. N. (2002, April). From broken promises to hope-filled realities: Developing success in African American males. Paper presented at the meeting of the American Educational Research Association, New Orleans, Louisiana.

Dillard, C. B. (2000). The substance of things hoped for, the evidence of things not seen: Examining an endarkened feminist epistemology in educational research and leadership. *International Journal of Qualitative Studies in Education*, 13(6), 661–681.

Fogelin, A. (2000). *Crossing Jordan.* Atlanta: Peachtree Publishers.

King, S. E., & Chepyator-Thomson, J. R. (1996). Factors affecting the enrollment and persistence of African-American doctoral students. *The Physical Educator*, 53, 170–180.

Johnson-Bailey, J. (2001). *Sistas in college: Making a way out of no way.* Malabar, FL: Krieger Publishing Company.

Joseph, G. (1995). Black feminist pedagogy and schooling in capitalist white America. In B. Guy-Sheftall (Ed.), *Words of fire: An anthology of African-American feminist thought* (pp. 462–471). New York: The New Press.

Lewis, A. E, Chesler, M., & Forman, T. A. (2001). The impact of "colorblind" ideologies on students of color: Intergroup relations at a Predominantly White University. *Journal of Negro Education*, 69(1/2), 74–91.

Matthews, W., & Jackson, K. W. (1991). Determinants of success for black males and females in graduate and professional schools. In W. R. Allen, E. G. Epps, & N. Z. Haniff (Eds.), *College in black and white: African American students in predominantly white and historically black public institutions* (pp. 197–208). Albany, NY: State University of New York Press.

McDowell, D. E. (1994). New directions for black feminist criticism. In A. Mitchell (Ed.), *Within the circle: An anthology of African American literary criticism from the Harlem renaissance to the present* (pp. 428–439). Durham: Duke University Press.

Mickelson, R. A., & Oliver, M. L. (1991). The demographic fallacy of the black academic: Does quality rise to the top? In W. R. Allen, E. G. Epps, & N. Z. Haniff (Eds.), *College in black and white: African American students in predominately white and historically black public institutions* (pp. 177–195). Albany, NY: State University of New York Press.

Morrison, T. (1994). Unspeakable things unspoken: The Afro-American presence in literature. In A. Mitchell (Ed.), *Within the circle: An anthology of African American literary criticism from the Harlem renaissance to the present* (pp. 368–398). Durham: Duke University Press.

Ross-Gordon, J., & Brown-Haywood, F. (2000). Keys to college success as seen through the eyes of African American adult students. *Journal of Continuing Higher Education, 46*(38), 14–23.

Scheurich, J. J., & Young, M. D. (1996). Coloring epistemologies: Are our research epistemologies racially biased. *Educational Researcher, 26*(4), 4–16.

Slaughter, J. B. (1989). Preventing the dwindling supply of Black Ph.D's. In J. C. Elam (Ed.), *Blacks in higher education: Overcoming the odds* (pp. 87–92). Lanham, MD: University Press of America.

St. John, E. (2000). More doctorates in the house. *Black Issues in Higher Education, 17*(10), 38–44.

Thomas, G. E. (1987). Black students in U.S. graduate and professional schools in the 1980s: A national and institutional assessment. *Harvard Educational Review, 57*(3), 261–282.

Washington, M. H. (Ed.). (1990). *Black-Eyed Susans/midnight birds: Stories by and about black women.* New York: Doubleday.

Wilson, R. (1992). [Review of the book *Fostering minority access and achievement in higher education*]. *Harvard Educational Review, 62*(1), 79–87.

Wilson, R. (1994). The participation of African Americans in American higher education. In M. J. Justiz, R. Wilson, & L. G. Bjork (Eds.), *Minorities in higher education* (pp. 195–209). Phoenix, AZ: Oryx Press.

Woodson, J. (1994). *I hadn't meant to tell you this.* New York: Bantam Doubleday.

Randal D. Pinkett, Ph.D.

Hometown: East Windsor, New Jersey

Current Institution: Massachsetts Institute of Technology

Department: Media Arts and Sciences

Personal Philosophy: Brothers and sisters, in life's travels there is no road. The road is made as one walks. Walk with God.

4

FIVE DEGREES AND A Ph.D.
POSITIVE DETOURS ALONG THE PATH
TO THE DOCTORATE

Rhodes to England

Ever since college, I have aspired to complete a Ph.D. My journey to
the degree began on October 4, 1994, when I left the United States for
the University of Oxford, England, as one of thirty-two U.S. Rhodes
scholars. I was the first African American ever to receive the prestigious
award from my alma mater, Rutgers University in New Brunswick, NJ,
and extremely proud to be among five African Americans recognized
that year. At Rutgers, my undergraduate major was electrical engineering. With an interest in both engineering and business, I arrived at
Oxford in pursuit of a Master's degree in Engineering, Economics and
Management (EEM). My intent was to complete this program and
attend the Massachusetts Institute of Technology (MIT), in Cambridge,
Massachusetts, where I had deferred admission to their graduate program in electrical engineering. However, shortly after settling into life
in Great Britain, I was informed by my academic advisor that EEM was
a three-year program. Consequently, I decided to change my direction
and pursue the British equivalent of the Ph.D., a D.Phil., in Computer
Science, as I was told it could be reasonably completed in the same
amount of time.

A Detour Along the Road

As I completed my first year at Oxford, I slowly came to realize two
things. First, I was not particularly happy living in Oxford. The City of
Oxford was essentially a small college town where drinking alcohol at
pubs was a centerpiece of social life. Having been a high jumper and long
jumper in college, I didn't drink and never enjoyed spending time at

smoke-filled bars. I preferred a good house party to a bar crawl, which made it somewhat difficult to fully immerse myself into Oxford's social environment. Furthermore, as an African American, I was a minority within a minority. Not including students attending Oxford on a junior year abroad, there were roughly ten African Americans at the University. And of the approximately 15,000 students at Oxford, approximately 100 were Black (less than 1 percent), whereas Africans, Caribbeans, and Britains were the largest contingents. Certainly, the highlights of my experience abroad included the opportunity to fellowship with and learn about these brothers and sisters across the African Diaspora, meet and interact with people from across the globe, and travel inexpensively to various parts of Europe. However, because my primary reason for being there was my academics, by the end of my first year even these benefits began to pale in comparison to my academic frustrations.

Second, I came to realize that Oxford's Computer Science department did not support my research interests. As an undergraduate, most of my electives were focused on digital signal processing (DSP) including speech compression, decompression, and recognition. As a relatively small department, there was a limited range of research areas supported by Oxford's faculty, and none dealt with areas I found engaging. Eventually, I settled on a hybrid research topic that examined how field programmable gate arrays (FPGAs), or reconfigurable hardware, could be used to implement DSP algorithms such as speech compression and decompression, through a software compilation, or design process. FPGAs and hardware/software compilation was a central theme to my advisor's work, making this research project interesting enough to garner his support. I spent my entire first year learning the basics of FPGA technology and examining how it could be applied to my personal area of interest, DSP.

In the middle of my second year, as I was supposed to begin preparing my D.Phil. proposal, I began having second thoughts about pursuing this line of research for another one to two years. While I was enamored with the idea of completing a doctorate in a relatively short period of time, I questioned whether I was trying to fit the department's round peg of FPGAs into my square hole of DSP. After much consternation, I approached my advisor with these concerns. We discussed the matter for a few weeks and reached the conclusion that it would be in my best interests to submit my work to-date as a master's thesis and pursue my Ph.D. back in the United States at MIT. Per the requirements of the department, I successfully defended my master's thesis, "Hardware/ Software Co-Design and Digital Speech Processing," in May 1996, and departed from England to begin classes at MIT one month later.

Dual Degree Then Ph.D.

My interest in engineering and management stemmed from my desire to eventually start my own technology company. For this reason, although I abandoned the EEM program, I maintained interest in an educational program that combined business and technology. Fortunately, when I applied to MIT a few years earlier as an undergraduate, I submitted applications to both the Department of Electrical Engineering and Computer Science (EECS) in the School of Engineering and the Sloan School of Management. This was done in conjunction with MIT's Leaders for Manufacturing Program (LFM), "a graduate level program in which students earn an MS in Engineering and an MBA. Established in 1990, LFM trains students to become industry leaders and agents for change" (Slavin, 2002). I was accepted to the LFM program as an undergraduate, and therefore my deferral afforded me the opportunity to return to MIT as a participant in this two-year, two-degree program. My thinking at the time was twofold. First, I figured I would be able to obtain an engineering degree and a business degree in the same amount of time it would take me to complete either one. Second, I anticipated I would be able to transition directly from the masters in EECS to the Ph.D. program without losing any time. It seemed like the perfect opportunity.

A Rude Awakening

MIT turned out to be of a rude awakening for me. My program at Oxford was strictly research, no classes. Overseas, I had plenty of time to travel and pursue other interests as long as I made steady progress in the lab. My first three semesters at MIT were not only primarily based on coursework, they also required an unusually high number of credits, which typically included two engineering classes and four business classes. Moreover, MIT, as well as graduate-level study in general, were far more demanding than my undergraduate experience.

In the business program, my primary challenge was time management. I was routinely assigned for more work, especially readings, than could be managed reasonably. It was an ongoing game of wait-and-see as to whether or not I had covered enough of a case study to offer remarks that were insightful enough to earn points for class participation. In the engineering program, my primary challenge was the level of expectation from my professors and overall rigor they applied to assignments. It wasn't enough to simply understand what was being taught, that is, if I could understand what was being taught. Rather than being asked to digest and regurgitate information, I was expected to take what I had learned in one domain and apply it to another. This was the case for problem sets, quizzes, and tests.

Initially, I approached my studies at MIT the same way I approached my studies at Rutgers where I maintained a 3.9 GPA. Only this time the formula didn't work. Whereas in college, mastery of the material would suffice, in graduate school I had to extend my thinking not only logically but creatively to solve problems. I recall my first test in the graduate DSP course. I had a longstanding habit of beginning tests with the easiest problem, whether it was the first problem or not. I didn't know where to begin on this test. In fact, I looked up after reading through all of the questions to make sure I was in the right room and see if anyone else had the same look of dismay that I did. I received a "C" on my first DSP test, which signaled to me that it was time for a change.

One of the first issues I had to address was finding other people to study with. During my first semester, particularly in my engineering classes, I studied alone. I believed I could conquer MIT on my own. I thought wrong. In my business classes, this wasn't a problem because we were arranged in teams and I had the added benefit of my LFM cohorts who were required to take many of the same classes. In my engineering classes, this was indeed a challenge because I was almost always the only black face in the room and a complete stranger to my classmates. At Rutgers, there were close to 200 African Americans in the College of Engineering. Many of these students were either in my classes or had taken my classes, which made it possible to form study groups among my people. This was not the case at MIT. At MIT, there are approximately 126 African American graduate students across thirty-seven programs and departments in a given year. Consequently,

I had to align my study efforts in engineering with people of different backgrounds, regardless of whether I enjoyed their company.

Another strategy I found useful was obtaining the course materials from previous years—problem sets, solution sets, examinations, and so on—inasmuch as they were available. At MIT, collections such as these are referred to as "Bibles." So-called Bibles were helpful if the materials were from the same professor teaching the course that year. Not surprisingly, several groups on campus such as ethnic communities, fraternities, and sororities maintained their own private libraries of course materials. The Minority Business Club (MBC) at Sloan conducted a similar practice for MBAs. The Black Graduate Student Association (BGSA) at MIT endeavored to do so for graduate students, but often found it difficult given the relatively low numbers of Black students in each department.

After a turbulent start, I emerged from the fall semester with a 4.9 out of a possible 5.0 as a result of these strategies, a lot of late evenings studying, a few all-nighters, and a renewed commitment to hard work. Thereafter, each semester became increasingly easier to manage as I came to understand what was required of me and settled into a routine that could meet those expectations.

A Detour Along the Road . . . Again

As I approached completion of my master's program, I began to do some soul searching and questioned whether I wanted to pursue a Ph.D. in Electrical Engineering specifically. Leading up to this point in my career, my engineering experiences were largely based in Corporate America. I had worked at General Electric, AT&T Bell Laboratories, and, more recently, Lucent Technologies as part of my LFM internship, but wasn't fulfilled with the notion of applying my talents for the profit of others. Furthermore, since I was more interested in business than academia, a career path as a professor wasn't really an option either. I was approaching four degrees and began to wonder whether it was worth my time to spend another three to five years pursuing a fifth. I pondered whether a Ph.D. in Electrical Engineering better prepared me for a job as a researcher in industry rather than a career as an entrepreneur.

At the same time, I also questioned whether I had a passion for Electrical Engineering. While I recognized I had a God-given talent in electrical engineering, an interest in DSP, and even enjoyed learning about these fields, I wasn't passionate about this work thus far. I was passionate about business school and I could immediately see how it applied to my long-term goals and objectives. I wanted to pursue my Ph.D. in an area I was equally passionate about, believing I could identify market opportunities to apply my expertise once the degree was completed. Consequently, as the second and final year of my master's program winded down, I came to a crossroads in determining the appropriate direction for me to move forward. So, I did what most graduate students do: I read through the research interests of various faculty, set up meetings to discuss their work, and gave serious thought to whether or not anything sparked my interest. Unfortunately, these efforts afforded me no greater insight on how to proceed.

One day I was talking with a friend, Greg Gunn, the only other African American in my LFM class and a fellow Rhodes Scholar, about my dilemma. Greg, who was familiar with my interest in community service and the African American community, suggested I arrange to meet with one of his master's thesis advisors, Professor Mitchel Resnick, at the renowned MIT Media Laboratory, to learn more about his work. He explained that Mitchel was instrumental in establishing a network of afterschool technology centers for inner-city youth, now known as the Intel Computer Clubhouse. This sounded interesting to me so I took Greg's advice and scheduled a day and time to meet with Mitchel Resnick.

Stumbling on an Advisor and an Opportunity

The Media Lab is one of the most intriguing laboratories at MIT. An aesthetically distinct building located on the eastern side of campus, it is widely recognized for producing cutting edge technologies. The Media Lab's agenda involves "a growing focus on how electronic information overlaps with the everyday physical world" (MIT Media Laboratory, 2002). Students there pursue graduate degrees in Media Arts and Sciences, a program of study that is unique to MIT and "signifies the study, invention and creative use of enabling technologies for understanding and expression by people and machines" (MIT Program in Media Arts and Sciences, 2002). Mitchel was the head of the Epistemology and Learning Group, which "explores how new technologies

can enable new ways of thinking, learning, and designing" (MIT Epistemology and Learning Group, 1998), and has as one of its sub-foci the
role of technology in underserved communities.

When I met Mitchel in his office I immediately noticed his personable and down-to-earth demeanor. He presented himself as someone
who was interested in doing good research while at the same time making a difference in people's lives. Prior to the meeting I had reviewed his
website and read some of his academic papers as well as a few papers
from members of his group, so I was familiar with their areas of inquiry.
For about an hour, we discussed each other's experiences and interests,
his group, and the activities at the Media Lab. Interestingly, the topic
that sparked the most conversation was the Computer Clubhouse.

Mitchel describes the Computer Clubhouse as a learning environment where "youth learn to express themselves fluently with new technology" (Resnick & Rusk, 1996) and "young people become designers
and creators—not just consumers—of computer-based products"
(Resnick & Rusk, 1996). During our conversation, he explained the
concepts underlying the Clubhouse and related research projects by
past graduate students such as Dr. Alan Shaw and Dr. Paula Hooper,
whose work I was familiar with from the group's website. I, in turn,
offered some of my ideas for possible projects and articulated my initial interest in conducting similar types of work. We ended the meeting
with Mitchel extending an invitation to me to visit the Computer Clubhouse in the near future.

A few weeks later, I accepted Mitchel's invitation and traveled with
him on a Saturday afternoon to visit the Clubhouse. There, I saw a
number of kids, many who came from local underserved communities,
producing digital music, artwork, videos, graphics, animations, and
more. I was fascinated. I also met several students, mentors, and staff
working on various projects and observed Mitchel working directly
with a small group of kids to create a programmable Lego-powered
device using technology designed by his group.

My exposure to the Clubhouse and Mitchel's research definitely
peaked my interest. In particular, I was excited about the idea of com-
bining community and technology, because I was previously unaware
of efforts to do so. Dating back to high school, I had always been
involved with organizations focused on communities of color as well as

various forms of community service. Similarly, I had spent years obtaining training and professional experience in areas related to technology. Until I stumbled on Mitchel's work, I regarded community work and technology development as existing in separate, distinct spheres. Now, my eyes were being opened to the possibilities between the two domains. I was also experiencing a renewed sense of optimism as I considered the fact that working with Mitchel could be just the opportunity I was looking for.

New Department, New Possibilities

I had sat through dozens of workshops on the importance of selecting a good thesis advisor and the critical decision factors such as their tenure status, number of students they advise, management style (e.g., hands-on or laid-back), and the scope of their research. Other than the fact that Mitchel was still one year short of tenure review, he met almost all of my criteria. Most importantly, I felt that our personalities meshed. I saw him as an excellent person to mentor me through the doctoral process.

During the winter break just prior to my final semester, I came to the conclusion I wanted to transfer out of the Department of Electrical and Computer Engineering and pursue a Ph.D. in Media Arts and Sciences. To my chagrin, this required that I resubmit a completed graduate school application including letters of reference, transcripts, a personal statement, and more.

The Media Lab is like a number of competitive graduate programs in that the admissions process is based not only on what you know but also who you know. I often describe the admissions process to others as beginning with the separation of applications by faculty into two piles: (1) "known quantities" or people they are familiar with, and (2) "unknown quantities" or people they are unfamiliar with. I go on to say that the known quantities pile is reviewed first and those applicants are selected to fill the available slots, while the unknown quantities pile is reviewed after the first pile has been completed, and those applicants are selected to fill the remaining slots, if any. While this is somewhat of an exaggeration, it does capture the spirit of how candidates are evaluated. The better someone knows you, the better your chances of being accepted. Unfortunately, I wasn't aware of this dynamic. Fortunately, I was very interested in getting to know Mitchel and the members of his group to solidify my decision. This was also time well spent in light of the fact I was already on campus and could easily arrange to meet with them. Consequently, I scheduled time to eat lunch with nearly all of his graduate students, attended various functions at the Media Lab such as sponsor events, and met with Mitchel one-on-one to talk. As a by-product of these efforts and despite my ignorance, I established a decent relationship with Mitchel and his students which I surmise, in retrospect, moved my application closer to the known quantity pile.

At the same time, I also submitted an application to the Ph.D. program at the Sloan School of Management, proposing to study the role of technology in inner-city economic development. However, I failed to reach out personally to faculty or students in the same manner as I did at the Media Lab. While preparing my application to Sloan, I sought the advice of a minority recruiter there. He gave me horrible advice, recommending I connect with an adjunct faculty member who shared a tangential interest in my proposed area of research, rather than more senior faculty with the wherewithal to advise students and actually influence the admissions decision-making process. And so, despite my qualifications and preexisting relationship to the school, my application to Sloan was rejected. Soon after I received the rejection letter, I belatedly paid a visit to a few faculty members to discuss the reasons why I wasn't accepted. They explained something about a "poor fit" between my interests and the department's research, which I interpreted to mean that none of the faculty took an interest in my proposed work or a personal interest in me, that is, if they read my application. After meeting with one faculty member who appeared interested in my work, I was contacted by the chair of her research group. If I wanted them to reconsider my application, they would be willing to do so. He said there was a good chance their original decision would be reversed. I declined their offer for reconsideration because I had recently received a verbal commitment from Mitchel that he was going to accept my application to the Media Lab and I felt his group was best suited to my needs. A few weeks later I was ecstatic to receive a letter in the mail confirming my acceptance, which also signaled the beginning of my final road to the Ph.D.

Paying Dues and Establishing Credibility

The Media Lab has a policy that all graduate students must be admitted to the master's program. Under rare circumstances, if a student already holds an advanced degree, they can transfer to the Ph.D. program after one year of satisfactory performance as evaluated by their advisor. At the time I joined Mitchel's group, he had a student who was pursuing a *second* Ph.D., and even he was required to start in the master's program. Given his experience, I knew that my three master's degrees would not be enough to justify entering the Ph.D. track directly. Yet, I had every intention of demonstrating my abilities to Mitchel and the other members of the group so that, one year later, I could transition directly to the doctoral program. This meant paying my dues and establishing credibility.

During the summer before I officially joined the Media Lab, I attended an annual group camping retreat. While I have never been a fan of camping, I saw this as an opportunity to get to know Mitchel and my colleagues in an informal environment. Once the fall semester arrived, I sat down with Mitchel and discussed some initial activities I could get involved with. I knew I wanted to craft a research project that applied technology for the benefit of low-income residents. However, none of the members of my group were working on similar endeavors. The majority of the members of the group were working on educational, not community technology projects. Mitchel suggested I align myself with one of the existing research projects in the group, not necessarily with the expectation it would evolve into my thesis project, but because it would contribute to the group's overall efforts at a time when I was still refining my own research agenda. As a result, I worked with my officemate, Rick Borovoy, writing code and helping him prepare a software demonstration for the first sponsor meeting at the lab.

Mitchel also suggested I enroll in the class he was teaching that semester. This was an excellent idea both from the perspective of building our relationship as well as learning more about his interests. Lastly, he suggested I volunteer at the Computer Clubhouse as a way to explore possible ideas. This made sense, given the close relationship between the Clubhouse and my proposed area of work.

During the summer after completing my first year, I spoke with Mitchel and he agreed he was comfortable transferring me to the Ph.D.

program. In retrospect, I'm sure the ongoing cultivation of our relationship and my contributions to the group, although not explicitly on the critical path to completing my degree, positively contributed to his decision.

Selecting a Thesis Topic

To inform my thinking about a possible thesis topic, I arranged meetings with a number of individuals, many of whom were recommended to me by Mitchel. He did an excellent job of introducing me to people with similar interests to my own. This included Professor Brian Smith, a recent graduate of Northwestern University's program in the Learning Sciences and the only African American faculty member at the Media Lab, and Dr. Alan Shaw and Dr. Paula Hooper, past graduates from the Media Lab and the two most recent African American Ph.D.'s from our group, graduating in 1995 and 1998 respectively. Alan's thesis focused on the deployment of a computer-based networking system called MUSIC (Multi-User Sessions in Community) in two low-income communities (Shaw, 1995). Paula's thesis focused on children's exploration of computational ideas at an African-centered school (Hooper, 1998). Clearly, their insight resulting from their thesis projects could help inform my thinking. I also met with Professor Ceasar McDowell, the Director of the Center for Reflective Community Practice (CRCP) in MIT's Department of Urban Studies and Planning (DUSP). I enrolled in his course, "Media and Technology," during the spring semester of my first year. CRCP "offers the opportunity to link students and faculty at MIT with community partners for mutual benefit, and to help develop the resource and leadership capacity of low-income communities and communities of color" (MIT Center for Reflective Community Practice, 2002). Once again, Ceasar was an excellent contact given the similarities between his work and my interests.

Based on conversations with these and other individuals, I continued to reflect as to what might be a suitable thesis topic. In the middle of the spring semester 1999, Mitchel invited me to meet with Professor David Gifford, another MIT faculty member and a friend from his alma mater, Princeton University. Dave had been volunteering at Mission Park, a housing development in Roxbury, MA, helping them establish a computer community technology center (CTC). Mission Park's CTC served the residents of the development by offering technology courses and related programs and activities. As a follow-up to establishing the CTC, Dave wanted to raise money to provide residents with home computers. He contacted Mitchel because he was looking for a researcher with an interest in studying the impact of such an initiative. Recognizing that I might be interested in getting involved, Mitchel invited me to meet with Dave. This sounded like the perfect opportunity.

A few months earlier, Ceasar had invited me to a conference on campus focused on women of color and technology, called "Cyber Sisters." There, I met Richard O'Bryant, a graduate of Howard University in Computer Engineering, a Ph.D. candidate in DUSP, and one of Ceasar's part-time assistants at CRCP. Soon after the conference, Rich and I met for lunch and discovered our mutual interest in technology and low-income communities. After Dave invited me to meet with the residents and CTC staff at Mission Park, I invited Richard to accompany us. Richard and I began cultivating a relationship with the residents at Mission Park by visiting the development on a weekly basis with Dave. By the end of the semester, we were working with Dave and Mitchel to write a grant proposal for the project and Dave agreed to help us show the proposal to potential funders.

I achieved another major breakthrough in my thesis project's development when Mitchel asked me to sit in for him at a conference in Chicago, sponsored by a nonprofit organization, the Community Technology Centers' Network (CTCNet). CTCNet had invited Mitchel to participate in a roundtable discussion of leaders in the field of community technology. He was unable to make it and asked if I would consider attending on his behalf. At first I declined his offer stating that I was too busy. On second thought I recognized it was an honor to have the opportunity to be there in addition to the fact it was in my best interests to be there. As fate would have it, Mitchel's placard was placed next to Dr. Gail McClure's, a Vice-President at the W. K. Kellogg Foundation, one of the largest foundations in the country. Throughout the meeting, I offered my insight on various issues related to community and technology. During one of the meeting breaks, Dr. McClure asked, "So, exactly what are you doing?" I replied, "I'm looking to raise money for a research project that would investigate the positive uses of technology in the homes of low-income residents." She said, "Interesting. How much are you looking for?" Lacking an in-depth familiarity with the project's budget, I guessed and replied, "About $250,000." She responded, "I think we could do that." I was floored. I thought to myself that she must be kidding. Immediately after the conference, I contacted her and she instructed me to get her a proposal as soon as possible outlining the project's overall scope, intended outcomes, and budget. Richard, Dave, Mitchel, and I proceeded to edit our current proposal and by the time the fall semester of 1999 arrived, we received a letter from the W. K. Kellogg Foundation stating that our grant proposal was approved!

Creating Community Connections

Around the time the grant was secured, it turned out that Mission Park was not a suitable location for conducting the research project. This was primarily due to the lack of necessary wiring and infrastructure to support high-speed Internet access at the development. Consequently, during the fall semester of 1999, Richard and I approached the tenants' association at Camfield Estates, a newly renovated, predominantly African American, low- to moderate-income housing development also in Roxbury, MA. They expressed an interest in working with us. During the spring semester of 2000, Richard and I embarked on the Camfield Estates-MIT Creating Community Connections Project, which has as one of its goals to establish Camfield Estates as a model for other housing developments across the country to help individuals, families, and a community make use of information and communications technology to support their interests and needs.

With the grant from the W. K. Kellogg Foundation in hand, we secured additional grants from Hewlett-Packard (computers), RCN Telecom Services (cable-modem Internet access), Microsoft (software), and others, totaling more than $250,000 in monetary and in-kind contributions. With these resources, we were able to offer every family at Camfield a new computer, high-speed Internet connection, and comprehensive courses at the CTC already on the premises. I began working with residents to design and implement a web-based, community building application called the Creating Community Connections (C3) System, to help facilitate connections between residents, local organizations and institutions (e.g., libraries, schools), and neighborhood businesses. I also worked with residents to develop a community building agenda to leverage this infrastructure and study the impact of these activities on the community. Similarly, Richard worked with residents to help them achieve greater levels of empowerment and self-sufficiency through the use of technology, and study their progress along these lines. In other words, while I was interested in the role of technology at the community level, Richard was interested in these same issues at the household level. Overall, the project was exactly what I wanted—a combination of community and technology.

Reaching Milestones in a Timely Manner: The General Examination and Thesis Proposal

In the midst of becoming a project manager, fund-raiser, and community liaison, I still had a number of academic milestones to achieve in order to remain on schedule in my degree program. My first milestone was the general examination. MIT's Program in Media Arts and Sciences is an interdisciplinary program that requires each doctoral candidate to identify three fields of study (and three faculty members in each of these fields), which constitute the basis for a written and oral general examination. This includes a "main" area, typically covered by the student's advisor; a "technical" area, typically an engineering discipline, computer science, or some other field related to technology; and a "contextual" area, typically a nontechnical field such as education, cognitive science, or social science, which provides a grounding human or social context for the degree. Once three or more faculty members are identified for the exam, the student works directly with them to generate a reading list for each area that is approved by the department. The student must complete both the written and oral components of the general examination within three months of receiving approval for their proposal from the department.

The department encourages students to begin preparing their general examination reading list *after* completing a mandatory doctoral seminar that is held during their first semester as a Ph.D. candidate. However, because the proposal can be submitted anytime after the seminar is completed, I began preparing my general examination reading list *while* I was in the seminar. Furthermore, because the departmental committee that reviews general examination proposals only meets a few times during the semester, it is easy to miss a scheduled meeting and have to wait until the subsequent meeting to submit a proposal. I wanted to avoid this at all cost. I promptly submitted my reading list to the department for review within weeks of completing the doctoral seminar. Clearly, the lesson here is to research and clearly understand the doctoral process to avoid wasting time.

My main area was related to education and learning in communities. Mitchel administered this written examination, which required that I submit a paper of publishable quality for his review. My technical area focused on technologies and architectures that specifically support communities and included software engineering, web and database design, and networking. Brian and Professor Walter Bender jointly administered this written examination which consisted of a twenty-four-hour take-home exam. My contextual area included community building and community development in the tradition of Urban Studies and Planning. Ceasar administered this written examination which also consisted of a twenty-four-hour take-home exam. Mitchel, Brian, Walter, and Ceasar facilitated my oral examination. It consisted of a twenty-minute presentation, which included an overview of my assigned readings, followed by roughly two hours of questions and answers.

To prepare for my written and oral examinations, I employed a number of strategies that enabled me to make more efficient use of my time. First, during my second semester, I enrolled in a course offered by my research group consisting of weekly discussion of papers considered to be core readings in our field of educational technology. A considerable number of these readings comprised the basis for Mitchel's reading list so that very few of the items on his list were new. Second, during my third semester (the semester leading up to my written and oral examinations), I worked very closely with Richard to study and prepare. I had learned from the lessons of my master's program that I did not want to go this alone. Richard and I arranged to receive credit for an independent study. We then spent the semester reading and discussing papers that could help inform our theoretical and practical approach to the Camfield-MIT project. We developed individual syllabi for the course, whereas my syllabus was primarily based on the readings from my general examination reading list. Twice a week, both Richard and

I prepared and delivered a PowerPoint presentation that summarized the major points from our readings and then conducted an in-depth question and answer for each reading, which hopefully mocked the oral examination. I've often been told that the best way to learn something is to teach it to someone else. This could not have been truer for the two of us. By requiring that we not only summarize the readings but also explain them to each other, we significantly increased our comprehension, retention, and understanding of the material. As a result of these strategies, I successfully passed my oral examination on May 16, 2001, just before the summer of my second year.

My second major milestone was the thesis proposal. Each student in the Media Arts and Sciences program is required to submit a thesis proposal that identifies their dissertation committee and documents their literature review, research question and hypothesis, research design and methodology, proposed time line, and required resources. Once approved by the department, the dissertation committee is then empowered to determine if and when a student has met the final requirements of the degree. Once again, I took very deliberate and proactive steps to reach this milestone. First, I used the grant writing process as an opportunity to establish the beginnings of my thesis proposal. This enhanced my ability to frame the issues I was seeking to understand, both from an academic and practical standpoint. Second, as I was preparing for my general examination during the fall semester of 1999, I enrolled in a "Research Design and Methodology" course in DUSP along with Richard. Given my background in Electrical Engineering, Business Administration, and Computer Science, I had a relatively weak set of skills in Social Science. This course not only strengthened my abilities in this area, it also required a thesis proposal as a final deliverable. Consequently, at the end of the semester as I was finishing the general examination process, I was also completing a full thesis proposal that could serve as the basis for my formal thesis proposal.

The Best Thesis Is a Completed Thesis

The two most significant tasks in connection to my thesis proposal were defining the scope of work and selecting a dissertation committee. To this first item, one of my mentors at AT&T Bell Laboratories once told me that the goal of a Ph.D. is not to save the world but to graduate. He said the Ph.D. is a means, not an end, and I should avoid the pursuit of an elaborate, groundbreaking research endeavor, and instead focus on what is needed to earn the degree. Similarly, Brian once told me that the best thesis is a completed thesis. Needless to say, their words resonated with me when I was preparing my thesis proposal and during conversations with Mitchel about the project's scope. My research question focused on the ways in which community social capital could be increased and community cultural capital could be activated through a comprehensive approach to community technology and community building. My hypothesis was that these outcomes could be achieved through the participation of residents as active agents of change, rather than passive beneficiaries, and as active producers of technology, as opposed to passive consumers. In order to obtain the necessary data to prove my hypothesis, I proposed in-depth interviews with each of the participating families in a pre/post fashion, beginning in August 2000 (pre) and ending in August 2001 (post). Obtaining approval for my thesis proposal with this time line was significant because it placed a time limit on what was required of me. Earlier in my tenure at the Media Lab, I was told the thesis proposal is like a contract. Once the committee signs it and the department approves it, it represents an agreement between all parties of what is expected in order to graduate. This time line meant that as long as the project remained on schedule and I was prepared to conduct interviews in August 2000 and August 2001, I would be in a position to finish sometime in the fall of 2001.

To the second item, I wanted a committee that was knowledgeable about my area of research, genuinely interested in my development, but also committed to completion of the degree. Mitchel also informed me it was good practice to have at least two faculty from the Media Lab on a dissertation committee to neutralize any possible departmental politics. I contacted a number of individuals to join my committee, including a well-known community researcher/practitioner at Northwestern who worked with Nicol Turner, the instructor for my software engineering course, and even a former professor at Sloan with a related interest in technology and organizations. In the end, Mitchel was, of course, selected to chair my committee, whereas the remaining four members of my committee were all African American, including Brian,

Ceasar, Alan, and Dr. Holly Carter, the second African American woman to earn a Ph.D. from MIT and the former executive director of CTCNet. I chose these individuals for two reasons. First, they were impeccably qualified to advise my doctoral research. All of them were recognized as having direct, relevant experience with issues concerning community and technology. Second, they represented a nice combination of academics (Mitchel, Brian, and Ceasar) and practitioners (Alan and Holly), as well as a necessary mix of individuals with direct ties to the Media Lab (Mitchel and Brian as professors, and Alan as a graduate) and MIT (Ceasar as a professor and Holly as a graduate). I must admit I was also extremely proud that a committee consisting of predominantly African Americans was even possible.

Unfortunately, my thesis proposal was rejected. This concerned me because, as I mentioned earlier, the thesis proposal represented the last opportunity for the department to exert any influence in determining my fate. Once it was approved, the dissertation committee then had the power to designate me as Dr. Pinkett. After receiving word from Mitchel and meeting with him to discuss what changes needed to be made, he suggested I meet with one of the members of the departmental committee to better understand why my proposal wasn't approved. The feedback I received was that my committee was too large and I needed to submit additional documentation explaining why such a large committee was required. I was also told that my research methods were not well defined enough and somewhat skewed toward quantitative versus qualitative methods. Always mindful of timing and deadlines, I made sure I had a revised version of the proposal that addressed these concerns ready by the next departmental committee meeting. In my updated proposal, I explained that, given the nature of my research project, I needed broad representation on my committee to address both the academic and practical implications of my work. I also provided a more elaborate description of the quantitative and qualitative data collection and analysis techniques I would employ to prove my hypothesis. Two months later, my second thesis proposal was submitted to the department and approved.

My third major milestone was completing the design and implementation of the C3 system. Once again, I used my coursework as a means to reach another milestone. During the fall semester of 1999, I registered for a software engineering course in the Department of Electrical Engineering and Computer Science. This course focused on web applications. For my class project, I designed a prototype of the C3 system and worked with an African American female Ph.D. student at Northwestern University, Nicol Turner, to deploy the system at a housing development in Chicago, IL (Turner & Pinkett, 2000). One year later, I used this prototype as the basis for a second version of the system that would eventually be deployed at Camfield.

During the summer of 2000, I worked with a team of Camfield residents to gather content, redesign the system, and introduce additional functionality. I also spent countless hours at the Media Lab writing code and testing modules, oftentimes spending consecutive evenings camped out in my office. I completed the second version of the system in the fall of 2000, just one month after my thesis proposal was approved. Furthermore, I worked with the same resident team and Richard to administer a preliminary survey instrument in August 2000, thus remaining on schedule. This meant that as the New Year was ushered in for 2001, the only remaining tasks for me to complete were follow-up interviews in August 2001 and writing the dissertation.

Discipline: The Thesis Draft

In essence, I started writing my dissertation the moment after I identified my thesis topic. My strategy throughout my doctoral program was to use every opportunity to write about my work as a means to contribute to my thesis.

My proposed thesis was made up of ten chapters. Before I officially sat down to start writing these chapters, I had half of the document already written. Chapter 1, the introduction, Chapter 2, which included background information and a literature review, and Chapter 4, which described my research design and methodology, were all extracted from my publishable-quality general examination paper and thesis proposal. Chapter 3, which described my theoretical framework, was based on a paper I presented at the 2000 Annual Meeting of the American Educational Research Association (AERA) (Pinkett, 2000). Chapter 6, which analyzed the data from the preliminary assessment, was based on a paper I presented at the 2001 Annual Meeting of AERA (Pinkett,

2001). Clearly, the benefit of this approach was that it allowed me to pace my writing over a long period of time, as opposed to condensing it to a confined period or delaying it until the end.

To remain disciplined, I used a tip I picked up from a time management workshop: make deadlines public. I informed my dissertation committee and told my family and friends I wanted to have a draft of the first six chapters of my thesis completed by June 1, 2001 (the five chapters previously mentioned, and a sixth, Chapter 5, which described the C3 system architecture). While the June 1 date was somewhat arbitrary, I figured if I had a draft in my committee's hands by the beginning of the summer, I would have more than enough time to edit and revise these chapters. I would continue to work on the remaining four chapters, which included Chapter 7, an analysis of the post-assessment, Chapter 8, case studies of selected families, Chapter 9, lessons learned and recommendations, and Chapter 10, the conclusion. By making it public, the people were close to me kept me focused by checking on my progress and being mindful of my time as the date gradually approached. This strategy proved to be effective. Working almost around the clock from the living room of my apartment in Somerville, MA, and surrounded by an infinite number of academic papers and books spread across my table and floor, I delivered an initial draft of my thesis to my committee on June 1.

Writing, Writing, and More Writing

While most of my summer was focused on managing the Camfield Estates-MIT project, in July I began scheduling one-on-one meetings with the members of my committee to solicit and document their feedback on my initial draft. This was a timely and helpful endeavor. Timely, because a sufficient amount of writing still remained, and if I had to adjust my focus or writing style, it could still be done without having to rewrite the entire thesis. Moreover, because I had yet to conduct the post-assessment, I could ensure that the follow-up interviews covered the areas of importance to my committee. This was helpful because I was able to hear, firsthand, their thoughts about the project and the current direction of my thesis. This enabled me to structure the remaining chapters in a way that addressed their concerns. For example, most of my committee members expressed an interest in the attitudinal changes taking place among residents as a result of their participation. They regarded positive changes along these lines as contributing to the community's health, something I hadn't previously considered. Consequently, based on their feedback I modified my theoretical framing to include a discussion about these outcomes and added questions to the post-assessment survey instrument and case study protocol to sufficiently explore them as a line of inquiry.

In August, I began the arduous tasks of revising the initial draft, administering the final interviews, conducting in-depth interviews as a basis for developing case studies, analyzing the post-assessment data, and writing the remaining five chapters of the thesis. These tasks were performed with the ambitious goal of completing them by September 1, 2001. Once again, I notified my committee, family, and friends of my target date, even discussing with my girlfriend the possibility of having the entire month to focus solely on finishing. Once again, I worked almost literally around the clock, writing, writing, and writing.

Fortunately, MIT has an Undergraduate research opportunities program (UROP) that allows undergraduate students to contribute to research projects either for pay or for credit. During my last semester, I hired two undergraduates to assist me with developing computer programs to compile the survey data and generate tables, charts, and graphs. I also enlisted the help of my college roommate, Jeffrey Robinson, a Ph.D. candidate at Columbia's Business School. He gave me a crash course in statistics and how to use the Statistical Package for the Social Sciences (SPSS) to perform regressions and other data analyses. Without their combined help, I would have had to spend a larger amount of time shifting through data and determining an appropriate means to analyze it.

As a result of sheer determination and will, I missed my target date by only three days. I submitted a complete draft thesis to my committee on Tuesday, September 4, 2001, coincidentally, exactly one year from my first day as a graduate student at the Media Lab.

A Coming of Age

Holly strongly suggested I convene the entire committee to review and discuss this latest draft. This meeting took place on Friday, September 28, 2001. Prior to the meeting, Mitchel gave me the green light to poll the committee for potential defense dates. I interpreted this as a good sign I was nearing completion. The committee agreed to a tentative defense date of Monday, October 22, 2001, pending the results of the meeting.

I was incredibly nervous prior to the meeting because I recognized its significance. Would they like the draft? Would I be asked to obtain more data? Would my scheduled defense date hold? A few days before the meeting, I found out Mitchel had serious concerns about my theoretical framework and worried that it might come under scrutiny. At the Media Lab, thesis defenses include a public component, which includes a forty-minute presentation and questions and answers, followed by a private component, which includes questions and answers and deliberations by the committee only. Mitchel worried I might be challenged during the public question and answer period. As the chair of my dissertation committee, it was incumbent on me to address his concerns. To Mitchel's discredit, he shared his thoughts with the other members of the committee prior to the meeting, unbeknown to me and to some extent, undermining my credibility. I later discussed my frustrations at this move with one of the other committee members who calmly instructed me to stay focused on what needed to be done to overcome this hurdle and worry about Mitchel's maneuvering after a successful defense. To Mitchel's credit, he later affirmed his commitment to fully supporting me during the defense. He explained that his concerns were based on my (and his) best interests and his desire for the defense to be a positive experience with minimal problems.

The meeting lasted approximately three hours. Throughout the conversation, I was reminded of something Dr. Peter Henry, another fellow Rhodes Scholar and MIT Ph.D. in economics, told me when I bumped into him on campus shortly after his defense. He said, "In order to graduate, they [the members of your committee] have to see you as their equal. They have to believe that they can learn something from you, just as you have learned from them. Once they see you as an equal, you have won the hardest battle." During the meeting, I reminisced over Peter's words as I was constantly challenged by my committee and asked to defend the arguments laid out in my thesis. I came to realize that the real defense was taking place in that room and that the formal defense would be merely a rubber stamp once I made it through this process. Feeling myself moving closer to the culmination of my journey to the Ph.D., I grew more and more confident in defending the work I had so passionately pursued for the past three years. And during that conversation, I believe my committee began to truly see me as their equal.

The Final Stretch: The Defense

Despite positive, constructive feedback from the committee, the meeting ended with each member outlining required changes, including a complete rewrite of the introduction and conclusion, the addition of an eleventh chapter focused on the challenges and opportunities related to the project, and a reframing of my theoretical framework per Mitchel's concerns. Additionally, despite their confidence in my ability to produce quality work quickly, the committee did not believe I could complete these edits and obtain their feedback in time for an October 22 defense. Mitchel suggested December as a possible date to reschedule the defense. Not wanting to delay the event any longer than necessary, I argued my case for an earlier defense. With unwavering support from the other committee members, I was granted a defense date in early November. The October 22 date was then changed to a follow-up committee meeting to discuss the revised draft.

I spent the next three weeks feverishly working around the clock to edit the thesis based on the committee's feedback and produce a final draft. At the follow-up committee meeting in October, despite Mitchel's continued concerns about my theoretical framing, the November date stood and I was poised to complete the degree.

On November 5, 2001, I successfully defended my thesis in the presence of colleagues, family, and friends. As I had anticipated, the private segment was more congratulatory than deliberative. It also turned out that Mitchel's concerns, although appreciated, were unwarranted. I made it through the public question and answer period practically unscathed.

At the end of the private session with my committee, Mitchel told everyone the story of what his advisor, Professor Seymour Papert, said to him after his defense. Seymour told Mitchel about the thesis defense of Dr. Aaron Falbel, one of his students at the time. After Aaron's defense, Seymour said to him, "I would like to officially welcome you to the community of scholars." Aaron responded by asking, "What, I wasn't a member of the community of scholars before today?" Seymour replied by saying "No, you weren't welcome." Seymour then proceeded to say to Mitchel, "Welcome to the community of scholars Dr. Resnick." Similarly, Mitchel then proceeded to say to me, "Welcome to the community of scholars Dr. Pinkett," and on June 6, 2002, it was official.

References

Hooper, P. (1998). They have their own thoughts: Children's learning of computational ideas from a cultural constructionist perspective. Unpublished Ph.D. Dissertation. Cambridge, MA: MIT Media Laboratory.

MIT Center for Reflective Community Practice. (2002). CRCP Website. http://web.mit.edu/crcp/

MIT Epistemology and Learning Group. (1998). Epistemology and Learning Group Website. http://el.media.mit.edu

MIT Media Laboratory. (2002). MIT Media Laboratory Website. http://www.media.mit.edu

MIT Program in Media Arts and Sciences. (2002). General Information for Applicants. Cambridge, MA: MIT Program in Media Arts and Sciences.

Pinkett, R. D. (2000). Bridging the digital divide: Sociocultural constructionism and an asset-based approach to community technology and community building. Paper presented at the 81st Annual Meeting of the American Educational Research Association (AERA), New Orleans, LA, April 24–28. http://www.media.mit.edu/~rpinkett/papers/aera2000.pdf

Pinkett, R. D. (2001). Community technology and community building: Strategies for active participation in a low-income community. Paper presented at the 82nd Annual Meeting of the American Educational Research Association (AERA), Seattle, WA, April 12–15.

Resnick, M., & Rusk, N. (1996). Access is not enough: Computer clubhouses in the inner city. *American Prospect*, 27, July–August, 60–68.

Shaw, A. C. (1995). Social constructionism and the inner city: Designing environments for social development and urban renewal. Unpublished Ph.D. Dissertation. Cambridge, MA: MIT Media Laboratory.

Slavin, L. (2002). "Massachusetts Institute of Technology Honors Randal Pinkett, LFM Graduate, with MLK Leadership Award." Press Release, February 8.

Turner, N. E., & Pinkett, R. D. (2000). *An asset-based approach to community technology and community building.* Proceedings of Shaping the Network Society: The Future of the Public Sphere in Cyberspace, Directions and Implications of Advanced Computing Symposium 2000 (DIAC-2000), Seattle, WA, May 20–23. http://www.media.mit.edu/~rpinkett/papers/diac2000.pdf

PART II

ADAPTING TO THE ACADEMY

Stephen Hancock

Hometown: Richmond, Virginia
Current Institution: The Ohio State University
Department: Teacher Education
Personal Philosophy: Without the struggle to embrace the unknown, there is no progress toward freedom.

5

BALANCING ACT
A REFLECTIVE PRACTICE

A Family Affair

The alarm goes off at 7:00 A.M. and our day gets off to its normal routine. I move about the room in a methodic dance preparing to leave for work. My wife is up already because our 7-week-old son needs his 6:00 A.M. feeding, and our 3-year-old has preschool today so I must get her ready. It's been three months since I've ended my research and started data analysis and writing. I thought I had a foolproof plan to stay focused and write. Yet, I haven't written a thing in seven weeks. We've been busy with the daily and wonderful task of taking care of a new baby and a preschooler. Who has time, energy, focus, and the nerve to work on a "third child"—the dissertation?

My wife and I knew that our new baby would present additional challenges to completing the dissertation. We were also aware that my time and energy would have to be divided into two distinct groups—family and dissertation. However, in order to maximize family and writing times we reflected on the goals and purposes of our family and what it would take to complete the dissertation. Our reflective practice revealed that in order to complete this dissertation as a family we must first understand the sacrifice, workload, and energy required to complete our various tasks. In an effort to understand the requirements of writing a dissertation, my wife sat in on the dissertation workshop provided by the university. To hear others lament, discuss, and inquire about pathways to completing a dissertation was helpful in her understanding of what I must endure. To understand what it takes to take care of two young children, household chores, and keeping me abreast, I spent time with the children and managed the house. Our participation in each other's world brought about deeper and more personal understanding of what is required of each of us.

Participating in reflective practice also revealed that we must not only understand each other's tasks but also respect the time, needs, and energy required to complete the work. To provide my wife with time and relaxation, our preschooler and I have planned activities out of the house every Monday evening. On Tuesday and Thursday my wife leaves for an hour-long water aerobics class. On these three occasions during the week I spend quality time with our children to continue developing healthy relationships. The times set aside for me to work on my dissertation are on Wednesday from 4:00 P.M. to 6:00 P.M. After dinner on Wednesday evenings, our family prepares to go to our 7:00 P.M. bible study. Friday afternoons from 4:00 P.M. to 7:00 P.M. and Saturday mornings from 9:00 A.M. to 12:00 P.M. are also times when I work on my dissertation. On Friday nights my wife and I try to spend time together (however it rarely happens). Saturday and Sunday afternoons are family times, and if energy and interest abound I'm usually up until 1:00 A.M. on any given night working on my dissertation.

Although it's sometimes hard to convince a 3-year-old that what I'm doing is for our family's benefit, difficult to stop playing with a 7-week-old to edit a paragraph, and down right cruel to leave a beautiful woman in a warm bed just to finish a chapter, we all believe that the sacrifice will be worth it in the end.

A Reflective Practice

I do not believe that I would be able to take this academic journey without God, my wife and children, my mother and siblings, friends, and the practice of critical self-reflection. If you can imagine a seesaw, with the plank or board holding school and job on one end and family, church, and social life on the other end—what balances these two sides is reflective practice. Reflective practice is a process of deep thinking about what, why, and how we are doing (Hunt, Touzel, & Wiseman, 1999). It is also the practice of critical self-analysis that leads to a series of questions that challenge current beliefs, attitudes, and practices (Stremmel, 1997). I have found reflective practice to be a force of autonomy and the ultimate balancing act in my life as a graduate student.

In this chapter I express how reflective practice has and continues to be an integral process in my development as a teacher, student, and person. In the first section I describe how reflective practice created a space for me to begin a journey from my comfort zone to the process of embracing challenge and autonomy. In the second section I describe how as a graduate assistant and supervisor of student teachers I had to find balance in my desire to educate student teachers and their naïveté, lack of desire, and inability to see themselves as effective teachers of diverse students.

It is my hope that as you read this chapter you will find a sense of relevancy that can enable you to balance the chaos that comes from inner convictions and external realities.

A Narrative Vignette: When I Look Back Over My Life

As an African American man in a Predominately White Institution (PWI), there is a need to be accepted and affirmed for how I perceive the world. Having gone through the culture shock of a PWI as an undergraduate, I was experienced in finding and securing cultural affirmation at church, work, and even in the academy. Entering the doctoral program at The Ohio State University, however, posed a greater dilemma. Not only did I have to carve out an academic place for myself, I also had to deal with the reality that I was a Black man in an "Ivory Tower"—not a physical "tower," rather, the ivory tower as a psychosocial reality of Eurocentric ideology. The ivory tower ideology creates conflicts with the nature of African American reality. The thought that I would have to assimilate into this elite and exclusive reality strove against my ideals of reciprocity toward my community. I began to ask such agonizing pathos as: How can I balance my inner convictions and still be an academician? Do I have to compromise my beliefs and values to be heard? Are the experiences of African American people valued and affirmed in the academy? These questions hurled me into a reflective journey as to how, why, and who I was becoming.

Surprisingly, after two courses, I found that my experiences and participation was a valued asset in class discussions. For the first time in my graduate career I had balance with my inner convictions and my expressions of them. I remember participating in a class discussion on teachers and the concept of multiculturalism. Unfamiliar with the term reflective practice, I rambled on to express the notion that teachers must know their own biases and prejudices before they can effectively meet the needs of a diverse student population. I went on to say, "One of the best ways teachers can know themselves is through a critical analysis of self." At that moment, I felt liberated and empowered. I was able to academically express myself without compromising my convictions. I've learned through this experience that although I may have to compromise the delivery for the sake of acceptance and professionalism, I don't have to negotiate the conviction that motivated the idea. From that moment until now, the process of being empowered through the act of reflective practice continues to keep me balanced.

The Autonomous Self

In life through personal, professional, and academic pursuits there is an inner longing to be needed, accepted, and affirmed for who we are, why we are, and how we are. Who we are is an intricate weaving of self-perceptions, gender, family dynamics, and internal will. Why we are encompasses our compassions, convictions, integrity, and beliefs. How we are involves our attitudes, perspectives, ways of knowing, and socially constructed behavior patterns. These concepts are all woven into the notion of self. A need to know self as we relate to people, places, and experiences compels us to move toward a place of affirmation, acceptance, and usefulness. It is in our quest for an autonomous self that hurdles of ignorance, fear, selfishness, and greed often hinder our desire to "know as we are known" (Palmer, 1993). Nonetheless, our inner longings never cease striving, forging, and pushing us toward a place of congruency—a place where self finds wholeness, and the wonder of who, what, and why we are is manifested and realized in its most excellent form. When we are able to grow, reach beyond the glass ceiling, and soar above pretentious expectations into a realm of freedom and liberation, then we will find our autonomous selves.

> To be autonomous is to be self-directed and responsible; it is to be capable of acting in accord with internalized norms and principles; it is to be insightful enough to know and understand one's impulses, one's motives, and the influences of one's past. (Maxine Greene, 1988, p. 118)

It is the journey of our lives to arrive at a place where we can congruently coexist with our internalized norms and principles as well as the external norms of society. However, this requires that we move from a place of interpersonal safety and begin a process of intellectual and cultural transformation. We must embrace the notion of change and allow it to walk us through phases of life that will bring us from the safe self to the autonomous self. In order to move beyond our comfort zones and places of complacency we must first engage in intellectual and cultural challenges. These challenges will begin a process of transformation that can bring us to a place of wholeness. Maxine Greene (1988) describes this place as autonomous. This autonomous self signifies that we have moved beyond fear, insecurities, racist ideals, and self-pity into a reality that fosters freedom, power, and internal peace. Here we occupy a place where we live, move, and can be without the manipulation of some external factor or alternative motive. In a place of authentic living, our inner thoughts, convictions, beliefs, and desires are congruent with the world around us. Authentic living is a reality where we neither compromise nor negotiate our fundamental principles and values for the sake of external appeasement. Greene (1988) contends:

> Values like independence, self-sufficiency, and authenticity are associated with autonomy, because the truly autonomous person is not supposed to be susceptible to outside manipulations and compulsions. Indeed, he/she can, by maintaining a calm and rational stance, transcend compulsions and complexes that might otherwise interfere with judgment and clarity. (p. 118)

This place houses the voice of freedom and self-assurance. It's a place of comfort, not complacency; a place of revolution, not militancy; a place of dignity, not denial; a place that embraces process, not attainment. Here in this reality, we emerge from the safe self and venture into a transformative process that produces an identity poised for unfettered consciousness. As a result, we are able to live in an ever-changing and complex reality where our intellect and culture can coexist simultaneously and in harmony. An "autonomous self" neither exists with chains of intellectual elitism nor lives tied to a monolithic perspective of culture. Rather, an autonomous conscious is able to make peace within, in an effort to make changes without.

Finally, in an effort to nurture an unfettered consciousness, as students, teachers, and researchers we must find balance with the academy and life. This balancing act must create a place where we become learners for our lives and not merely academics for the sake of the academy. In our pursuit of graduate degrees we must participate in reflective practice by asking ourselves this question: Am I being trained for the academy or educated for life? Na'im Akbar (1998) explains the difference between being trained and educated in this analogy:

> The dog that learns how to bark to scare away its enemies (predators), to defend itself by biting its attackers and to hunt and to feed itself is an *educated* dog. The dog that learns how to stand on its hind legs and wear a dress and dance to the music of its trainer is actually a *trained* dog. Despite how impressive the dancing dog may appear to the human observer, this dog has been trained away from its nature . . . . Such a dog is what Dr. Woodson described as being miseducated because the dog can perform at someone else's command but cannot effectively command itself to do what is required for its life and enhancement. (p. 2)

I believe that it is the duty of us all to give back and to enhance the life of our brothers and sisters. However, if we allow the academy to train us for the sake of spinning intellectual wheels in the Ivory Tower, we will lose our autonomy and smother our convictions. It is the challenge for us all to find ourselves in a place where our inner purpose matches our graduate and postgraduate work.

A Narrative Vignette: Made Me Wanna Holler

It had been three months into my sabbatical from my career as a kindergarten teacher and as many months as a university supervisor of student teachers. Residency at Ohio State was a busy yet exhilarating experience of balancing university teaching, being a student, and supervising student teachers. Supervising student teachers was a wonderful opportunity to learn and teach. I was assigned six students who were placed in the Columbus Public School district. I often thought and never took lightly the possibility that my guidance could influence a prospective teacher and have an affect on her future students.

As a supervisor of student teachers and observer of cooperating teachers, I was afforded opportunities to hear, see, and address issues that occurred in the day-to-day dynamics of classroom life. The number one issue that plagued most of my student teachers was discipline. One student said, "I just don't know how to handle this age group." Another student confessed, "They're (African American students) not like the students I had in summer camp." After addressing their lack of disciplinarian skills with articles, books, and conversation concerning African American children and school, I decided to model how I would handle the class.

A week later, I was perplexed to see that the student continued in her previous manner. When I asked her if she was trying to practice culturally relevant disciplinary methods she said, "It's not me, I can't do what you did, and I can't relate to some of the articles." While I dealt with this as a supervisor of student teachers, students in my course were complaining that Black parents didn't care, poverty was the cause of bad behavior, and many other uninformed complaints for their lack of discipline. "It made me wanna holler and throw up both my hands" (McCall, 1994, p. 404).

I pondered how I would usher these prospective teachers into a place where they could begin a journey into self in an effort to understand others. I decided to do research and produce a paper to introduce my class and student teachers to the idea of reflective practice. Being aware of my audience, I delivered this paper with an academic voice and the convictions of one who believes that if we don't reflect on our own prejudices, ignorance, and fear we will be ineffective teachers for diverse student populations.

Reflective Practice Meets Teacher, Student, and Teacher Education

The term *reflective teaching* has been embraced by teachers, researchers, and teacher educators all over the world (Zeichner, 1994). On the surface, reflective teaching purports that teachers are salient components in formulating the purpose and ends of their work, and that teachers must become leaders in curriculum development and school reform (Zeichner, 1996). However, Zeichner (1996) has found that "in reality one cannot tell very much about an approach to teaching or teacher education from an expressed commitment to the idea of teachers as reflective practitioners" (p. 200).

Zeichner (1996) warns us "that all teachers reflect in some sense" (p. 207). He further contends that we cannot focus on reflective teaching as a new phenomenon or support it with dogmatic definitions. Rather, Zeichner and Liston (1996) believe that teacher education programs must begin to ask what types of reflection teachers are practicing, what teachers are reflecting about, and how they are going about reflecting. These questions create critical perspectives that enable teachers opportunities to process reflective teaching on a metacognitive level. Zeichner (1996) believes that without a critical perspective on reflective teaching, teachers and teacher educators should not be given responsibility for reforming curriculum, instructional design, and teacher education programs.

In this discussion of reflective practice, I have grounded my perspective with researchers, theorists, and educators who support an approach of reflection that is sensitive to students' interests and emancipatory and critical of self (Zeichner, 1996). It is my belief that the social reconstructionist tradition of reflective practice has great benefits for students, teachers, and teacher education programs. "Its commitment to collaborative modes of learning indicates a dual commitment by teacher educators to an ethic where social justice on the one hand and care and compassion on the other are valued" (Zeichner, 1996, p. 208).

Cruickshank (1987) argues that teacher preparation programs must produce high-quality teachers that have the ability to critically examine their actions in an effort to enhance or change their teaching practices. "Reflective teachers think deeply about what they are doing; reflective teachers are thoughtful, analytical, self-critical, and informed decision makers" (Hunt, Touzel, & Wiseman, 1999, p. 6). Woolfolk (1998) suggests that "reflective teachers think back over situations to analyze what they did and why and to consider how they might improve learning for their students" (p. 8). Finally, Schon (1983) concludes that reflective teaching is reflection-in-action. Reflection-in-action is an active process where the teacher reflects on his or her knowledge in an effort to discover limits and pursue growth.

In an effort to reform the teacher education program at the University of Florida, Ross and Bondy (1996) investigated how reflective teaching was a salient component in the Elementary PROTEACH program. In stage two of PROTEACH, students were assisted in understanding what reflection looked liked, how to reflect, and the value of

personal and professional reflection (Ross & Bondy, 1996). In addition, prospective teachers were exposed to ideas that "teaching implies
mastery not only of performance and procedure, but also of content
and rationale; the teacher should employ reasoned judgment rather
than just display prescribed behavior" (Rud, 1992, p. 46). Ross (1989)
contends that faculty viewed reflective teaching as "a way of thinking
about educational matters that involves the ability to make rational
choices and to assume responsibility for those choices" (p. 26). For
both prospective teachers and teacher educators, reflective teaching
"involves high level thought processes where practitioners recognize
and possess skills, competencies, and knowledge essential to effective
practice" (Hunt, Touzel, & Wiseman, 1999, pp. 6–7).

The main focus of reform in the PROTEACH program was "to clarify the nature of reflection and to find ways to help students become
more reflective" (Ross & Bondy, 1996, p. 65). The faculty introduced
prospective teachers to reflective practice in their initial semester
through "a variety of strategies, such as reflective writing, curriculum
development and analysis, development of action research projects, and
faculty modeling" (Ross & Bondy, 1996, p. 65). The focus on teacher
preparation reform was so extensive that Ross and Bondy (1996)
report additional strategies that guided the focus on reflective teaching:
"(1) use of collaboratively developed core courses to increase programmatic coherence, (2) provision of training for supervisors of field experiences to foster coherence between course work and field experience,
and (3) the provision of ongoing support to program graduates" (p. 65).
These additional strategies proved imperative in the development of traditions and values that help prospective teachers and teacher educators
form programmatic cohesion (Conway, 1990).

Any discussion that focuses on reflective practices in the preparation
of prospective teachers must provide discourse on the relationship
between teacher and student (Schon, 1983). In the social reconstructionist traditions of reflective teaching the teacher and student interactions are a core component (Zeichner, 1996). It is important to highlight
that reflective teaching lessens the rewards of authority, "the freedom
to practice without challenges to competence, the comfort of relative
invulnerability, and the gratifications of deference" (Schon, 1983, p. 299).
Prospective teachers and university professors must be aware that

reflective practice as a reform effort in teacher education compels teachers to rethink personal perspectives, invite student empowerment, and challenge status quo teaching methods (Schon, 1983; Zeichner, 1996). In an effort to effectively deliver curriculum to a diverse population, teachers are challenged to build critical relationships based on reflective practice (Schon, 1983). Noddings (1992) contends that students are set free to pursue their own growth when reflective practice is a factor in the student-teacher relationship. Schon (1983) provides a critical perspective on how universities with and without reflective practice prepare teachers for professional relationships (see Table 5.1). Schon (1983) uses the term *expert* in reference to attitudes and beliefs that knowledge is elitist and exclusive. He counters this perspective with

Table 5.1   The Reflective Practitioner (Schon, 1983)

Expert	*Reflective practitioner*
I am presumed to know, and must claim to do so, regardless of my own uncertainty.	I am presumed to know, but I am not the only one in the situation to have relevant and important knowledge. My uncertainties may be a source of learning for me and for them.
Keep my distance from the client (student) and hold onto the expert's role. Give the client a sense of my expertise, but convey a feeling of warmth and sympathy as a "sweetener."	Seek out connections to the client's (student) thoughts and feelings. Allow his respect for my knowledge to emerge from his discovery of it in the situation.
Look for deference and status in the client's response to my professional persona.	Look for the sense of freedom and of real connection to the client, as a consequence of no longer needing to maintain a professional façade.

the notion of reflective practice and the need for inclusion and creation of genuine connections. Although "teacher-student relation is, of necessity, unequal" (Noddings, 1992, p. 107), teacher as a reflective practitioner enables students and teachers the opportunity to nurture mature connections and freedom of discovery (Noddings, 1992; Schon, 1983).

Just as reflective practice demands alternative competencies and interactions for the teacher, it also changes and challenges the traditional concept of students (Schon, 1983). When teachers become reflective practitioners they compel students to be responsible for and contribute to their own growth (Noddings, 1992). And, although "the contributions of teachers and students are necessarily unequal, they are nonetheless mutual; the relationship is marked by reciprocity" (Noddings, 1992, p. 108). Schon (1983) suggests that when students are participants in reflective practice they must be able to challenge expert knowledge without causing hostile or defensive attitudes. Noddings (1992) says that students must not be passive spectators; rather, they must accept responsibility for communicating their intellectual, social, and personal needs to teachers.

It is evident that the reflective practice movement as related to teacher education reform produces challenges, insight, and new perspectives on teaching and learning. Stremmel (1997) believes that these challenges, insights, and perspectives should not only compel teachers to alter teaching strategies and methods, but they should also engage teachers in a journey of self-awareness and cultural sensitivity.

The concept of reflective practice brings about a deep understanding of one's own experiences, which then gives a slow but purposeful birth to true consciousness (Ahlquist, 1991). Stremmel (1997) argues that prior to the use of reflective practice as a means to understand diversity, teacher education programs must expose prospective teachers to the many cultural and historical experiences that shape their own reality, teach them that child development occurs in a sociocultural context, and reveal to prospective teachers that diversity awareness is a lifelong, dynamic process that moves us from mono-perspectives to multiple perspectives. In an effort to become sensitive to multicultural issues, teacher education programs must also systematically and critically explore their attitudes, beliefs, and practices in order to move toward cultural awareness and multiculturalism (Stremmel, 1997). Smyth

(1992) claims that teachers should ask these questions as they begin the process of reflective practice:

- What do I believe?
- How have I come to believe this? Where do these beliefs come from?
- What do my daily actions say about what I believe and value?
- What contributes to the tenacity of my beliefs? (What has influenced me to maintain certain beliefs?)
- How do my beliefs constrain what is possible (i.e., restrict my freedom to make choices and take actions that would move me toward greater multicultural understanding)?[1]

The use of these questions in reflective practice is essential to the development and nurturing of multicultural teachers. Stremmel (1997) argues:

> . . . teachers thoughtfully and carefully examine their own system of values, attitudes and beliefs, they cannot begin to understand and be responsive to the perspectives and needs of diverse children. Self-reflection is advocated as an ongoing and deliberate means to help teachers develop cultural self-awareness and to critically examine how their cultural realities may influence their teaching practices. (p. 364)

It is incumbent upon teacher education programs to provide prospective teachers with the practical and applicable tools of reflective practice so that they will become aware of the degree of their beliefs, actions, and patterns as they relate to diverse student populations (Smyth, 1992).

Conclusion

In the process of reflective practice, as we seek to become better students, spouses, parents, and employees, our goal must drive us to a place of autonomy and liberation. I have found that this walk through the hallowed walls of the ivory tower (literally and figuratively) required me as an African American man to know who, how, and why I am in order to navigate racism, fears, and ignorance. Although self-reflection is not embraced by everyone, I concur with Stremmel (1997) that

> Self-reflection is a dialectical mental process that allows one to challenge, reinterpret, reframe, and reconstruct assumptions, attitudes, beliefs, and values. Through reflection, individuals subject their action and belief systems to critical assessment. Because reflection invites self-examination, it may lead to greater self-awareness, open-mindedness, introspection, and an enlightened attitude. (p. 369)

Self-reflection has enabled me to position myself in the academy where I exist harmoniously. As a candidate venturing into the realm of dissertation writing, the act of balancing my life has and will continue to come through self-reflection.

Note

1.   These questions are found in Stremmel (1997) pp. 369–370.

References

Ahlquist, R. (1991). Position and imposition: Power relations in a multicultural foundations class. *Journal of Negro Education, 60*(2), 158–169.

Akbar, N. (1998). *Know thyself.* Florida: Mind Production and Associates, Incorporated.

Conway, J. (1990). Organization rites as culture markers of schools. *Urban Education, 25*(2), 195–196.

Cruickshank, D. (1987). *Reflective teaching: The preparation of students for teaching.* Reston, VA: Association of Teacher Educators.

Greene, M. (1988). *The dialectic of freedom.* New York: Teachers College Press.

Hunt, G., Touzel, T., & Wiseman, D. (1999). *Effective teaching: Preparation and implementation.* Springfield, IL: Charles C. Thomas Publisher, LTD.

McCall, N. (1994). *Makes me wanna holler.* New York: Random House, Incorporated.

Noddings, N. (1992). *The challenge to care in schools: An alternative approach to education.* New York: Teachers College Press.

Palmer, P. (1993). *To know as we are known: Education as a spiritual journey.* San Francisco: Harper Collins Publisher.

Ross, D. (1989). First steps in developing a reflective approach to teaching. *Journal of Teacher Education, 40*(2), 22–30.

Ross, D., & Bondy, E. (1996). The continuing reform of a university teacher education program: A case study. In K. Zeichner, S. Melnick, & M. Gomez (Eds.), *Currents of reform in preservice teacher education.* New York: Teachers College Press.

Rud, A., & Oldendorf, W. (1992). *A place for teacher renewal: Challenging the intellect, creating educational reform.* New York: Teachers College Press.

Schon, D. (1983). *The reflective practitioner: How professionals think in action.* New York: Basic Books.

Smyth, J. (1992). Teacher's work and the politics of reflection. *American Educational Research Journal, 29,* 267–300.

Stremmel, A. (1997). Diversity and the multicultural perspective. In C. Hart, D. Burts, & R. Charlesworth (Eds.), *Integrated curriculum and developmentally appropriate practice: Birth to eight* (pp. 363–388). New York: State University of New York Press.

Woolfolk, A. (1998). *Educational psychology* (7th ed.). Boston: Allyn & Bacon.

Zeichner, K. (1994). Conceptions of reflective practice in teaching and teacher education. In G. Harvard, & P. Hodkinson (Eds.), *Action and reflection in teacher education* (pp. 15–34). Norwood, NJ: Ablex.

Zeichner, K. (1996). *Educating teachers for cultural diversity.* East Lansing, MI: National Center for Research on Teacher Learning.

Zeichner, K., & Liston, D. (1996). *Reflective Teaching.* Mahwah, NJ: Erlbaum Associates.

Catherine Cushinberry

Hometown: Memphis, Tennessee
Current Institution: University of Missouri at Columbia
Department: Human Development and Family Studies
Personal Philosophy: I'd rather be hated for who I am, than to be loved for who I am not.
—Anonymous

6

MAINTAINING MY IDENTITY

ENHANCED BY THE SYSTEM, BUT NOT LOST IN IT

I am the product of the prayers, discipline, love, and hope of my mother, extended, and church family. I am a dream realized. As a qualitative researcher, I believe it is important to know biographical information about the writer. From biographical information, you gain a perspective of what frames my interpretations of my experiences as a single, African American woman at my traditionally Predominately White Institution.

I am the first in my family and my church to pursue a doctorate. I mention both my blood and fictive families because similar to many single-parent African American households, my mother had the support of others. Extended family and fictive kin support is a strength of many African American families (DeGenova, 1997). Both families were instrumental in nurturing me.

Religion and my religious beliefs guide many of my decisions and my worldview. I do not believe that my life is without the guidance and leadership of God. I believe that there is nothing too hard for me to deal with, regardless of the circumstances. Among the many white faces at my institution, I know that I am not a stranger to God, nor is He deaf to my voice. My extended family, particularly, my maternal side, continuously supports my academic goals. I cannot recall a time in my life when I was told that I could not achieve a goal or dream. It is from that perspective that I work toward a Ph.D. in Family Studies in a department where I am one of three African Americans at an institution where less than 4 percent of the graduate students are African American.

I have learned as an African American doctoral student that lack of adaptation is futile in academia. Basic junior and high school biology note that certain animals and species thrive under certain conditions. When placed in a different environment, adjustments to new surroundings are critical to survival. The institution of graduate school was not developed for the African American scholar, and it has become particularly evident to me that I am embedded in a system that demands that I adapt or fail.

Resolving the Question, "Am I in the Right Place?"

Throughout my collegiate career, I have attended Predominately White Institutions. The universities where I received my bachelor's and master's degrees pale in comparison to the rigor of the graduate program at this Research One institution where research is highly emphasized.

When I received word that I was accepted into the program, I was so excited because I could tell both families that I was going back to school to get the coveted doctoral degree. I knew I was embarking on a wonderful experience that would propel me among an "elite" group of African Americans. My excitement eventually turned into reevaluation. When I arrived and began interacting with the graduate students in my department, I found myself surrounded by White graduate students, many of whom were Ph.D. students either trained at other research universities or former master's students from our department. I was intimidated by the level of knowledge they had of the field. They all seemed so confident. I knew it would be a challenge for me to get to where many of them were academically.

I was learning a new field. The faculty was aware of my limited research background and knowledge of family studies. They designed my first semester of course work so that I could become acclimated to the field. The first semester I took two undergraduate courses. When they informed me of this schedule, I felt awkward, and a little prideful, but I knew it was in my best interest, and it was.

As I sat in courses and exposed myself to readings outside of the classroom, over time I began to gain more knowledge of the field. When my preliminary courses were completed, I began taking graduate courses. My feelings of inadequacy were soon dissolved. I noticed that students who I thought to be confident were unsure of themselves. They questioned their abilities and shared those concerns with me.

Over the past three years some of the students who I considered exceptional writers and researchers dropped out of the program. Initially I had made myself believe that at some level, they were better or more worthy than me of a Ph.D. A valuable lesson was learned. I have come to realize that graduate school is not a race against others, nor is it about who is the "smartest," but rather a challenge of personal persistence. It is an individual endurance race.

Overcoming the Language Barrier

In addition to dealing with the question of whether I belonged in a Ph.D. program, I had to readdress the issue of language and power. Philosopher Michael Foucault stated that those who control language have power over what is acceptable and unacceptable. Those who create language and ways of speaking can create contexts that are specific to their experiences. People who are not exposed regularly to that language or involved in the development of that language are excluded and may be perceived or may perceive themselves as inferior.

I grew up in a Southern, predominately African American neighborhood where slang and what has now been termed ebonics, was a part of everyday language. Although my mother is an educator, she worked mostly with African American elementary students and was not immersed in the language adopted by higher education. One challenge in graduate school is understanding, accepting, and adopting jargon that is commonly created and used among White academicians within each field and within the institution as a whole. For me, terms such as "dovetailing," "comparing apples to oranges," "pigeon-holing," and "tongue in cheek," were foreign.

My first introduction to jargon was during my master's program. I sat in a rhetoric class and I was the only African American (which was usually the case), and my White professor and my White classmates kept using the phrase "tongue in cheek." I was completely lost. I did not have a clue what they meant. I tried to gather contextual clues, but they all appeared to be using the phrase in different ways. Finally, I asked what they meant by the phrase. Three people gave three completely different answers. One stated that the term meant that they were speaking without total certainty. Another used it to mean that it is to say something lightheartedly. The third person could not give a concise explanation of their use of the phrase. They were all using the term, but failed to recognize that they were using it differently.

I had sat in the class feeling subordinate to them because I did not understand the phrase, but by asking for clarity, I gained a stronger sense of self-confidence. That was my first experience with White peers and a White professor using jargon that was unfamiliar to me. The use of that language initially excluded me from the discussion, but I learned that terms are used as ways of exercising what to some is perceived as intelligent talk. As a doctoral student, I am inundated with jargon from peers and professors. I do not, however, allow myself to feel less intelligent than my White colleagues. I ask questions and sometimes challenge the language that excludes those of us who were not raised in an academic environment. Other obstacles that occurred were research topics and interests. Research studies discussed in the classroom can often be critiqued based on the lack of racial and ethnic representation. Particularly in my field, many of the studies use White, middle-class families as samples. Theories, concepts, statistical measurements, and training in those three areas are handicapped and submersed in the White, middle-class perspective. Often racial and ethnic discussions are neglected in the classroom. They are usually absent from course content unless the course is about multiculturalism or race. White peers have alluded to me that everything is not about race. I disagree. Many issues in the academy are the result of bias because of race whether it is methodological or theoretical. Ignorance and denial of that reality further infects the institution with a White ethnocentric view of the world.

The African American Female Student and White Male Advisor Relationship

Mentoring is described as a positive socializing experience between a novice and a wiser person for the purpose of learning traditions and frameworks of a profession (Brown II, Davis, & McClendon, 1999). In a case study of women doctoral students, Bruce (1995) noted a supportive mentor offered opportunities for overall personal and professional growth. Doctoral advisors usually serve as mentors. I believe the most effective advisor–advisee relationships must encourage, promote, and incorporate a mentor–mentee relationship into the advising environment.

There are some African American doctoral students with African American advisors, but that has not been my experience. My advisor is a White, middle-class, male. Researchers have noted that advisor–advisee relationships are problematic when the advisor is a White male and the advisee is an African American female (Bruce, 1995). When I entered my program, there was only one African American professor, and she and I do not share similar research interests. I was not going to choose an advisor based on race. I desired to have a positive, healthy, and supportive relationship with whoever would serve as my advisor. I had encountered a professor during my master's program who did not want me to change advisors. She saw me as a commodity and ignored that we had dissimilar interests. Thankfully, I followed my instincts, made the choice to change advisors, and stood firm on my decision. I was determined to make the same decision as a doctoral student if necessary. I had decided that if I did not feel comfortable with and have confidence in my advisor, I would select a new advisor.

In my department, advisors are assigned, but only as a way of helping students immediately connect with the department. During my visit to campus prior to joining the department, I met with professors and the man who would become my advisor. When I first met him, I wanted to be open-minded despite my reservations. He and I sat and talked. I asked questions about his expectations of students and what he has observed as characteristics of successful students in the department. I shared my experiences at my past institution. When he shared that the department encourages students to change advisors if interests change or personalities are not a good fit, I felt a sense of relief.

He was personable and had a rich sense of humor. Those two characteristics are important to me. I felt comfortable with him. I was not sure how the relationship would change over time, but we had gotten off to a good start. I admit that I am not exempt from stereotypes, nor am I oblivious to the words shared by others that a White, male advisor would not be supportive of me, an African American female. However, my options were limited and I knew that I would help mold the relationship to something that would be beneficial for us both.

I have been proactive in building a working relationship with my advisor. Over the past three years, I have made him aware of my interests to publish and work with him on projects. Embedded in our doctoral program are six hours of research practicum time. We have the opportunity to work with faculty on research projects. I was determined to work with my advisor for a practicum. I e-mailed him constantly and met with him weekly to stay abreast of projects he was working on. I would remind him of my desire to work on projects. In response to my requests, as projects surfaced that matched my interests, he would solicit my participation. He included me in on a collaborative research project for a poster to be presented at our national conference, the National Conference on Family Relations (NCFR). He was co-editing a book and asked me to co-author a book chapter with other graduate students. I am currently working on an article with him and preparing to begin a second.

He introduces me to others in the field during national conferences. Although I make efforts to meet scholars at the conference, I appreciate his efforts to make me visible and comfortable in professional settings. My advisor is respected in our field and contributes through publications and academic addresses. I am fortunate to have him as an advisor and mentor.

I encourage constant and constructive feedback from him. He has been an outstanding motivator, critic, and sponsor. Through our regular meetings he has become familiar with my personality and vice versa. It is with his guidance that I am growing as a scholar and researcher. Our relationship has blossomed into one of mutual respect and admiration. He challenges me, and I respect his professional and personal opinions.

Supportive mentors are said to offer opportunities for growth of self-awareness and identity, inspiration, and to assist with professional development by offering visibility, protection, and sponsorship (Bruce, 1995). My advisor embodies those characteristics. I continue to be proactive in maintaining a healthy relationship with him. He recognized my sincerity and desire as a student, and has unselfishly reciprocated.

Striking a Balance

I try to keep my advisor marginally aware of personal matters that may influence my performance. I believe there is a fine line between advisor/ advisee relationship and being close personal friends. He is my advisor. If, however, there is something occurring in my life that hinders or affects my performance in any way, I make him aware. Otherwise, my personal life is mine. I do not feel like my entire life should be made available to him or my department. Having a life outside of the department helps me maintain a sense of balance between my school and personal lives.

I admit that with my advisor I do think about how he perceives me as an African American student. I do not want to be seen as a slacker or a whiner. Nevertheless, I balance those thoughts with the reality that there is life after graduate school, and trying to carry the weight of being the "perfect little African American doctoral student" is not worth my sanity or sense of self-worth. I attended a discussion on critical issues in higher education sponsored by our graduate school, and a speaker noted that the suicide rates of graduate students on predominately White campuses are higher than suicide rates for nongraduate students. I take my program seriously, but I do not sacrifice my mental well-being. There is a great deal of liberty in the schedule of a full-time graduate student. I try to enjoy my time and use it wisely.

Service and Involvement—"Am I a Token?"

I have been offered opportunities to teach, serve on committees, and participate in university events. There is currently a movement on college campuses to discuss diversity and the need for diversity. I say "discuss" because that seems to occur more often than actions toward diversification. Initially, I dealt with the question of whether I was a "token" for the diversity picture the university or department wanted to paint. In 2000, I was awarded a scholarship. I thought my academic performance for my first year was mediocre, so I wondered why I was offered a scholarship. I called my mom because I thought there were others who were more deserving than I, in my opinion. I knew my mom would offer sound advice and wisdom. Referring to our religious beliefs, she quickly helped me dispel my concern about tokenism. She reminded me that I am fearfully and wonderfully made, and that it is God who promotes. I am thankful and grateful for the support of my mother. As an aside, my mother has a saying "bring that college home," which translates into "bring that doctoral degree into our family." Her words ring in my head daily and motivate me and remind me that I am worthy of this and other opportunities.

When asked to serve on committees or in other areas where I would be the only person of color, I try to balance common sense with assessments of professional development opportunities when making my decision. For me, the question of whether I am a token is a matter of perception. If there are opportunities that are beneficial to me as a professional, I participate. I do not, however, serve on committees just to serve. I must believe that my ideas and concerns will be given merit. When I do not feel that my suggestions will be considered, I decline to participate. As a matter of perception, if I have no voice, I am a token. I choose to have a voice.

Creating Opportunities

Many valuable opportunities lie in wait in departments. As students, with bills and other obligations, we often search out assistantships, grants, and fellowships. We seek established, paid teaching and research positions. Those paid positions often serve dual purposes. They provide financial support and add to our professional credentials. I regularly review my curriculum vita, often referred to as a CV. The curriculum vita is similar to a resume except it emphasizes academic experiences over work experiences. I refer to my CV to see if goals I have set for myself are reflected in that document.

If there are areas that are underdeveloped, I contemplate ways to fill those gaps. For example, next semester, there is a course offered in my department that focuses on my research interests. It is a graduate-level course, co-taught by two of the leading researchers in stepfamily research, one of whom is my advisor. In our department, graduate courses rarely have graduate assistants because money is usually not allocated for those courses in part because of the small class sizes. I contacted the professors teaching the course and offered my services as a graduate assistant, free of charge, in exchange for adding it to my CV. Although it is at some cost to my time, I believe the benefits outweigh the costs.

In my department, we are offered opportunities to teach undergraduate courses. I have taught three courses for my department, and am preparing for a fourth. Two of the three classes I taught were large lecture courses with over 120 students enrolled. Over 97 percent of my students are White. I recognize that solely based on my race, students may perceive me as incompetent. However, I also recognize that for many of my students, I am the first African American that has been in a direct authority position over them. Despite what I believe their perceptions are of me, I tactfully blend professionalism with my personality. I walk into each teaching situation with my head held high, and the expectation of being respected by my students.

I bring to the classroom new perceptions, ideals, and experiences that are unique to the student population here on my campus. Many of the students come from White middle-class families. Some are oblivious to the realities that other families experience. Although initially I battle with how students perceive me as an instructor, I slowly integrate aspects of my personality and life experiences into the classroom. I blend academic discussions with phrases that help me stay real to who I am, and also allow my students to learn more about me and my background. This teaching strategy is comfortable for me. At the end of the day I am not drained and left feeling as if I have to search for my identity. I teach, talk, and act like myself, and include personal references of my grandmother and great-grandmother, who were not college educated, into my classroom. My applicable experiences help bring class discussions to life for my students.

During one class, we were discussing the role of the extended family (i.e., cousins, aunts, grandparents). As an example, I drew a brief genogram. A genogram is similar to a family tree, except specific signs are used to represent gender, relationships, and family processes. It also includes more information than a family tree by including birth dates, death dates, and causes of death. After drawing the diagram, I explained to my students how my great-grandmother raised three of her grandchildren and my great-aunt had adopted one of her great-nephews. I also explained how my grandmother cared for me and two other cousins while our mothers were working or in school. My students were intrigued by these explanations of how our extended family contributed to our holistic family functioning. After class, I had a White young lady approach me and thank me for sharing my life and family with the class. She said she was raised in a very sheltered household and had no idea these type of family systems existed. In my student evaluations, students consistently note their appreciation of being exposed to new ideas and experiences.

Similar to some Latin families where dichos (short phrases) are used to socialize and teach children (Chahin, Villarruel, & Viramontez, 1999), my grandmother and other family members would use phrases to promote what they called "common sense" development. My grandmother would say, "What good is book sense if you don't have common sense." For my family, common sense meant being able to think rationally about the consequences of our actions by thinking before we act. To promote common sense or to socialize us, my grandmother would use phrases to illustrate her point or help us recognize the ignorance of our decisions. There are times in the classroom when I use my grandmother's phrases.

My students had a paper due, and I explained to them that late papers were unacceptable, and any attempts to turn in a late paper would not result in conversation, but a zero. I emphasized that point by sharing with them something my grandmother used to say. Whenever she felt that we didn't believe something would happen, she would say, "You don't believe fat meat is greasy." For those who don't know, fat meat is very greasy! In essence, you don't believe the truth. I explained it to my students. I felt good because I was being true to myself while introducing my students to something that represents a part of who I am. They smiled, and complied.

The Challenge of Research in the African American Local Community

My institution is located in a predominately white, mid-sized, Midwestern city. The African American community within the city is small. African Americans make up 8.5 percent of the county (University of Missouri, 2001). For researchers wanting to study the African American population, statistically, it is difficult to get a large sample from this population, but more importantly, getting this population to participate in research is an even greater challenge. African Americans are hesitant to participate in research studies in part because of mistrust of the researchers (St. John, 1997). I had a firsthand experience of this lack of trust toward researchers.

A qualitative research course required that I conduct a small-scale exploratory study. I chose to research the nature of the relationship of African American stepdaughters and their stepparents. I needed participants. Several African American professors were recommended as contacts or gatekeepers to current African American female research participants. As a new and inexperienced researcher, I did not think it would be too difficult to get participants, especially African American women because I am an African American woman. They would want to help support me as an African American student, or so I thought. I contacted one professor and she made me aware of some truths regarding researching African Americans within this particular community.

She kindly shared with me that she had been here for five years, and had just gained the trust of African American women in the community. She said that the community does not trust the university or those affiliated with the university. She emphasized the need for African American students to become involved in the community, attend churches, and make contributions to begin bridging that gap between the African American university community and the African American community at large. As I attempted to solicit participants for my study, her words rang true. Potential participants were skeptical about my intentions and how the information gathered would be used. Because they didn't know me, they did not feel comfortable being interviewed by me. Eventually, I had to have a woman from the community serve as a "go-between" for me and the participants. She was someone they trusted, and thankfully I was able to conduct the study. It was from that experience I learned that there is a gap that exists in the overall African American culture often dividing college-educated from the non-college educated. I am, at some level, distanced from the larger African American community because of my collegiate experiences, particularly my experiences at Predominately White Institutions. I consider this a cost of this educational experience.

Community with Other African American Graduate Students

Approximately 4 percent of the graduate students are African American. It has been through the Association of Black Graduate and Professional Students (ABGPS) that I have come to establish a close knit family of friends and associates. When I came here, I was 24 years old. I feared that I would not meet others in my age range. To my surprise there were quite a few African American graduate students of my age and younger. They were hip, creative, vivacious, and social. They have been a blessing to me. They are my sounding boards for research ideas. Although I can talk to my friends back home, the graduate students here share in similar experiences and offer perspectives unique to our shared experiences. As I see other graduate students matriculate and graduate, I am inspired to persevere. Although the African American graduate students in my age group are a larger group than I expected, the "dating" options are limited.

Some African American graduate male and female students feel comfortable dating undergraduates. That is not a comfort I share. I simply do not want to see any of my male friends sitting in my class. The African American male population is low among graduate students and in the community. I see my presence here as temporary; therefore, finding a mate is not a priority for me. I was aware before I came here that there is a limited number of males. However, some women were not armed with that information, and I have seen women almost reach the point of depression and despair because of the lack of available, and I must add, dateable, men. There are some who propose that I date interracially; however, that is not my preference. My goal here is to matriculate through this system and be hooded as a Ph.D. Some women desire both, but for me, I only seek the Ph.D. If I meet someone I will not oppose it, but my goals are focused on my program and professional development.

Deciding for the Future—PWI or HBCU

Over the next few months, I have to decide about employment options. If I choose to be a teacher/researcher, the question becomes where I want to apply. To some the answer is obvious when the options are narrowly confined between a Predominately White Institution and a Historically Black College or University. For me, the choice is not a simple one. I have never attended a HBCU. My experiences have been with PWIs. I cannot with certainty say which is my preference. I know that there are African American students at PWIs that long to see an African American professor and crave a relationship or a connection with one. There are White students at PWIs who benefit from their interactions with and teachings from African American professors. On the other hand, my experiences and knowledge gained at this university will be beneficial to African American students at HBCUs. They are just as deserving of the connection with

African American professors as those at PWIs. I have a love for students and learning. I sincerely want to use my gifts in the place or places where they will be most beneficial to the students, university, and community at large. Regardless of my decisions, I have been fortunate to be trained by an outstanding advisor/mentor, to gain valuable experiences through the university and the African American graduate student population, and to learn about how this system works. But more importantly, I have learned how I can work within the system. I chose to be persistent and survive!

References

Analysis (2001, July). *Boone MO: Racial composition 1999–2000.* Retrieved April 22, 2002, from the Office of Social and Economic Data Analysis Website: http://oseda.missouri.edu/counties/racepop/29019.html.

Brown II, M. C., Davis, G. L., & McClendon, S. A. (1999). Mentoring graduate students of color: Myths, models, and modes. *Peabody Journal of Education, 74,* 105–118.

Bruce, M. A. (1995). Mentoring women doctoral students: What counselor educators and supervisors can do. *Counselor Education and Supervision, 35,* 139–149.

Chahin, J., Villarruel, F. A., & Viramontez, R. A. (1999). Dichos y refranes: The transmission of cultural values and beliefs. In H. P. McAdoo (Ed.), *Family ethnicity: Strength in diversity* (2nd ed., pp. 153–170). Thousand Oaks, CA: Sage.

DeGenova, M. K. (1997). *Families in cultural context: Strengths and challenges in diversity.* Mountain View, CA: Mayfield Publishing.

St. John, E. (1997). A prescription for participation. *Black Issues in Higher Education, 14,* 18–23. University of Missouri, Columbia, Missouri, Office of Social and Economic Data.

Felicia Moore, Ph.D.

Hometown: Selma, North Carolina
Current Institution: Florida State University
Department: Science Education
Personal Philosophy: My faith grounds me; my family inspires me; my hope encourages me; and life fulfills me.

7

IN THE MIDST OF IT ALL

A FEMINIST PERSPECTIVE ON SCIENCE AND SCIENCE TEACHING

Introduction

After taking a graduate course entitled Education and Culture, I thought about how culture influences the way students learn science and how I am influenced in teaching it. The course not only enlightened me to a new area of focus for science education but also broadened my perspective as to how I could become a more effective educator. As a requirement for the course, I was expected to conduct an independent research project or fieldwork that involved some aspect of a cultural issue. I was interested in cultural capitol. The concept of cultural capitol is defined by Pai & Adler (2001):

> Cultural capitol refers to the ability to understand and practice the norms, discourse patterns, language styles, and language modes of the dominant culture. This is, given that the cultural forms of our society are dominated by white middle-class norms, behaviors, and language, individuals who lack the knowledge and skills associated with these norms and behaviors are denied access to success. (p. 72)

It is applied most often as "the general cultural background, knowledge, dispositions, and skills that are passed from one generation to the next, where some people's culture are more valued than others within the context of schooling" (Obidah, 2001, p. 48). I knew that I wanted to look at the concept of cultural capitol in the context of a public school. I was asked to assist a first-time science teacher at a local middle school. While assisting him, I started collecting probable research data through observations, surveys, and conversations, and a theme eventually emerged. I started to look more closely at cultural capitol in terms of educational resources and student access within the school science program. I concentrated on how science was taught in the classrooms I was observing.

From weekly observations and conversations with school personnel, students, and teachers, the issue that became more apparent was the organizational structure of the science program within the school. After further dissecting the school science program, I unveiled a larger context of tracking or ability grouping as an entire school practice. I completed the project and learned a great deal about school structure, teacher and student attitudes as a result of tracking, the quality of science teaching within the science department, and the value placed on some children's schooling and not others. I was a little surprised by my findings but not totally shocked. I did not like tracking practices prior to doing this research project, and I was convinced more than ever that it was not a good system of education, especially for African American students and other ethnic groups. Tracking is a system that maintains inequality and further marginalizes minority populations for access, knowledge, and resources in education, and perpetuates social stratification (Gamoran, 1992; Hallinan, 1992; Lee & Bryk, 1988; Oakes, 1994).

After completing the paper, I could not help but reflect on my experiences in school, my education in science, and the way teaching and learning science is taught to children of color. Through much of what I observed and have learned over the past year and a half, I understand better what my experiences were like in learning science, and what things were expected of me as an African American female in science. After being asked to contribute to this book, I felt compelled to reexamine my experiences more critically. Therefore, this chapter addresses my past experiences in science as an undergraduate student and my current experiences as a doctoral student in science education.

Undergraduate Experiences in Science

I attended a Predominately White Institution. In choosing to attend this university, I knew that the number of African American students enrolled at the university was less than 10 percent of the more than 22,000 student body. I had attended a rural high school of approximately 1,200 students. I was accustomed to being the only one or one of no more than four African Americans in my classes throughout my entire high school. Thus being in the context of a larger Predominately White University was not a distressing experience. As an undergraduate student, I encountered many obstacles during my four years of study. I was, however, quite naïve to what was actually going on. As Fordham (2000) said of her experiences, "growing up female and African American in American society, I never quite trusted the validity of my personal experiences" (p. 331), and I was reluctant to put racism, prejudice, and discrimination on my experiences. Today, I have more mature eyes and can see that I experienced oppressive and discriminatory acts as a female and an African American student in science.

Because I initially wanted to be a medical doctor, I majored in science (biology). I had loved science since I was a young girl, and still do as a young woman. But being a female in science was difficult and it was not what I expected. I expected to be one in a small number of other African American science majors. I expected the program to be challenging. I expected that learning science would be exciting and interesting. I expected to be successful and to become a doctor. My expectations met reality my freshman and sophomore years of college.

My reality was that I often felt marginalized because of my female status within the science department and because of my race and my gender. Reflecting back on my experiences, I remember the networks of male study groups versus female study groups. When I was a member of a study group, it consisted mainly of other females, mostly Caucasian, and I was the only African American. I remember not getting much out of these experiences and feeling more confused than when I joined the group. I remember spending long hours in the library studying the textbook and seemingly longer hours in laboratory completing four- and five-hour experiments, while most of the male students in their laboratory groups completed their activities seemingly in record time. They would either leave the laboratory early or would hang around to talk with the laboratory instructors, who were also male and Caucasian. It was almost a given rule to treat the females within the department a certain way. Likewise, they treated minority students in the same manner. There were certain social structures within the science department that were not inviting of women and minorities. Mostly I spent a great deal of time not knowing what was going on. Other than attending lectures and laboratories, I typically found myself outside of the culture of science. Therefore, I experienced a double-edged sword of subordination because I am African American and a female in science.

Specifically, in my organic chemistry class as a sophomore, I had difficulty following the lecture format and teaching style of my professor. He attended class, worked a few problems very quickly on the board, answered very few questions from the class, assigned the next set of problems from the text, and then would leave the large lecture hall of more than 150 students. He was a very stern, Caucasian, elderly man, and a veteran professor of chemistry at the university. He gave only two exams for the entire semester, one midterm and one final. I went to his office for assistance after failing the midterm, which meant I had only one more opportunity to pass the course. When I finally gained enough confidence to approach him and went to his office for assistance on completing some chemistry problems, his comment was "use more paper and pencil." This comment I will never forget. He was condescending, unapproachable, and not at all interested in helping me learn chemistry. Needless to say, this was the first course I had ever failed.

My challenges with organic chemistry and this professor can be analyzed by using a feminist science education perspective, which "seeks to challenge the ideologies that justify power inequalities and utilizes that knowledge to break silences, disrupt power relations, articulate what is possible, construct different realities, and experiment with alternative ways of learning and knowing" (Calebrese-Barton, 1998, p. xx). At that time in my life, I had no power; I had no voice; I had no alternative way of learning and knowing science. Additionally, there was no way that my former chemistry professor saw me as an equal to him so that I could begin to understand how power is distributed between professor and student. He had all the power. I had none. When I entered my professor's office, I was simply looking for assistance and expecting respect from him. I expected him to respect me as a person and to value my desire to have an education. How many other students were made to feel as I did when they were only seeking some assistance with a science problem? Furthermore, the course was designed to "weed out" students from majoring in science. To me, I became aware of subtle and not so subtle practices of sexism, racism, and elitism in science.

As a result of both gender discrimination and racial prejudice, I learned science from a distance and maintained my interest in science despite the opposing forces within the system. Adia Hurtado (1996) discusses how women of color withdraw as a means of coping with social structures, and women of silence who obtain knowledge "return to their own safe communities to share what was learned and to verify the accuracy of their observations" (p. 382). To extend these notions, I withdrew from the structural conditions of the university science department. I spent a great deal of time studying alone in the library, learning in silence, and at the same time being very observant, making sure that what was expected and required of me as a science major were done. This form of accommodation and resistance, learning science in the public sphere of the institution, while developing for myself private thoughts and beliefs became a well-skilled process of my learning science (Anyon, 1983). This form of learning and knowing was still quite diminishing because in order to pass I had to learn the subject matter even if I did not understand it. I had to attend classes but only associated with very few people. This was how I functioned within a community that did not want me there. As a high-achieving Black female, I worked hard and kept quiet/silent (Brickhouse, Lowery, & Schultz, 2000; Fordham, 2000). These behaviors allowed me to develop my own sense of identity as a female science major.

I found science to be very interesting yet challenging, not so much as to content, but in understanding scientific language and concepts. For example, I would read pages over and over again, trying to understand what the information meant. Once I felt I understood it, it made sense, but I thought it could have been written in an easier way. Or I would go through the process of problem solving, using formulas, and drawing conclusions and then would think completely opposite of what I thought to get the "right" answer. This process served me well, yet I felt somewhat inadequate. The information was there for me to accept, to agree with, but my own way of thinking was not considered. Similarly, I questioned findings, thought of alternative solutions to problems, and wondered how they (scientists and professors) got the "right" answer but mine had to be "wrong". Needless to say, objective forms of assessment made me feel like I had to agree with information I really did not agree with, while essay-type assessments allowed me to voice/write my opinion with alternative ways of answering a question. I would write what I thought and still receive partial credit for not getting the "right" answer. Even now, I know the "right" answers but I still maintain my own thoughts as also "right". Calabrese-Barton (1998) explains her experiences in the same way: "When my wants, needs, and beliefs were in contrast with either school or science, then it was my ideas that were somehow faulty; and when my wants, needs, and beliefs were aligned with school or science, then they were somehow right" (p. 23). I learned that this is just one way to know and learn science. I had to suppress my ways of knowing.

My junior and senior years were less discordant. I developed some friendships, another African American female biology major, a couple of European American females, but mostly European American males. These few friends, associates, and I successfully overcame the "weeding out" process to become full-fledged science majors. These friends and associates accepted me into their community as I accepted them into mine. The barriers located within the institutions of racism, gender bias, and educational opportunity were coming down. I had found myself in predominantly white and male laboratory classes and groups. Although we were still reproducing knowledge of our professors and subjects/ textbooks, I had the opportunity to share in scientific discourse in small groups. Though my association with other science majors was allowing me to reclaim my childhood interests, science still remained virtually closed. In this sense, I speak of science almost as a separating force between me and it. I never entered that domain my junior year.

As a senior, full of excitement, mainly for anticipating graduation, I entered an imaginary door into science. I got a research assistant position in the genetics department, where I worked under the supervision of a senior researcher. During this time, I was able to discuss with him his research projects, conduct experiments, work on a team of other scientists and students, and contribute to his research efforts. (I still have an ambition to get a degree in genetics, one day.) Appreciatively and for the first time, after several years of being on the outside, I was in. The professor agreed to give me an independent study for the last three hours to complete my degree requirements. I worked with Drosophila melanogaster (fruit flies) and mated them for induced mutations. Exciting! It had taken my entire undergraduate career for the door to be opened. I was prepared. This positive experience within the Genetics department encouraged me to continue my education in science. I think now that had I given up prior to this point, or had lived up to expectations that African American women "cannot and do not do science" I would have missed many opportunities and future chances, such as contributing my story to this book.

As a result of my early college years, I learned that science has different forms of domination that have produced for me both oppression and opportunity (Zinn & Dill, 1996). Karen Meyer (1998) explains the kind of attitude you must have when oppression and opportunity are displayed as contrary forces that you must contend with:

> Access means entrance, opportunity, the ticket in. The opposition is retreat, withdrawal, the closed door. One direction moves forward; the other recedes inward. At the heart of this duality are perceptions of be-longing or mis-fit, the social act of participating or not, and the communication in a particular or silence. Within the learning context are situated constructions of meaning that are dependent upon the surrounding discourse. Therefore, access hinges on taking up, becoming fluent in that discourse; retreat rests on silent nonparticipation. (p. 467)

Meyer (1998) concludes that one goal of science is to turn from application toward implications of science. This will mean discussing "social and political sensibilities, science as a cultural institution situated in various allegiances, limitations and privileges, but also identifying myths of its objective value-free nature and its metaphors of control and domination" (p. 470). She declares that the crisis of "pervasive mythical perceptions is the inaccessibility of science to cultural diversity and multiple perspectives" (p. 470).

Calebrese-Barton (1998) says that "the shift is to challenge accepted definitions of school and science, deconstructing an ideology of white, male, middle-class privilege, and establishing purposes and goals for science education for critical self awareness rather than accumulating facts" (p. 33). Ideally students should not have to learn science from the outside. There should be plenty of room to learn inside. The issue, however, is getting the gate open, or opening doors for women and others to enter. How you do this may have to come from your own interventions, your determination to hold on, or a gentle push, until the gate opens, or at least a small enough (or big enough) crack for you to get your foot in. But I have learned that you cannot retreat in defeat if science has chosen you.

I have gained many insights, some by direct instruction, but mostly through observation and interacting in the community of science and science education. Calebrese-Barton (1998) speaks of "positionality" as knowing how gender, race, class, and other socially significant dimensions influence how one constructs knowledge. Because of these multiple contexts, I have become skilled at shifting consciousness by having more than one voice and developing the ability to talk to different audiences (Hurtado, 1996), to understand various perspectives, and to move back and forth between different contexts. I am certain that my experiences have enabled me to see science and teaching differently. I view science as holding a set of values, beliefs, standards, and worldview that seek to answer questions pertaining to the world around me. It is a study of phenomena that answer questions systematically through experimentation, observation, measuring, collecting, and reporting; then it uses this knowledge to revise and revalidate. Science is dynamic and multidimensional. At the same time it is limited and limiting. Though science presents itself as being positivistic, male-oriented, exclusive, and nonaccepting of multiple views of representing reality, there are ways I have positioned myself in it while still holding on to my own values and worldview. Still, "learning science also means learning about the norms, beliefs, values, discursive practices, and ways of acting and reasoning that are acceptable within the community of science" (WISE, 1994, 1995, as cited by Calabrese-Barton, 1998, p. 12).

Lisa Delpit (1995) suggests that students be "*taught* the codes needed to participate fully in the mainstream of American life . . . while learning the culture of power . . . the arbitrariness of those codes and about the power relationships they represent" (p. 45). I believe that students should be taught and be expected to know the canon of science or the most acceptable scientific knowledge of leading theory, principles, and research so that they can direct themselves within scientific discourse. I learned a great portion of it by engaging myself, reading, completing laboratory exercises, and conducting small experiments through supervision so that I could communicate in classes, labs, and with others in the community of science. "Science knowledge is a gate to power; students have to be taught the canons, no matter how oppressive or exclusive" (Calabrese-Barton, 1998, p. 93). However, I believe that there are multiple ways of obtaining and understanding that knowledge without having to follow many of the strict, one-dimensional, mandated ways of doing science that leave many of the marginalized out of and away from scientific knowledge and discourse.

Furthermore, Delpit explains that "acquiring the ability to function in a dominant discourse need not mean that one must reject one's home identity and values, for discourses are not static, but are shaped, however reluctantly, by those who participate within them and by the form of their participation" (1995, p. 163). I have developed a view of science that does not contradict my beliefs or my views. Nevertheless I understand the history and nature of science and can negotiate the invisible, though explicitly real, boundaries of science. You cannot function as a member of the community without knowing it. One goal is to tread new ground in science through science education research that addresses how science doors can be opened for others, more easily than they were for me.

In all honesty, the weight of negative experiences, the alienation, and the discrimination I have endured are far less than what I have gained in overall compensation for diligence, determination, and belief in myself. In spite of how I learned science, the subject matter was the reason for my majoring in it and holding on to it. I graduated from the university and immediately went into a master's program at a Predominately Black University. However, because of my love for science and learning, I took an alternate route—education/teaching—that has set my life in a new and exciting direction. I am so blessed to be here at this juncture in my life. I not only have maintained my passion for science but also have incorporated teaching and research into it. From this point on, I will discuss how the integration of science and teaching has been shaped by attending yet another Predominately White University.

Graduate Experiences in Science Education

I arrived at Florida State University in the science education program, with a continued strong desire to learn science and education. I came with a goal to become both a more effective educator and a researcher. I wanted to be in a better position to have an impact on my family and my community. I had no reservations about coming to a Predominately White University. For my first year, I was the only African American student in my department. My sense of community comes from two other African American women who work in the main office of the department, the memberships I hold in church and in organizations, the service I do in the community, and the communications I have within my department.

I was ambitious enough to leave my family and friends in North Carolina and to move to Florida to begin what I call a "new" life. All of my past experiences were the lessons that helped me to be here at this particular point in my life and to benefit from whatever adverse and positive conditions I had previously encountered. What I have gained from those experiences has helped me tremendously to advance in my program. My focus is still on science, but it is also on education and research. Just as there are fewer numbers of African American women and men and other ethnic groups in science, there are despairingly lower numbers of us in science education.

In my program I am presented with questions such as these: Can science and science education shift from a traditional, exclusive, male-dominated paradigm to one that is inclusive and gender and culture sensitive? Can students who have been historically and presently marginalized from teaching and learning science now have access to power and knowledge? Can science be taught so that it accepts multiple ways of knowing and accommodate multiple representations for all races and females? To answer these questions, I am finding that the things that were once deemed negative in science are being positively received in science education. Through the concerns I have for science—how it is taught, to whom, and for what purposes—I am able to contribute my perspectives and insights into the arena of science education and research. In my graduate program, I am encouraged not only to dismantle many of the walls that science has built up but also to reconstruct notions of what science is and how it is taught and learned. With particular emphasis on my experiences, I am able to analyze concepts from multiple perspectives.

I believe science should be learned in very practical ways so that people can apply concepts in real-life situations. Then the teacher can progress to teaching more concrete and more traditional science—laws, formulas, terminology—because learners have prior knowledge or a foundation on which to build more science. Learners should be expected to know this information, or the traditionally accepted claims of scientific understandings, so that they are able to communicate successfully in the science community, to make decisions related to having adequate knowledge of scientific principles, and to think about issues that directly affect society. However, students having their own cultural capitol are also invited into the science classroom, to contribute their experiences, and to learn science on their terms. In science teaching, I think students should develop the capacity to think about others and the world around them in much broader terms than how science is taught today.

For example, in Gale Seiler's (2001) study of inner-city African American youth, he formed a science lunch group where males discussed scientific concepts that were generated from their daily activities. Students discussed physical factors related to how a drum sounds, and gathered evidence, created graphs, worked statistics, and videotaped arguments for discourse in a debate about basketball. The students also learned concepts in physics such as motion and force by dropping basketballs and tennis balls. Seiler (2001) envisions a "student-emergent science curriculum" where students are involved in creating curriculum and have opportunities to express themselves in ways that may broaden their conceptions of science and their position in science.

In other words, science is not learned the way I learned it, nor is it taught the way it was taught to me. Students are not "received knowers" who listen to authorities, soak up information, remember and reproduce knowledge, or seldom speak up or give opinions (Stanton, 1996, p. 31). When students are able to use their voice, are included in the learning of science, are able to discuss their ideas, and are encouraged to do so openly and honestly, then teachers do not perpetuate the alienation, domination, and oppression that are often associated with learning science in the traditional sense.

The "framework shifts from a science-driven education, where science is unproblematically imposed from the outside, to a student-driven education, where science and the self-in-science are continually and simultaneously examined, challenged, and articulated" (Calabrese-Barton, 1998, p. 128). I would encourage beyond this point, a "subject-centered" learning (Palmer, 1998, p. 118). The driving passion for learning is to acquire knowledge of the subject. Students are able to build their own understandings and personal interpretations of science that are meaningful and useful to them. Knowledge grows out of students' interests and backgrounds, which will be highly individual and culturally specific. My hope here is that when students engage in science in this way that they become interested, motivated, and excited. This is where our future scientists and science educators will come from.

As a graduate student I am able to validate my experiences as mine and participate "inside" the community of science education with professors and colleagues in my program as well as in departments across campus. There were some small bumps that I had to go over, but I attribute these to being in a new environment and having to learn the culture of science education and the dispositions of my professors and peers. I found that it was not as difficult as my transition and eventual acceptance into science during my undergraduate years. Then again, I am sure a degree of comfort, confidence, and competence have joined me in making this transition unproblematic. I had to contend with professors' prior expectations and them not knowing me as a student and a person. I have since my first year developed relationships with my professors that are mutually accepting and supportive of my ambitions. In a very significant way, my current experiences are definitely different from my undergraduate years in science.

Another aspect of my graduate learning is the time I spend in reflecting about the world. My program requires a great deal of mind work, which I am sure is true of other Ph.D. programs in general. bell hooks (1995) in her book, *Killing Rage: Ending Racism,* discusses how a "significant part of her intellectual work is critical engagement of ideas" (p. 228). This is expected in my program. I am constantly thinking. A peer of mine said, "Your head is a very busy place." hooks affirms that "there is necessarily a private solitary dimension to intellectual work" (p. 229) and that "intellectual work need not be done solely in academic settings" (p. 238). "The mark of an intellectual is time to reflect. As a result they bring to black liberation struggle a radically new vision of social change" (p. 239). I believe in reflection, contemplation, and intellectual endeavors. I think this element is important in thinking of alternative ways to address "issues raised by marginalized discourses" (Norman, 1998, 365).

The Explicit Gender Perspective

The gender perspective is valuable for analyzing my experiences in science and science education. I conceptualize science and science education in broader perspectives, and view the power and privilege dynamic active in the world. There are constraints in science and science education, and my focus is to make a difference in the system, either large or small, as I contribute to changing existing inequalities in it.

From an academic standpoint, I am encouraged to voice my concerns so that science is taught "equitably" and "equally" (Atwater, 2000a). My views as an African American in science and in science education have to be voiced more openly so that misconceptions about African American women, and other marginalized groups, are addressed and resolved. From a pedagogical standpoint, how will teachers, or myself, teach increasingly diverse populations of students in the classroom without considering the cultural, social, and educational backgrounds of the students we are teaching? Therefore, the gender perspective speaks to the marginalized race, ethnicity, gender, and economics in the classroom. It persuades teachers to address issues that affect student learning as well as influences teachers' professional development. In my case, who would know more about me as an African American female, my learning, my culture, my thinking, and my experiences in science, science education, and society, except someone sensitive to cultural and gender perspectives? The gender perspective speaks directly to my experiences and my view of the world, and it is inclusive of my experiences.

I do not perceive the gender perspective in science education as strictly feminist or of a feminine view but one that is inclusive of males, females, various ethnic groups, and those who have been prevented access to science. The "gender- and culture-sensitive" movement for inclusive science education is about creating "equitable opportunities for all students to develop scientific literacy" (Calabrese-Barton, 1998, p. 91). However, a curriculum of science education that is inclusive is necessary for closing the gap between scientific knowledge, literacy, power, and privilege. I know that everyone cannot be a scientist, but I want everyone, including those deemed by society as nonprivileged and less powerful, to have every opportunity to learn and to experience quality science teaching and learning.

Feminist science education affords learners an opportunity to validate their thinking, to question science, and to receive assistance in thinking about science content, problems, and information. Students should not take for granted everything that is presented to them by an instructor or the textbook. I am not saying that everything that is written in the textbook is true or false, but by providing learners with an opportunity to question and think critically and to develop alternative solutions, they will be well prepared and equipped to function in a technologically advanced society. "Given the enormous authority that science exercises in our culture, it is crucial that citizens in a democratic society not only be aware of the role that ideology plays in shaping science, but that they also learn to critically evaluate the ideological implications of individual science claims and practices" (Norman, 1998, p. 365). Therefore, learning environments constructed so that students have opportunities to discuss science in this way are excellent for exposing cultural, social, and historical dimensions of scientific knowledge.

Conclusion

I have been influenced by traditional understandings of science teaching and learning, both inclusive and exclusive, meaning that I have experienced both physical and philosophical obstacles to accessing science. Presently I find myself in the midst of both science and science education, and even more recently science education research as I approach my dissertation. Science, science education, and research have to meet somewhere. Science has to be seen as a means of including different perspectives on how phenomena are studied and reported; science teaching should allow for students' own experiences to be shared in the classroom, for students to make their own multiple ways of learning science; and research has to be about giving voice to those who have been traditionally marginalized from discourse, race, class, and gender.

I could have written this chapter from almost any perspective— transformatory, which challenges some of the key assumptions that scholars make about knowledge and some of their major paradigms, findings, theories, and interpretations (Banks, 1995); or multicultural, which involves thinking through and analyzing the situations of different people (Grant & Gomez, 2001). The topics of gender and feminism usually center on issues related to what it means to be a female. Atwater (2000b) explains that females are a diverse group of people with similar and dissimilar problems in a male domain. "These females face problems related to not only gender, but class, ethnicity, language, lifestyle, and religion" (p. 386). Therefore, a feminist/gender perspective enables me to view science through multiple lenses that connect to my experiences, past and present. This perspective works to "uncover, understand, and transform gender, race, and class oppression and domination" (Mayberry, 1998, p. 444). With the confidence I have gained from my oppression and privilege in science, I can challenge structures that hinder those historically denied access to science.

My educational experiences at Florida State University (FSU) have been very rewarding. I have learned a great deal by becoming acclimated to the culture of science education and teacher education. I am confident that my time at FSU has fully prepared me for a future teaching and research position. And I still have more learning to do! I am focusing on students' learning of science, teachers and their practice, and trying to make connections to theory and practice for research and science learning. By working with elementary, middle, and high school science teachers, I am thinking about how to get them to reflect more on their practice, and assisting them in making relevant and effective changes in their practice to improve science teaching and learning.

Finally, I offer five small bits of advice to share with students in general, whether high school students trying to graduate, college students finding themselves challenged by academic standards, graduate students in the middle of their programs, or those desiring to enter higher education. After writing this chapter these points seemed to stand out in my mind:

1. *Be true to yourself.* The faith that you have in yourself really did not come from you. It came from God who watches over you and wants to see you succeed. A Yoruba proverb says, "When you stand with the blessings of your mother and God, it matters not who stands against you."

2. *Make development a personal goal.* In whatever circumstances in life you find yourself, expect to learn something from them. Anticipate learning so that you can integrate past, present, and future circumstances in order to reach perfection, and to assist others in this same goal.

3. *Understand history.* Whether it is yours, your family, your subject, your world, know your history; understand it.

4. *Choose your battles.* Know when to speak, how to speak, and the purpose for which you are speaking. Not everything is worth the

fight, but some things are definitely worth fighting for. (I know this is an area that I will continue to grow in.)

5. *Make your own "science."* As you work out your own course of life, it may involve negotiation, redirection, solitary moments, and patience. You have a voice, a mind, a heart that is valuable and worthy of acknowledgment and respect. Make things happen and work for you.

References

Anyon, J. (1983). Intersections of gender and class: Accommodation and resistance by working-class and affluent females to contradictory sex-role ideologies. In S. Walker & L. Barton (Eds.), *Gender, class & education* (pp. 19–37). Taylor & Francis: Philadelphia.

Atwater, M. M. (2000a). Equity for black Americans in precollege science. *Science Education, 84,* 154–179.

Atwater, M. M. (2000b). Females in science education: White is the norm and class, language, lifestyle, and religion are nonissues. *Journal of Research in Science Teaching, 37*(4), 386–387.

Banks, J. A. (1995). Multicultural education and curriculum transformation. *Journal of Negro Education, 64*(4), 390–400.

Brickhouse, N. W., Lowery, P., & Schultz, K. (2000). What kind of girl does science? The construction of school science identity. *Journal of Research in Science Teaching, 37*(5), 441–458.

Calabrese-Barton, A. (1998). *Feminist science education.* New York: Teachers College Press.

Delvit, L. (1995). *Other people's children: Cultural conflict in the classroom.* The New Press: New York.

Fordham, S. (2000). Those loud black girls: (Black) women, silence, and gender "passing" in the academy. In Bradley A. U. Levinson, Kathryn M. Borma, Margaret Eisenhart, Michele Foster, Amy E. Fox, & Margaret Sutton (Eds.), *Schooling the symbolic animal: School and cultural dimensions of education* (pp. 327–343). Lanham, MD: Rowan & Littlefield Publishers, Inc.

Gamoran, A. (1992). The variable effects of high school tracking. *American Sociological Review, 57* (December), 812–828.

Grant, C. A., & Gomez, M. L. (2001). *Campus and classroom: Making schooling multicultural.* Upper Saddle River, NJ: Merrill Prentice-Hall, Inc.

Hallinan, M. (1992). The organization of students for instruction in the middle school. *Sociology of Education, 65*(2), 114–127.

hooks, b. (1995). *Killing rage: Ending racism.* New York: Henry Holt & Company, Inc.

Hurtado, A. (1996). Feminists of color theorize the production of knowledge. In N. Goldberger, J. Tarule, B. Clinchy, & M. Belenky (Eds.), *Knowledge, difference, and power: Essays inspired by women's ways of knowing* (pp. 372–388). New York, NY: Basic Books.

Lee, V. E., & Bryk, A. S. (1988). Curriculum tracking as mediating the social distribution of high school achievement. *Sociology of Education, 61* (April), 78–94.

Mayberry, M. (1998). Reproductive and resistant pedagogies: The comparative roles of collaborative learning and feminist pedagogy in science education. *Journal of Research in Science Teaching, 35*(4), 443–459.

Meyer, K. (1998). Reflections on being female in school science: Toward a praxis of teaching science. *Journal of Research in Science Teaching, 35*(4), 463–471.

Norman, O. (1998). Marginalized discourses and scientific literacy. *Journal of Research in Science Teaching, 35*(4), 365–374.

Oakes, J. (1994). More than misapplied technology: A normative and political response to Hallinan on tracking. *Sociology of Education, 67*(2), 84–91 in Exchange.

Obidah, J. E. (2001). In search of a theoretical framework. In R. O. Mabokela, & A. L. Green (Eds.), *Sisters of the Academy* (pp. 42–54). Virginia: Stylus Publishing, LLC.

Pai, Y., & Adler, S. A. (2001). *Cultural foundations of education* (3rd ed.). Upper Saddle River, NJ: Merrill Prentice-Hall.

Palmer, P. J. (1988). *The courage to teach.* San Francisco, CA: Jossey-Bass Inc.

Seiler, G. (2001). Reversing the "standard" direction: Science emerging from the lives of African American students. *Journal of Research in Science Teaching, 38*(9), 1000–1014.

Stanton, A. (1996). Reconfiguring teaching and knowing in the college classroom. In N. Goldberger, J. Tarule, B. Clinchy, & M. Belenky (Eds.), *Knowledge, difference, and power: Essays inspired by women's ways of knowing* (pp. 25–56). New York: Basic Books.

Women in Science Education [WISE]. (1994). Revisioning boundaries in science education. Symposium conducted at the meeting of the American Educational Research Association, New Orleans.

Women in Science Education. (1995). Revisioning boundaries in science education from a feminist perspective: Continuing the conversation. Symposium conducted at the meeting of the American Educational Research Association, San Francisco.

Zinn, M. B., & Dill, B. T. (1996). Theorizing difference from multiracial feminism. *Feminist Studies, 22*(2), 321–331.

Anthony Graham

Hometown: Kinston, North Carolina
Current Institution: University of North Carolina at Greensboro
Department: Curriculum and Instruction
Personal Philosophy: Every man has two educations: that which is given to him and the other that which he gives himself. Of the two kinds, the latter is by far the more desirable.
　　　　　—Carter G. Woodson

8

PRESSING TOWARD
THE MARK

AN AFRICAN AMERICAN MAN'S
REFLECTION ON THE DOCTORAL
PROCESS AT A PREDOMINATELY
WHITE INSTITUTION

Introduction

What makes a graduate student successful at attaining a terminal degree? What are the right ingredients that must be mixed together to create that perfect recipe for a well-seasoned doctoral candidate? What is the correct mathematical formula that a doctoral student must use to calculate how much work will be needed while subtracting excess activities to yield a well-deserved product? These types of questions are often played out in the minds of graduate students across the nation when contemplating for which doctoral program to apply.

For some African American graduate students like myself, however, the most serious question to ponder is perhaps the most life altering. Many prospective African American doctoral students will struggle with the question: Should I attend a Predominately White Institution (PWI) or should I attend a Predominately Black Institution (PBI)? While on the surface the question seems an easy one, for those African American graduate students contemplating the answer, it is not so easy. After a long, grueling, internal decision-making process, justification for attending the chosen school must appease family, peers, colleagues, and enemies since there will be critics and naysayers from each group for either path—a path that will become either a wonderful experience of learning and exploration or a horrific experience of politics and frustration.

In this chapter, I wish to reflect on my experiences as a young African American doctoral student at a Predominately White

Institution. Before addressing my experiences in the program, I think it is important to explain my reason for wanting to pursue a doctoral degree. This information is essential to understanding why I chose my current university. Then, I will begin to reflect on my experiences as a 26-year-old African American male in my third year of a doctoral program with very few African American students and even fewer African American faculty.

I Don't Want to Be Heard—I Want You to Listen!

The Ph.D. means many things to many people: a license to speak freely with credibility; a marker of expertise in a given field or discipline; a symbol of knowledge, power, and status; an impossible dream; a degree that signifies that a person has the rhetorical tools to "pile it on higher and deeper." To those graduate students pursuing the doctorate in graduate programs across the world, many come to realize why it is often termed a "terminal degree," as life seems to come to an end while tirelessly pursuing it. Regardless of what the doctoral degree means to various people, graduate and undergraduate students around the world view it as the ultimate educational prize, a grandiose symbol that acknowledges that a student has reached the highest peak conceivable in the schooling realm. No longer is the graduate student an apprentice but an expert in the chosen field, or a "doctor," with the capability to ask the right question, to examine the situation based on that question, and to remedy the situation while providing prescriptions on how to eliminate the problem forevermore.

I realized the importance of the doctoral degree while student teaching as a graduate student at a high school in North Carolina. I had been assigned several classes of students who were identified as low achieving by the educational system, and the majority of those classes consisted of a disproportionate number of African Americans. As I taught, I became more interested not only in teaching these students but also in understanding who they were and what they wanted in life.

My interest in the labeling of African Americans as low achievers made me turn to the library to find literature on low achievers and African Americans, and I slowly began to learn more about the overrepresentation of African Americans in low-achieving classes (Fordham &

Ogbu, 1986; Jencks & Phillips, 1998; Oakes, 1985; Steele, 1992). However, I was dissatisfied with all the statistical information and theoretical jargon that cluttered many of these articles and books. My students had taught me that they had stories that needed to be shared, and in some cases, unbelievable tales of hardships. I wanted these students to be heard, but what I would soon find was that no one wanted to listen to them or, for that matter, me.

After the 10th grade End-of-Year Writing Test given to all North Carolina sophomores, I had a sudden epiphany. If I truly wanted to be an advocate for these students, I needed a microphone that could reach thousands of people to share these students' stories and experiences. I realized that without a doctorate, people would not hear me. With a doctorate, people would listen, and I understood the difference clearly.

Facing the Odds

When I began researching doctoral programs across the United States, I was not totally sure that it was my time to pursue a doctorate. After all, at the time, I was 23 years old. If that fact was not insurmountable enough, I knew that the schools to which I applied would notice two other characteristics that would surely catch their attention and return a letter of denial: (1) African American and (2) male. These characteristics led me to apply to one predominately Black doctoral program because I felt it was a "safe" choice. I felt comfortable that my people would not turn me away because I was a young African American male destroying all the stereotypes typically held by people of all races. I also decided to apply to two predominately White doctoral programs, including where I attended as an undergraduate and where I was attending as a graduate student for the master's degree.

The Black school, which I counted on for admission, sent me a letter of rejection. Having not heard from the White universities at that time, I resumed my job search for a public teaching job in the area. Several days before committing to a job as a high school English teacher and assistant football coach, I received in the mail a letter of acceptance to the doctoral program in curriculum and teaching at the traditionally White institution where I did my undergraduate studies. Truly elated at the time, I failed to realize that a second letter was hiding underneath the other mail from the Curriculum and Instruction program at the other traditionally White institution in which I was currently enrolled. As I read, the first line stated simply:

> Your application to the Graduate School has been reviewed with careful attention given to the credentials you submitted. I am pleased to inform you that you have been granted admission (assuming successful completion of the master's program) to the Doctor of Philosophy degree program in curriculum and teaching.

Needless to say, I was perplexed by the acceptance letters to the predominately White schools and the rejection letter from the predominately Black school. I felt certain that I had the academic credentials to be accepted to all three programs and not just two. I completed my undergraduate career by making the Dean's List two consecutive semesters; I maintained a 4.0 grade point average throughout my forty-eight-hour graduate program in English Education; I worked two jobs during the graduate program as a librarian and as a computer lab assistant on campus, assisting undergraduates in their academic pursuits every day; I volunteered as a tutor in the community; and when I taught high school English, my students achieved when people doubted their ability, and I consistently scored superior on my teaching evaluations whenever I was observed. The end result of my efforts was that I had been accepted to two doctoral programs.

In the Beginning: My First Class as a Doctoral Student

Upon entering my first class, a research methodology course required of all newly admitted doctoral students or aspiring doctoral students, I sat in the back of the class so I could take it all in. Immediately I began to count the number of African Americans in the class, a habit I picked up as an undergraduate student. I had grown so accustomed to being the only "one" that I was trained to expect no one else. Yet, to my surprise, there were five of us—three women and two men—in a class of roughly twenty-eight students. I would not discover until much later during that semester that only two of us had been accepted to the doctoral program. One young woman was a master's student taking the class as an elective. The other two had applied but had not been accepted. These four African Americans would become my initial support group, as I was still unsure if I belonged.

As the class progressed over the course of the semester, I began to feel more comfortable with the course requirements and the even playing field that was apparent due in large part to the instructor's grading style. If a paper was submitted that was not thoroughly detailed or lacked attention to detail, it would be given back with a simple red mark of "NY" in the upper right corner, meaning "not yet." Every week the papers would be handed back, and students would groan and complain when the "NY" was visible. We all supported one another and encouraged one another to keep trying until the "NY" would no longer be visible.

My "NY's" slowly began to stack up, and I noticed that other people were moving on to the next assignment successfully. I noticed at the end of the weekly three-hour class period that certain students would always approach the instructor with questions and would talk with the instructor until a satisfactory answer would be given. Slowly I began to figure out that those students who spoke with the instructor on a regular basis were the same students not having troubles with the "NY." For the first time in my collegiate career, it dawned on me—talk with the instructor. I was spending so much time with my support group (i.e., the Black folk) that I was ignoring the one person I needed to understand and who needed to understand me the most, the instructor. As I began to get more comfortable with asking questions and asking for guidance, the "NY's" quickly disappeared. The lines of communication had been established, and my support group began to expand. I had limited myself to the African Americans in the class when, in fact, I needed to open myself up to the other people in the class.

As I reflect now on the beginning of the program, I understand and appreciate the lesson that I learned from the author of one of my favorite books. I can relate wholeheartedly to Rose (1989) when he realized the following:

> We live, in America, with so many platitudes about motivation and self-reliance and individualism . . . that we find it hard to accept the fact that they are serious nonsense. To live your early life on the streets . . . and to journey up through the top levels of the American educational system will call for support and guidance at many, many

points along the way. You'll need people to guide you into conversations that seem foreign and threatening. You'll need models, lots of them, to show you how to get at what you don't know. You'll need people to help you center yourself in your own developing ideas. You'll need people to watch out for you. (pp. 47–48)

I became so wrapped up in trying to succeed by myself or relying on those who looked like me that I almost missed the big picture of the doctoral process. The doctoral process teaches you to gather information from others and to discuss the issues with others without regards to race, gender, or class. Moreover, I learned that I needed to understand the language and the thoughts of the academy, as well as the behavior of academicians. I needed that instructor to guide me, to mentor me, and to introduce me to the academy.

Keeping It "Real": Representing African American Men

Coming from a predominately White undergraduate program in the English department, having three or four other African Americans in a class with me was more than pleasing. In fact, it was borderline utopia. However, the one thing that would remain the same from those undergraduate days was the fact that I would be the only African American man in the majority of my classes. Yet, I expected this scenario since the number of African American men graduating with doctorates held consistent between 1.8 percent; and 2.0 percent; between 1995 and 1997 (Jones, 2000).

Being the only African American man in doctoral classes has been much more intimidating than being the only African American man in an undergraduate course. As an undergraduate, I felt on the same level as my peers. I believed that we were learning the same information at the same rate, and I felt comforted knowing many of us had no work experience to complement our intelligence. With doctoral classes, it has been much different. My peers are only my "peers" because we are doctoral students. For the most part, that is where the similarities end. Many of my colleagues are ten to fifteen years older than I, and they have worked in the field for many more years. Not only do they have the intelligence to do the work, but also they have the experience to supplement that knowledge. For that reason, I feel as if I am on another level than my colleagues, a lower level, and I feel intimidated in many classes.

Because of this environment, I often feel pressured when engaged in philosophical class discussions. Steele and Aronson (1998) refer to this pressure as *stereotype threat*. Stereotype threat is a condition that ethnic minority students experience when being tested or examined in the presence of Whites. In this type of environment, minorities "must deal with the possibility of being judged or treated stereotypically" and they experience extreme pressure because they fear "doing something to confirm the stereotype" (Steele & Aronson, 1998, p. 401) that may be held by Whites. I perceive the Ph.D. as the ultimate test of intellectual ability; consequently, I often feel inadequate when discussing what I found in the text or when sharing my view of the readings or when presenting in class.

On the other hand, this stereotype threat motivates me as well. Although no one has ever directly stated that I represent African Americans and African American men all across the United States, I truly believe it deep down inside. As a representative of African American men, I feel the need to demonstrate to my intellectual colleagues, who may have limited contact with African Americans, that we are more than capable of learning and comprehending. I feel that I have to dispel myths and media images about young African American men that suggest we are only capable of singing, rapping, dancing, playing sports, disrespecting women, chasing the "bling bling," being lazy, or creating babies. I want to show my colleagues and instructors that African American men are capable of leading and not simply following, that African American men are capable of speaking the language of intellectuals, and that African American men are capable of thinking in an abstract manner.

Throughout the program, I have suffered from what W. E. B. Du Bois termed "double consciousness," or the "sense of always looking at one's self through the eyes of others, of measuring one's soul by the tape of a world that looks on in amused contempt and pity" (Lee, Jarrett, & Mbalia, 2002, p. 301). I have constantly looked at myself through the eyes of White people, and I have attempted to answer those questions that I believed Whites would pose. I have learned and accepted quite a bit about White culture, but I have also made it my business, if not my duty, to introduce the African American culture, beliefs, and values to my White colleagues.

While I have had to avoid confirming negative stereotypes to my White colleagues, I have also had to prove to my fellow African Americans that I have not lost myself and changed. This line has been a fine and delicate one to walk. In the classroom, I have had to prove my intelligence and my place to my colleagues. Outside the classroom, I have had to prove my Blackness to friends and associates. I have had lifelong friends accuse me of changing when, in fact, I have not had the time to spend with them as in the past. I have had other African Americans that I have met for the first time search me from head to toe, trying to find some fault in my character. As daunting and frustrating as the task of walking this line has been, it has been the easiest one for me. I have remained constant in all areas of my life by being myself at all times and by keeping it real. I have dealt with this double consciousness by being consistent in my actions, my beliefs, and my values, and I continue to move forward every day in the face of criticisms and in the presence of doubters.

Ph.D.: The Playa Hatin' Degree

Being a young African American man in a doctoral program has been quite interesting. I have received utmost respect and admiration from my undergraduate students, my friends, and my peers because of my age and because of my accomplishments thus far. As a young African American in quest of the doctorate, I am often encouraged by the comments that I hear from many of my African American peers. I often hear comments that range from "You the man, dog" to "I want to be like you when I grow up" to "You are my inspiration, Mr. Graham." These comments are frequent reminders of how important it is to complete the doctoral program because so many other young African Americans want and need to see that this goal is possible for a young person.

However, not all remarks and behaviors from African Americans have been positive or encouraging. In fact, the biggest and most painful barrier that I have faced throughout my pursuit of the doctoral degree has been the conscious and unconscious discouragement from some African Americans. Dealing with them has been far worse than any instance of overt racism that I have ever experienced throughout my life. Ironically, many who have discouraged me to aspire toward a doctoral degree have been those African Americans with education, the ones who would seemingly be supportive. What really hurts me, though, is not that they are highly educated, but that many of them attend the National Association for the Advancement of Colored People (NAACP) meetings, that many of them are members of Black sororities and fraternities, and that many are people who donate money to the United Negro College Fund or other fund-raising activities that promote African Americans to pursue higher education. These are the people who preach Black unity and equality, yet who do not practice what they preach. These are the people who are my worst critics and who question my intelligence and ability. These are the people who criticize me for pursuing a doctorate at "such a young age." These are the people who seemingly attempt to keep me down while I continue to strive for the top. These are the people who "playa hate" while smiling falsely in my face and stabbing me in the back.

To further illustrate my point, allow me to recall an incident that occurred. Upon meeting a fellow educator, a middle-aged African American woman who was interviewing for a faculty position, I was introduced to her as an instructor, as a new father, and as a doctoral student. Her response is one of many that I shall remember for the rest of my life. She replied in a very straightforward manner:

> Aren't you too young to be working on a doctorate? You look like a college student yourself. Perhaps you should consider focusing on being a daddy right now and go back for your doctorate a little bit later. They give you about ten years to finish, you know?

While I believe her remark was made with good intent, it was the fact that the comment was made at all that bothered me the most. Why not encourage me to achieve in spite of this new obstacle? Why not provide advice on how to handle this new situation while working toward the completion of the degree? Why not wish me well with my academic pursuits?

Race Still Does Matter

One of the mistakes that I admittedly made upon applying for doctoral admissions and upon entering the program was separating the doctoral process from campus life. When I thought of the doctoral program,

I only thought of the coursework, the comprehensive exams, the dissertation process, and all the challenges that existed within that context. The idea of the doctoral process limited my vision and my thought to focusing only on the larger concern, the dissertation. This tunnel vision led me to divorce the doctoral program in Curriculum and Instruction from the School of Education and from the campus. What I failed to realize was that there would be challenges that would await me on the campus of this traditionally White institution that cared not that I was a doctoral student or that I was educated.

What I have rediscovered during the doctoral program is race still does matter. While professors and peers alike have done a wonderful job of understanding and accepting the nuances of African American culture, certain aspects of the Predominately White Institution have not been so kind. Not all librarians within my "second home," as I so affectionately call the library, have been extremely forthcoming with assistance. Not all campus staff have been extremely helpful when a question was asked or a concern was raised.

Allow me to share one incident that occurred during the summer of my first year in the doctoral program while taking a writing workshop course at night. After the class meeting one night, I walked back to my dormitory. I can vividly recall wearing black pants and a green short-sleeved shirt. Since the class was an evening class lasting from 5:30 P.M. to 8:30 P.M., it was dark outside. As I had done several weeks before this particular night, I allowed my girlfriend to remain in my room with my dorm key in case she wanted to leave and return for any reason. When I reached the dorm, I used the callbox to phone the room so I could enter the dorm, but there was no answer. Fearing that I would not be able to enter the dorm, I called a friend who lived in the basement to open the door. I walked from the front of the building to the side of the building where my friend lived to gain entry.

As I prepared to enter the dorm, a White cop and his partner-in-training ran up behind me, asking for my college identification. At that time on the campus, we had experienced a series of muggings from an unknown man the students referred to as "BOLO" ("Be On the Look Out"), which was the heading of the posters across the campus. Immediately I cooperated with the White officers, asking if another assault had taken place, but I was given no answer. The officers asked me to come with them, and I cooperated fully with no resistance, but I continued to ask questions, trying to get an idea of what had happened. Eventually, the officers informed me that I should not throw rocks at the windows to gain entrance into the building. After pleading my case that I had thrown no rocks, the White officers informed me that I could be subdued for misconduct and for resisting them although I had remained absolutely calm. I asked one final question, which was "What was the description of the rock throwing assailant?" The officer responded with "a short Black man wearing blue jeans and a black shirt." At that point, it dawned on me that it mattered not that I was not wearing blue jeans, or that I was not wearing a black shirt, or that I was not short, as I stand six feet, two inches in height. What mattered was that I was a Black man, and I fit the description perfectly.

This experience led me to understand what young African American men all over the United States realize: that there are "police whose too frequent relation to black communities is a corrupted one of containment rather than protection" (Williams, 1998, p. 40). That incident led me to write in the margins of my paper while doing homework for the writing workshop class that night the following five-line poem:

> Because of my race,
> I must be kept in my place.
> "Forget your schooling, boy,
> For it is just a toy—
> 'Cause you're still a Black face!"

The bottom line is that I am an African American man at a Predominately White Institution living in a predominately White nation, as African Americans make up approximately 13 percent of the United States population (Williams, 1998). It matters not that I am pursuing a doctorate or that I am educated. Race still does matter in this world regardless of how many "baby steps" African Americans have taken since the Civil Rights Movement. At the end of every day, I am reminded that I am still an African American man just as Danny Glover and Cornel West came to that epiphany respectively as they stood on a New York street corner while attempting to hail a taxi cab. Race still does matter and it exists in spite of socioeconomic status, political affiliations, gender, and education, even if that education is in the form of a doctorate.

My Eyes Are Watching God

The doctoral program has seemed like a perpetual process. As I write this reflection, I am preparing to defend my dissertation proposal, and the initial feedback from committee members seems positive. I have come a long way in only a few years, but I have experienced quite a bit as an African American male doctoral student at a Predominately White Institution. At this moment, I am battling the nasty stigma of "ABD," which means "all but dissertation" to many people. To many doctoral students, "ABD" is equivalent to the Bermuda Triangle. Many students enter but very few exit, as they mysteriously vanish, never to be seen or heard from again. Being unique, though, I have placed a positive spin on the negative "ABD" stigma. Relying heavily on Southern dialect, I have changed the acronym from meaning "all but dissertation" to mean "Anthony's 'bout done." Instead of perceiving "ABD" as some negative symbol of disgrace, I wear it as a badge of honor. To reach this point in the doctoral program is quite an achievement in itself. Its sole purpose is to serve as a reminder that the real prize is at hand and should not be looked upon negatively.

For me, it has been imperative to approach not only the "ABD" but also the doctoral process with a positive attitude. In the face of the odds of being accepted to a doctoral program, in the face of overt racism at the onset of the doctoral program, and in the face of criticism from Whites and African Americans, I have consistently remained positive and optimistic. I could attribute this optimism to many things along the way—a wonderful support group of doctoral students consisting of White and of African Americans who have provided kind words of encouragement; knowledgeable professors who have provided endless guidance, who have made themselves available to answer questions, and who have offered valuable input and suggestions; a group of supportive colleagues at work who have cheered me on every day and reminded me that trouble does not last always; an extremely talented and wise "Ph.D." at work who has served as a mentor and guide, who has challenged me to look at issues in totality, and who has been a great friend; a wonderful and caring family that loves me regardless of how many times I fail.

It has not been any special recipe or some mystical mathematical formula that has catapulted me to this point. In fact, it has been nothing extremely special or profound that I have done. Through all my challenging coursework, through all the criticisms, and through all the odds, I have kept my eyes on God. His Word has provided strength when I have felt distraught, discouraged, and dejected. His Word has offered insight on problems that have led to solutions that I could never see. His Word has supplied encouragement and inspiration during the early morning hours when no one else has been present to assume that role. Every day I put His name and His Word before me, and I walk by faith in His footsteps. Positive things will continuously happen as long as my eyes are watching God.

References

Fordham, S., & Ogbu, J. U. (1986). Black students' school success: Coping with the 'Burden of Acting White.' *Urban Review, 18*(3), 176–206.

Lee, M. G., Jarrett, J. M., & Mbalia, D. D. (2002). *Heritage: African American readings for writing* (2nd ed.). Prentice Hall: Upper Saddle River, New Jersey.

Jencks, C., & Phillips, M. (Eds.). (1998). *The Black-White test score gap.* Washington, DC: Brookings Institution Press.

Jones, L. (Ed.). (2000). *Brothers of the academy: Up and coming Black scholars earning our way in higher education.* Sterling, Virginia: Stylus Publications.

Oakes, J. (1985). *Keeping track: How schools structure inequality.* New Haven: Yale University Press.

Rose, M. (1989). *Lives on the boundary: The struggles and achievements of America's underprepared.* New York: Free Press.

Steele, C. M. (1992). Race and the schooling of Black Americans. *The Atlantic Monthly, 269*(4), 67–78.

Steele, C. M., & Aronson, J. (1998). Stereotype threat and the test performance of academically successful African-Americans. In C. Jencks & M. Phillips (Eds.), *The Black-White test score gap* (pp. 401–427). Washington, DC: Brookings Institution Press.

Williams, P. J. (1998). *Seeing a color-blind future: The paradox of race.* New York: Noonday Press.

Terrolyn Carter

Hometown: New Orleans, Louisiana
Current Institution: University of Missouri at Columbia
Department: Rural Sociology
Personal Philosophy: The way I live and experience life can be reflected in one statement, a belief I'm thankful to my parents for instilling in me— "I can do all things through Christ which strengtheneth me."

     —Philippians 4:13

9

ENDURING THE RACE

A DIARY OF MY GRADUATE YEARS

> I will persist until I succeed. Always
> will I take another step. If that is of no
> avail I will take another, and yet another.
> In truth, one step at a time is not too dif-
> ficult . . . I know that small attempts,
> repeated, will complete my undertaking.
> —*Og Mandino*

When people learn that I am pursuing a Ph.D. in rural sociology, I am praised and congratulated for my successes. However, following this praise, I am immediately asked to define rural sociology and explain why I chose to get a doctoral degree in this discipline. Rural sociology is an applied sociology that links research to practice. Scholars in the discipline focus on a variety of societal issues that are not solely limited to rural people and their environments. For example, my research interests are related to educational achievement of minorities, in both urban and rural communities. Although I will be obtaining a Ph.D. in rural sociology, this was not my initial plan when I began graduate school. My plan was to pursue a doctoral degree in counseling psychology, but my preparation for graduate school as well as my experiences during graduate school have led me to my current degree program.

Preparing for Graduate School

My aspiration to attend graduate school was not fully realized until the end of my junior year in college. Thus, I had a very limited amount of time to prepare for graduate school. I immediately began my preparation by becoming a part of GradStar, a program at my undergraduate insti-tution designed specifically to help students who will pursue a Ph.D. As a participant in this program I attended monthly meetings that primarily focused on choosing graduate programs, the application process, and acquiring funding for graduate school. In addition, this program sponsored campus visits to a number of Research Extensive and Intensive universities. GradStar particularly assisted us with securing funds for graduate education. The director of GradStar informed me that acquiring funding for graduate school that covered both tuition and living expenses was significant to my attainment of a graduate degree.

Financial assistance became the deciding factor between the remaining two graduate schools of my choice. I had to decide whether I would pursue a graduate degree at a Predominately White Institution (PWI) or a Historically Black College and University (HBCU). Based on the amount of funding I received from each institution, I decided to attend the PWI. I was informed by the graduate school at the HBCU that financial assistance (teaching and research assistantships) were primarily awarded to students currently at the doctoral level.

I am fortunate to have received the type of preparation and assistance I needed to get into graduate school; however, I lacked the preparation that was essential to surviving the *process* of matriculating through a graduate program. My assumptions about graduate school were basically formed by observations I made of my mother and other family members who had attained post-baccalaureate degrees. Yet, their experiences would prove to be quite different from my experiences. There are a number of reasons why they could not prepare me for what I was to endure. These differences may be attributed to the timing of their attendance to graduate school (e.g., my mother attended graduate school to earn a master's degree in mathematics after marriage and creating family), the type of institution they attended (e.g., Research Extensive, Intensive, Comprehensive), and their discipline of study (e.g., Business, Mathematics). For example, before leaving for graduate school, one of my aunts believed that it should only take me eighteen months to complete the master's program. I immediately responded to her that the program I applied to required me to complete thirty hours of coursework and six hours of research and thesis writing in order to complete the two-year terminal master's program. Though I had applied to a terminal master's degree program, I had planned to continue my education and pursue a Ph.D. However, my plan changed after my first year in the master's program.

Transitioning from a HBCU to a PWI

The transition from a small, historically Black liberal arts university to a predominately White, Research Extensive institution was more challenging than I would realize. First, there was a change in the academic support system that I previously received at my undergraduate institution. Unexpectedly, I had entered a world in which students believed there was only one Ph.D., and we were all competing for that degree. Consequently, many doctoral students as well as master's students competed against one another for something that everyone could potentially attain. This was a challenge for me because how do you become acclimated into an environment without guidance and support from your peers. Furthermore, the limited number of African American students in the graduate program exacerbated the lack of support I received in the program. For example, during my first year, there were only three African American students (including myself) out of approximately forty graduate students in the graduate program. This number declined the following year to only two African American students in the graduate program.

The number of African American students in my graduate program was most likely representative of the percentage of African American graduate students attending the university. For example, during 1998, approximately 5 percent of the graduate student population at the university was African American (Office of Admissions and Registration). Since 1998, the percentage of African Americans pursuing a graduate degree at this institution declined. As reported by the university's office of admissions and registration, currently 4.2 percent of the graduate student population is African American. In comparison, 92 percent of the graduate student population is White American. The relatively low percentage of African Americans attending the university has also had significant implications for me socially.

My interaction with other African Americans outside of the university setting was limited because the surrounding city consisted of predominately, White middle-class families. African Americans made up only 11 percent of the city population. This includes African American students and faculty at the university. In response to this environment, African American graduate students, in many ways, were forced to build their own community through the Association of Black Graduate and Professional Students (ABGPS). For me, this organization became both my academic and social support system. Essentially, ABGPS became my family because it gave me (and still does) the emotional and sometimes financial support needed to matriculate through my graduate program. I was even more fortunate than other graduate students, because I had a close friend from college who was already attending the university. She assisted me in becoming acclimated to the academic and social environment. This relationship, in part to the support received from my family, played a significant role in my completion of the master's program.

Matriculating Through the Master's Program

My experiences during graduate school at this institution are primarily twofold because I earned a terminal master's degree in one graduate program, and will be earning my doctoral degree in another graduate program. As I look back throughout the years, I can say that my experiences as a graduate student drastically changed midway through my graduate career. During the first three years of graduate school, I entered a master's program in the Department of Human Development and Family Studies. I decided to obtain my master's degree in this program for a number of reasons.

Although I felt academically prepared for the course work in the master's program, I was soon proven wrong on the first day of class. In particular, my preparation for understanding research was not at the same level of other students who had previously attained their undergraduate degrees at research intensive institutions. My research experiences were limited to a part-time job as a research assistant in which I mainly entered data into a spreadsheet file and a psychology lab course that required me to design a basic research study. For example, I had no idea how to write a literature review, test the reliability and validity of measures, and even more so, I did not understand how to read and interpret empirical research articles. Understanding research articles was necessary to performing well in my courses because the majority of these courses required reading a large amount of research studies. Without asking other graduate students for assistance I continued to struggle through my courses.

My position as a teaching assistant (TA) only increased my academic load and demanded more time than I expected. As a TA, my duties were to teach two lab classes per week, grade papers and assignments for each student in those classes, hold office hours, attend the larger lecture classes, and attend weekly TA meetings. Despite this workload, I thoroughly enjoyed teaching. Teaching a small group of students gave me the opportunity to hone my skills as a future professor. I had fun finding new and innovative ways of teaching students theories and concepts about human development; this was a subject that students could easily apply to their own experiences. This experience was to prepare me for a position later as a graduate instructor (i.e., teaches own course without direct guidance) in the department. Yet, before this opportunity presented itself, other challenges emerged at the very end of my first year in the graduate program.

My advisor, whom I was just beginning to build a relationship with, decided to leave the university. He informed me that this would not affect the completion of my research and master's thesis. My anxiety escalated when other graduate students questioned me about the completion of my research study and which faculty member in the department would assist me through the thesis process. Before my advisor left, I asked him to identify a faculty member who would be most appropriate to serve as my new advisor and the chairperson of my thesis committee. I told my advisor that I really wanted someone who would work well with him. I decided to ask that question, in particular, because through conversations with other graduate students, I learned that it is good to have a committee that not only liked one another, but could also work well together.

During this time, I did not understand the significance and relevance of choosing an academic advisor. Even more so, I did not realize the significance of *every* choice I made in graduate school. Whether I was choosing to teach an extra lab class or work on a faculty member's research project, my choices would determine my paths. For example, choosing to work on a research project with my first advisor completely and forever changed my research interests.

As a part of my advisor's research project, I was primarily responsible for interviewing thirty African American male and female young adults. The overall goal of this research study was to collect quantitative and qualitative data on African American young adults' educational, occupational, and general life experiences as they transitioned into adulthood. Furthermore, we were interested in these young adults' conceptions of adulthood. I knew then, this would not have been my choice for a thesis topic because it was not my area of interest. I wanted to conduct research on African American teenage mothers. But, I had no idea how to tell my advisor that I was interested in researching this group of people. Without hesitation, I accepted this "great" opportunity (as people pointed out) to work with a well-published and established researcher in the field of adolescent development. Moreover, I was told by both faculty and students that using my advisor's data for my thesis project would make it easier to complete my master's program in two years. Of course, I agreed that this was a good idea for a number of reasons: (1) I would gain quantitative and qualitative research experience for the first time; (2) I would receive $15 per hour for conducting face-to-face interviews and passing out surveys; (3) I would complete the data collection for my thesis by the beginning of the next school year; and (4) I could conduct the research during the summer in my hometown. Nevertheless, each of these reasons alone would have convinced me to work on the project.

In actuality, it did not matter which part of the data I *wanted* to use because I did not *own* the data. My choices were limited in that I was told which part of the data I could use for my thesis. Again, I accepted this option as an easy way out and was very happy that I did not have to continue agonizing over finding a topic for my thesis project. Furthermore, if I did not accept the topic given to me, I would not have had data to analyze for my thesis. Choosing not to use this data could have also potentially added an extra year to my master's program.

As I finished the coursework for my master's program, I continued writing my thesis throughout the summer. I completed and defended my thesis the following fall semester. To me, this was a great achievement because I accomplished a task that many other graduate students who had begun the program before me did not achieve. Moreover, finishing my thesis determined, in part, my acceptance into the doctoral program. I decided that I wanted to remain at the university and obtain my Ph.D. in the same department. Applying to the doctoral program in this department may be to date one of my most challenging experiences in graduate school.

The process of applying to graduate school had begun again. Though I was seeking a doctoral degree in the same department, the application process remained the same. I was still required to complete an application, write a new statement of purpose, and submit new recommendation letters and Graduate Record Examination (GRE) scores. In essence, the requirements were the same, but the level of meeting these requirements had changed. My application for the doctoral program was "tabled."

Prior to learning about the department's decision regarding my application, my advisor discussed with me the faculty's decision concerning my application to the doctoral program. My advisor explained that she wanted me to be prepared for the letter I would receive in the mail and further stated that she, along with the departmental chairperson, supported me in my pursuit of the doctoral degree in the department. Knowing I had some support among faculty members influenced whether or not I would continue to pursue the doctoral degree. I also learned from other doctoral students that if my advisor wanted me in the doctoral program to work with her, then there was no doubt that I would be accepted. In other words, doctoral students who express an interest (in their statement of purpose) in conducting research with a certain faculty member have an increased likelihood of being accepted into a program. The applicant's chances of being accepted into the program are increased if a faculty member is willing to serve as that student's mentor throughout the doctoral process.

My advisor told me that she would support me and push for my acceptance into the program. However, I was unsure how much influence she held in the department. My advisor came into the department the same year I did, so she was still relatively new to the department and university. Although she entered the department as a tenured associate professor, being relatively new in the department might have weakened her ability to influence (which translates into power) other faculty members on the admissions committee to accept me into the

Ph.D. program. I truly believe this was the reason my advisor's influence was not effective.

I learned throughout the years in my master's program that power in the department solely resided in the hands of one person, the director of graduate studies. She was the deciding factor on my being accepted into the doctoral program. The director of graduate studies wanted me to retake the GRE because the scores I had originally submitted to the master's program did not meet the requirements for the doctoral program. The faculty informed me that I needed to retake the GRE and score at least within the 50th percentile rank in two of the three subject areas. If I attained this goal, then I would be accepted into the doctoral program. Again, this seemed unfair, because there were other graduate students at that time in the doctoral program who did not attain GRE scores in the 50th percentile rank. I was courageous enough to state this fact to the department's director of graduate studies because I did not understand why I had to retake this test. The director of graduate studies agreed that there were other students who did not attain the required scores, but because I did not "earn enough A's in my previous courses" to balance out my application packet, my GRE scores needed to increase substantially.

Preparing for the GRE was difficult because I was still a full-time student in the department. Though I had completed the master's program, I was advised and allowed to continue taking courses in the department because my advisor expected me to be accepted into the doctoral program. Moreover, the courses I was taking that year would later contribute toward the doctoral program. In addition, I was awarded a teaching position in the department. This position gave me the opportunity to teach a yearlong course that consisted of more than 120 undergraduate students. Typically, this position was reserved for doctoral students in the department. These commitments along with research limited the time I needed to study and prepare for the GRE.

After taking the GRE numerous times and spending hundreds of dollars, I finally achieved scores that reached the 47 percent percentile rank, a substantial increase from my original scores. Both my advisor and I thought this would satisfy the director of graduate studies and other faculty members; however, we were mistaken. It was then that my advisor asked me whether I had considered taking a break from graduate school. At this point, I began to feel as if she no longer had confidence in my ability to pursue the doctoral degree. As a result, I began to seek guidance elsewhere.

I decided to explain my situation to an African American professor at the university because I was interested in her perceptions of the situation. She also could not understand why the department placed so much emphasis on a test that does not determine an individual's ability to attain a Ph.D. She told me the large amount of money I had spent retaking the test and the stress that accompanied this process was not worth it. The professor advised me to really think hard about whether my career goals could be achieved by matriculating through another doctoral program. She suggested that I continue to strive for the Ph.D., even if it was not going to be in the department I was currently in.

Matriculating Through the Doctoral Program

The Department of Sociology seemed to be an appropriate fit for my research interests. I had become highly interested in the department when I took a course in sociology during my master's program. Yet, before I applied to the program, a close friend suggested that I talk to an African American doctoral student who was once in that department. After speaking with this student and other African American doctoral students, I decided not to apply to the doctoral program in the Department of Sociology. I was informed that graduate students, primarily African American students, were having a hard time passing the comprehensive examinations and completing the doctoral program. Because I was really searching for a program that would combine interests in teaching, research, and practice, one of those students suggested that I talk to a faculty member in the Department of Rural Sociology.

Like many people, I had never heard of Rural Sociology, so I was very apprehensive about applying to the doctoral program. I was fearful that a Ph.D. in Rural Sociology would not be prestigious enough for me to compete in the academic job market. These concerns faded when I learned about the marketability of the degree. When I met with the professor in that department, I learned more about the discipline and became excited, specifically about what the doctoral program in rural sociology could offer me academically and professionally. After the conversation with that professor (who eventually later became my doctoral advisor and mentor), I applied to the doctoral program in the Department of Rural Sociology and was accepted.

As a doctoral student in the Department of Rural Sociology opportunities for me to engage in research, teaching, and practice have been limitless. I was afforded these opportunities because my advisor in this department has motivated me to seek new and challenging experiences. For example, my first year in the doctoral program I served as a teaching assistant for one of his undergraduate courses, while I was a co-instructor for another of his undergraduate courses. Within that first semester, I was able to learn and experience teaching in two different environments at two vastly different levels. As a teaching assistant, I primarily graded papers and assignments and rarely facilitated class discussions. As a co-instructor, I assisted with the course design, facilitated class discussions, and evaluated and assessed student presentations and papers. Following that semester, I was able to participate in a community development project in which I served as a community development agent for a rural town in Missouri. During the length of this project, I took a course that assisted me with linking theory to practice. Making this connection between theory and practice was important to me because I was more interested in applied research than theoretical research.

The most challenging part of the doctoral process in Rural Sociology has been the coursework. My struggles in these courses are related to my comprehension of sociological theories and concepts that I have been introduced to for the first time in my academic career. Thus, keeping up with other classmates in my sociological courses has forced me to put forth double the amount of time needed for completing papers and other assignments. I shared with my advisor that when I listened to other students discuss the course material in class they seemed to comprehend and explain the material at a higher level. My advisor also explained to me that "sometimes graduate students try to impress professors by presenting complicated ideas and using big words." My advisor further stated that the goal of understanding complex theories and concepts is to break them down into simpler terms. He reassured me that I was accomplishing this goal because my grades reflected my performance in these courses. During times when I lacked confidence and experienced self-doubt about my intellect, my advisor gave me the extra support and motivation I needed to continue through the doctoral process.

My relationship with my current advisor has changed my life academically and personally. From the beginning of my doctoral program, he has continued to provide the support and attention I have needed to attain the Ph.D. This does not mean that my previous advisors did not provide me with support; they did, however, this support came at different levels. My advisor's rank as Professor in the department and university enables him to devote more time to his advisees than my other advisors who had not yet reached this level. There were many times when I have sat in my advisor's office and talked to him at length about any issue that was on my mind.

My advisor always encourages me and other graduate students to meet with him to discuss our coursework, potential research projects, and other issues that were pertinent to our matriculation through the doctoral program. For example, my advisor brought together his advisees once a week for an entire semester to give each student an opportunity to share their current research/dissertation projects with one another. When we presented at these meetings we were able to receive feedback from him as well as other graduate students. My advisor believed that presenting and discussing our research agendas was an important part of our professional development especially for graduate students who were interested in becoming faculty members.

Throughout the years, I have been very successful in acquiring experiences that I know will contribute to my success as a future professor. Particularly, my current assistantship as graduate coordinator of the Preparing Future Faculty (PFF) program has increased my understanding of the realities and expectations of the faculty role. The PFF program at my institution is part of the national PFF movement that was started by the Council and Graduate Schools (CGS) and the Association of American Colleges and Universities (AACU). It is a comprehensive program designed for Ph.D. students interested in an academic career. More importantly, the goal of this program is to ensure that graduate students are prepared for faculty roles in a diverse range of university settings (not only Research Extensive and Intensive institutions).

Although this program is limited to Ph.D. students nominated by the chairperson in their department, all graduate students benefit by attending a myriad of seminar sessions that include presentations by faculty and staff on topics ranging from teaching with technology to the realities of tenure and promotion. However, there always seems to be a very small number of African American graduate students who attend seminars such as those stated previously. Some people assume that African American students may not be aware of professional development opportunities at the university, but my membership in the Association of Black Graduate and Professional Students allows me to inform African American graduate students about these professional development events and activities taking place throughout the year. Notwithstanding my advocacy of such opportunities, the number of African American students attending professional development seminars continues to be significantly lower than White American graduate students. Low attendance among African American students at these seminars concerns me, especially since research indicates that minority graduate students, in comparison to their White counterparts, have fewer opportunities for professional socialization experiences (Perna, 1999). Moreover, doctoral students have been found to be unclear about faculty life.

Overall, my experiences attending a Predominately White Institution have been rewarding while at the same time challenging. I believe that in both my master's and doctoral programs, I have been afforded numerous opportunities to develop and enhance my skills as a researcher and teacher. The doctoral program has extended these experiences by introducing me to career opportunities outside of academia (nonprofit organizations, government positions). In addition, each course I have taken has equipped me with the knowledge necessary for understanding theoretical perspectives and concepts that would enable me to contribute to my discipline and area of research. The challenges I have encountered throughout this process have only reinforced my resiliency to survive and endure an academic career that will be laborious and demanding.

References

Minority Student Enrollment, Fall Semesters. (1998–2002). University of Missouri-Columbia, The Office of Admissions and Registration.

Perna, L. W. (1999). The role of Historically Black Colleges and Universities in preparing African Americans for faculty careers. Paper presented at the 1999 annual meeting of the American Educational Research Association, Montreal, Canada.

Jonda McNair, Ph.D.

Hometown: Macon, Georgia
Current Institution: The Ohio State University
Department: English Education
Personal Philosophy: Once you learn to read, you will be forever free.

10

"WALK TALL IN THE WORLD"

REFLECTIONS FROM A SCHOLAR OF AFRICAN AMERICAN CHILDREN'S LITERATURE

> The color of the skin is in no way con-
> nected with strength of the mind or
> intellectual powers.
> —*Benjamin Banneker*

"Walk tall in the world," says Mama to Everett Anderson (Clifton, 1974).

Several years ago as a graduate student pursuing a master's degree in elementary education at the University of Florida, I was encouraged by my advisor to apply for admission to the doctoral program in the College of Education. Upon submitting an application, I eagerly awaited a reply. I assumed that with a Graduate Records Examination (GRE) score of 1010 and a 3.5 GPA that my chances of acceptance were above average, with the only possible drawback being my lack of classroom teaching experience. One day at the end of a master's seminar, in which I was enrolled, the professor pulled me aside and explained that she was chairing the committee in charge of reviewing doctoral applications. She also stated that she believed I could successfully complete doctoral coursework but that I would experience difficulty when it came to the analysis stage of the dissertation, as if intellectually competent doctoral students dash through their dissertations trouble-free.

Noted historian, John Hope Franklin (1989), in his essay "The Dilemma of the American Negro Scholar" addresses some of the challenges that Blacks encounter in the world of scholarship and contends that one of the foremost challenges is that African Americans must constantly prove themselves to be intelligent and capable of scholarly work. The aforementioned quote by Benjamin Banneker is one that most African American scholars find themselves incessantly attempting to demonstrate. Franklin (1989) writes:

> At the very time when American scholarship in general was making its claim to recognition, it was denying that Negroes were capable of being scholars. Few Americans, even those who advocated a measure of political equality, subscribed to the view that Negroes—any Negroes—had the ability to think either abstractly or concretely or to assimilate ideas that had been formulated by others. (p. 297)

As an emerging critical race theorist, I now question the extent to which my skin color might have influenced this professor's notions in regard to my ability to engage in higher level, abstract thinking and whether or not a White student in my position would have received a similar response? Basically I took this conversation to indicate that I wouldn't be accepted into the doctoral program because she, the chairperson reviewing the applications, didn't think that I was fully capable of the analytical thinking required to complete a dissertation. Around this same time my advisor, all of a sudden, began to suggest that perhaps instead of applying to the College of Education, I should consider applying to the College of English in order to receive a doctorate in children's literature through that department. I "got the message" and realized that she had probably also been told by my master's seminar professor that my chances of being accepted into the College of Education's doctoral program were virtually nil. I was deeply upset by this experience but decided that maybe it wasn't a good idea to receive all three of my degrees from the same institution and that I did need experience as a public school teacher. I begin this article with a description of this experience in order to demonstrate that from the very beginning, my goal of acquiring a doctorate has been an uphill and challenging process.

Unfortunately, incidents such as the aforementioned are not atypical in the discourse related to the experiences of African American students attending Predominately White Institutions. African American students must negotiate and contend with the academic, emotional, financial, and psychological challenges that doctoral programs typically entail along with racism, therefore making a process that is already difficult enough even more so for them. In a qualitative investigation involving eight African American students pursuing doctoral degrees at Predominately White Institutions, researchers found a common thread to be the questioning of students' writing abilities by White professors (Patterson-Stewart, Ritchie, & Sanders, 1997). Similarly, in a research study involving African American women pursuing doctoral degrees at the University of Michigan, Woods (2001) contends that one of their most prevalent concerns was being perceived as unintelligent by faculty. This article offers an account of my experiences as one African American woman in pursuit of a terminal degree at a Predominately White Institution. I will also incorporate relevant research, which relates to my experiences as well as my interests in children's literature as a means of affirmation for African American children especially.

My Career Before Doctoral Studies

After the incident with the professor in my master's seminar course, I graduated a few months later from the University of Florida, receiving a "C+" in my master's seminar class. This would be the lowest grade that I would ever receive during my graduate coursework. Ironically, the master's thesis, for which I received this grade, was looked upon favorably by professors when I applied to enter the doctoral program in the School of Teaching and Learning at The Ohio State University in Columbus.

Upon graduation I returned to my hometown of Macon, Georgia, and acquired a position as an elementary school teacher. During my five years as a public school teacher there, I taught students in grades kindergarten, first, and second. As a graduate student at the University of Florida, I had specialized in children's literature and so books served an integral role in my pedagogical practices. I utilized children's literature to teach subjects across the curriculum, so for example, if my students and I were learning about the solar system, I made sure to incorporate an abundance of literature about the planets and famous astronomers such as Benjamin Banneker. In an attempt to incorporate technology, I also encouraged my students to utilize the Internet in order to browse the websites of well-known authors and illustrators (McNair, 2000).

I attempted to not only teach my students to read but more importantly to love reading by sharing books with them every day and encouraging them to view reading as a meaningful, pleasurable, and worthwhile activity. According to Morrow (2001), U.S. surveys indicate that approximately 60 percent of Americans don't even read one book after completion of high school while the remaining 40 percent read an average of one book each year. These statistics indicate that most Americans don't enjoy reading and are alliterate. As a teacher, I worked diligently to alter these discouraging figures.

After five years, I decided that it was time to refocus on my goal of obtaining a doctorate. In my experience as an elementary school teacher, I discovered that most teachers weren't as knowledgeable or as excited about children's literature as I was and I believed that if I were to receive a doctorate in reading and become a college professor, I could have a greater impact on children by teaching educators as opposed to children. I had kept in contact with my advisor over the years and so when I spoke with her about my plans to pursue a doctoral degree, she recommended that I attend The Ohio State University in Columbus, one of the few universities in the country to offer a doctorate in children's literature. She also told me about a highly regarded professor who specialized in African American children's literature, Dr. Rudine Sims Bishop, who would later become my advisor.

After flying to Columbus, Ohio, in April for a Friday afternoon interview with several of the faculty, I was accepted into the program and slated to begin in the fall of 1999. I resigned from my teaching position and made plans to relocate. Over the summer I struggled with leaving my family, my hometown, and my job and began to grapple with the realization that pursuing a doctorate would encompass a plethora of difficulties in addition to the common academic rigors such as completing coursework and writing a dissertation. My mother and I drove the 600 plus miles to Columbus before the beginning of the fall quarter to search for an apartment, and after getting lost a number of times along the way, as we approached Columbus, my Mama compared our difficult and long road trip to the journey that I would face over the next few years. She told me that at times it would be tough and that I occasionally might lose my way or think I was lost even when I was headed in the right direction but that if I was persistent and didn't

give up, I would earn my doctorate just as I had found my way
to Columbus.

Making the Adjustments

The first year of the doctoral program for me was extremely difficult
for a number of reasons. While teaching school I received a decent
salary and lived at home with my Mama, so I had very little expenses.
All of a sudden, I had taken an enormous pay cut and began to incur
bills such as rent and utilities. Pedicures, frequent hair appointments,
shopping sprees, and Bath and Body products went from being "sta-
ples" to becoming luxuries that I could no longer afford. Also, having
grown up in the South and attended college there as well, I had never
lived in another part of the country and I found myself experiencing
culture shock. My hometown of Macon, Georgia, is fairly small while
Columbus is one of the largest cities in the country. Frequently, after a
long and difficult day on campus, I would get lost on the way home,
only adding to my frustration level.

I was so challenged by the reading materials for my courses that I
once jokingly confided to my advisor that I was beginning to think that
I had a reading disability. This is a statement I would have never made
to a White advisor and it attests to the importance of having African
American faculty at Predominately White Institutions with whom
Black students can honestly confide and seek support without fear of
being perceived as lacking in terms of ability. Upon developing friendships with other White, Black and Asian doctoral students, I later
found out that all of them experienced similar feelings and problems at
the onset of their doctoral programs. As a result of these friendships,
family support, mentoring from supportive faculty, and God's help,
I eventually made the necessary adjustments and began to function successfully as a doctoral student.

In all fairness, I must say that as a graduate student at The Ohio
State University, my overall experiences with faculty members, of all
races, have been pleasant. The majority of the White faculty with
whom I have interacted is progressive and possesses what I call a
"social critical consciousness." Most of them acknowledge the benefits
that their "whiteness" affords them, conduct critical self-reflection in

regard to their socialization in a society that is fundamentally racist, and encourage their students to do the same.

Race [Always] Matters

After conducting a presentation on poetry at a state conference for early childhood educators held in Columbus, the moderator provided me with a few minutes to peruse the evaluation forms. As I browsed through them, I was pleased to see that I had received mostly marks of "excellent" and "good" along with encouraging and thankful comments. One evaluation that rated my presentation as "poor" caused me to stop and read it more carefully. The attendee to my session had written that I shouldn't have read only poems by African Americans and that in the future I should read more "general poems," as if the poems written by people of color were not "general poems." Even though this racist comment angered me, I wasn't overly surprised or shocked.

As I left the conference and drove to the public library to return some of the books, I reflected on whether or not I might have read more poems by African Americans than by people of other racial backgrounds. The fact is that even if I did read more poems by African American poets, this would hardly affect the dominance of White poets such as Shel Silverstein and Jack Prelutsky in the field of children's literature, and it would have provided much needed knowledge about literature that is not canonized in the same manner as books by White authors, such as J. K. Rowling and Eric Carle.

However, I do make a special effort to include literature written by people of color, so I had chosen books of poetry written by not just European Americans, but also Asian Americans, Latin Americans, Native Americans, and African Americans. As I walked into the library, I decided to sit down at one of the tables and categorize the poetry books that I had read by the race of the author. I discovered that I had shared nine books of poetry by European American authors, four books of poetry by African American authors, three books of poetry by Latin American authors and one book of poetry by a Native American. Then I proceeded to count up how many poems I read from each of the books to discover that I had read a total of nineteen poems written by Whites, seven poems written by African Americans, three poems written by

Asian Americans, five poems written by Latin Americans, and three poems written by Native Americans. Why is it that this attendee accused me of reading only poems by African Americans, when in fact I had read more poems written by Whites? More importantly, why did he or she resist exposure to literature written by African Americans of which most educators know little about? The answer is most likely racism.

This story illustrates the challenges that scholars of color often encounter when conducting work in their fields of study. We are situated as being overly biased and incapable of maintaining objectivity. The truth of the matter is that all scholars are biased and it could be argued that the word "objectivity" in itself is a misnomer. The fact that I chose to specialize in African American children's literature is influenced by my "Blackness" but I would argue that "Whiteness" impacted the decision of Charles Murray and the late Richard Herrnstein to write the controversial book entitled, *The Bell Curve,* which argues that there are measurable genetic differences between people of different races. According to the authors, on average, Blacks possess an IQ that is fifteen points below that of Whites. How likely would a Black person be to write a book that makes such outrageous, offensive, and racist claims? Are Charles Murray and Richard Herrnstein objective? I think not and I would argue the book they have written serves as an example of how the written word can serve to maintain and legitimize white supremacy while marginalizing people of color.

The racism that I have encountered as a doctoral student has been mainly on the part of White preservice teachers in an undergraduate children's literature course that I teach. The comments of the attendee to my poetry session echo the sentiments of many of the preservice teachers with whom I interact as an instructor. I utilize children's literature with preservice teachers to help them learn to read the word and, more importantly, the world, something that I neglected to do with my elementary school students (Freire & Macedo, 1987). I address issues such as White privilege and racism within the context of children's literature. In my two years of experience as an instructor of mainly white, middle-class preservice teachers, I have found that they exhibit an enormous amount of resistance when confronted with sociopolitical issues such as racism and they accuse me of talking about race "too much." When forced to participate in discussions involving racial bias and/or stereotypes in children's books they often engage in behavior labeled by Christine Sleeter (1996) as "white racial bonding." Sleeter (1996) states:

> By "racial bonding," I mean simply interactions in which whites engage that have the purpose of affirming a common stance on race-related issues, legitimating particular interpretations of groups of color, and drawing conspiratorial we-they boundaries. These interaction patterns take such forms as inserts into conversations, race-related "asides" in conversations, strategic eye contact, jokes and code words. (pp. 149–150)

An example of one of the books that I usually choose for the preservice teachers to read is entitled *The Watsons go to Birmingham— 1963* (Curtis, 1995), a story of an African American family visiting a relative in Birmingham, Alabama, when the Sixteenth Street Baptist Church is bombed, resulting in the death of four young girls. During class discussions of the book, I find it virtually impossible to completely ignore racism and its effects on people of color, which is a central issue within the book. Typically I find that White preservice teachers avoid discussing racial issues in their responses and often attempt to "deracialize" texts. Fortunately, I have come to an understanding of theoretical positions, such as critical race theory and social dominance theory, which offer explanations for the reluctance and or inability of many Whites to think critically in terms of racial issues. Critical race theory maintains that racism is a "permanent fixture" in American society and it is so pervasive that Americans tend to see the effects of racism as "normal" rather than deviant (Delgado, 1995). Social dominance theory contends that the way in which people view the world is shaped by their position of dominance within it (Howard, 1999). Therefore, because Whites are members of a dominant social group and are not subjected to racism in the manner in which people of color are, it is difficult for them to think critically about racial issues.

My Paradigmatic Shifts in Regard to Children's Literature

As I approach the completion of my doctoral program, I remain committed to the idea that children should be exposed to a wealth of children's literature and be encouraged by educators to view reading as a pleasurable and worthwhile activity. However, my position on children's literature has changed in many facets as well. For instance, I am now much more cognizant of the "politics" of children's literature and believe as Mem Fox (1993) states in an article that "There is no such thing as a politically innocent picture book" (p. 656). Children's books are political for a number of reasons. First of all, they are political in the sense that they aid in socializing children who will one day become adults, and they reflect the biases, values, beliefs, and worldviews of their creators as well as the time period in which they were produced (McGillis, 1996; Nodelman, 1996). Children's literature published in the early twentieth century such as *The Story of Little Black Sambo* (Bannerman, 1899; 1923), which depicted African American protagonists in stereotypical and demeaning ways, illustrates this notion. According to Williams (1977) literature also has the power to maintain and legitimize the hegemony of dominant social groups such as European Americans, males, and the middle class. I am also much more deeply committed to the notion that African American children's literature has the potential to provide Black children with affirmations of their cultural norms, experiences, and historical legacy.

It is of the utmost criticality that African American children be exposed to "culturally conscious" children's literature. According to Sims (1982), "the label culturally conscious suggests that elements in the text, not just the pictures, make it clear that the book consciously seeks to depict a fictional Afro-American life experience" (p. 49). The delightful series of books, by poet Lucille Clifton, featuring an endearing, vivacious African American boy named Everett Anderson are examples of "culturally conscious" children's books. For example, in *Some of the Days of Everett Anderson* (Clifton, 1970) the text reads, "'Afraid of the dark is afraid of Mom and Daddy and Papa and Cousin Tom. I'd be as silly as I could be, afraid of the dark is afraid of Me!' says ebony Everett Anderson" (unnumbered pages). Within this passage, the author, through the voice of Everett Anderson, defies the negative connotations generally attributed to and associated with the word "black."

Recurring features within the books include descriptions of skin colors, nicknames, and names that are common within the African American community as well as its historical and cultural traditions. African American children need books that affirm their language, skin color, hair texture, and their historical legacy. According to Rudine Sims Bishop, (1990) "such literature will reflect back to the children positive images of themselves, transmit some of the shared values of the African American community, and help them learn how to 'walk tall in the world' " (p. 563).

Racial Identity Development in African American Children

For African American children existing in a society that is fundamentally racist, the development of a positive and healthy sense of racial identity is no easy task. Alvin Poussaint (1974) states:

> The psychological development of black children is greatly affected by prejudice, discrimination and racial segregation. Black children, like all children, come into the world victims of factors over which they have no control. In the looking glass of white society, the supposedly undesirable physical image of "Tar Baby"—black skin, wooly hair and thick lips—is contrasted unfavorably with the valued model of "Snow White,"—white skin, straight hair and aquiline features. (p. 138)

According to Banks (1993), research studies conducted over a span of fifty years have consistently demonstrated that from an early age, children are aware of racial and ethnic differences and have often internalized the perspectives, worldviews, and cultural norms of the dominant societal group. Kenneth and Mamie Clark's (1947) research studies with young children involving racial preferences, racial differences, and racial self-identification are quite well known and cited frequently. In one of their research studies, the Clarks selected 253 African American students between the ages of 3 and 7 from nursery schools in Arkansas and Massachusetts and asked them a series of questions related to brown and white dolls.

The Clarks discovered that more than 90 percent of the children were able to identify the dolls based on their race. So, when asked by the researcher to point out the colored doll or the white doll, the majority of the children were able to successfully complete the task. Also, when asked which dolls they identified with, 66 percent of the children selected the color dolls while only 33 percent selected the white dolls.

The Clarks also found that when given a choice between the two dolls the majority of the children chose the white one. Fifty-nine percent of the children in the study thought the brown doll looked bad while only 17 percent thought the white doll looked bad. Banks (1993) states:

> The Clarks interpreted the tendency of African American children to make incorrect racial self-identifications and to prefer white to brown images as an indication that the children were aware of and had internalized the dominant society's attitudes, perceptions, and evaluations of blacks and whites. (p. 238)

Due to the research studies conducted by the Clarks and other researchers who confirmed their findings, social scientists began to presume that most Black children had low self-esteem and harbored negative feelings about being black (Banks, 1993). Recently, researchers such as William Cross have critiqued these studies for methodological weaknesses and reinterpreted their findings by suggesting, for example, that it is possible for Black children to exhibit a pro-white bias and still maintain a positive sense of self-esteem (Banks, 1993; Cross, 1991).

The Brownies' Book Magazine

Children's literature is one of the ways in which Black children can develop a positive sense of self-esteem. Children's literature is powerful in that it aids in socializing young children and helps to shape their values, beliefs, and worldviews. Fully cognizant of the power of literature, W. E .B. Du Bois (1921) wrote:

> Heretofore the education of the Negro child has been too much in terms of white people. All through school life his text-books contain much about white people and little or nothing about his own race. All the pictures he sees are of white people. Most of the books he reads are by white authors, and his heroes and heroines are white. . . . The result is that all of the Negro child's idealism, all his sense of the good, the great and the beautiful is associated with white people . . . . He unconsciously gets the impression that the Negro has little chance to be great, heroic or beautiful. (p. 63)

In an attempt to educate African American children and give them a sense of their beauty, importance, and cultural and historical legacy, Du Bois along with members of the National Association for the

Advancement of Colored People (NAACP) Crisis staff created *The Brownies' Book,* one of the first periodicals directed primarily at Black children. Du Bois articulated the following seven objectives that he hoped to accomplish with the publication of this magazine:

1. To make colored children realize that being colored is a normal, beautiful thing;

2. To make them familiar with the history and achievements of the Negro race;

3. To make them know that other colored children have grown into useful, famous persons;

4. To teach them delicately, a code of honor and actions in their relations with white children;

5. To turn their little hurts and resentments into emulation, ambition and love of their own homes and companions;

6. To point out the best amusements and joys and worthwhile things of life;

7. To inspire them for definite occupations and duties with a broad spirit of sacrifices (Du Bois, 1919, p. 286).

According to Bishop and McNair (2002), "these goals reflected Du Bois' recognition that the available literature about Black children neither affirmed them as human beings nor informed them about their history and culture" (p. 110). *The Brownies' Book* was published monthly for two years with Jessie Fauset, a Harlem Renaissance novelist, serving as the literary editor. It contained news pieces, games, fiction, columns, biographies, and folk tales that aimed to educate Black children (Johnson-Feelings, 1996). In spite of its significance, *The Brownies' Book,* for financial reasons, lasted only two years. Notable contributors to *The Brownies' Book* included Harlem Renaissance writers such as Langston Hughes and Nella Larsen.

Contemporary African American Children's Literature

Albeit *The Brownies' Book* was published over eighty years ago, its objectives and ideological underpinnings remain relevant and continue to be embraced, upheld, and extended upon by contemporary writers of

African American children's literature such as Patricia C. McKissack, Jim Haskins, Eloise Greenfield, Walter Dean Myers, Andrea Davis Pinkney, Angela Johnson, Joyce Carol Thomas, and Jacqueline Woodson. Patricia C. McKissack, for example, has written children's books about the Negro baseball leagues, the Tuskegee Airmen, the Pullman Porters, and African American whalers, scientists, and inventors. Their writing is also political in that it has the potential to challenge racist and uninformed misconceptions about African Americans and their culture.

Contemporary writers of African American children's literature are extending upon the objectives of W. E. B. Du Bois by openly confronting sensitive and controversial issues such as homosexuality, colorism, and mental illness. For example, *From the Notebooks of Melanin Sun* (Woodson, 1995) is pioneering in terms of its realistic and insightful portrayal of a young boy dealing with his mother's "coming out" as a lesbian. Contemporary writers are also beginning to embrace aspects of African American culture such as the black vernacular and nappy hair, of which Blacks have historically been made to feel ashamed. *I Love My Hair* (Tarpley, 1998), *Happy to be Nappy* (hooks, 1999) and *Nappy Hair* (Herron, 1997) are books that celebrate and affirm the normalcy and beauty of black hair. African American children's literature is important for all children, but I would argue that it is especially important for Black children who need to see positive and realistic depictions of themselves and their cultural norms. Black children need to also learn of the tremendous role that African Americans have played in helping America to become the country that it is.

Conclusion

As I approach the completion of my graduate work, I recognize that my trajectory through the doctoral program has been an enlightening, transformative, and difficult, yet necessary one. I believe that my voice needs to be included among the voices of scholars in the field of children's literature to challenge, expand, and "color" their perspectives. I am continually reminded of this when I read articles in professional journals or attend presentations by White scholars of children's literature that virtually ignore the existence of quality African American children's literature. I am committed to placing "culturally conscious"

African American children's literature at the forefront so that Black children can have opportunities to receive affirmations of themselves and their cultural and historical legacy and learn as Bishop (1990) stated earlier how to "walk tall in the world."

As I began to consider applying for teaching positions, I initially questioned whether or not I wanted to teach at a Predominately White Institution, being cognizant of the difficulties I will most certainly encounter as an African American professor with a "social critical consciousness" of mainly White students and having never in my entire life attended a Historically Black College or University. Because I enjoy conducting research and writing, I was particularly attracted to Research One institutions, which are mainly Predominately White Institutions. However, I think that there is a place for me at Predominately White Institutions, since there will be African American students, if only a few, for whom I can serve as a role model and mentor. As I think back on my encounter with the professor of my master's seminar who told me that I wouldn't be able to engage in the analytical thinking required for completing a dissertation, I know that this is most certainly happening to other African American students. I want my office door to be open to students, to whom this occurs, so they can come in and have a talk with me after having had a talk with someone who tells them that they can't, so I can tell them that they can. I want to share the negative experience that motivated me to relentlessly pursue my goal of obtaining a terminal degree and help future African American scholars of the academy learn how to "walk tall in the world."

References

Banks, J. (1993). Multicultural education for young children: Racial and ethnic attitudes and their modification. In B. Spodek (Ed.), *Handbook of research on the education of young children* (pp. 236–250). New York: Macmillan.

Bishop, R. S. (1990). Walk tall in the world: African American literature for today's child. *Journal of Negro Education, 59*(4), 556–565.

Bishop, R. S., & McNair, J. (2002). Centennial salute to Arna Bontemps, Langston Hughes and Lorenz Graham. *The New Advocate, 15*(2), 109–119.

Clark, K., & Clark, M. (1947). Racial identification and preference in Negro children. In T. M. Newcomb & E. L. Hartley (Eds.), *Readings in social psychology* (pp. 169–178). New York: Holt, Rinehart & Winston.

Cross, W. (1991). *Shades of black: Diversity in African American identity.* Philadelphia, Pennsylvania: Temple University Press.

Delgado, R. (1995). Introduction. In R. Delgado (Ed.), *Critical race theory: The cutting edge.* Philadelphia, PA: Temple University Press.

Du Bois, W. E. B. (1919). The true brownies. *Crisis, 10*(10), 285–286.

Du Bois, W. E. B. (1921). The grown-ups corner. *The Brownies' Book, 2*(2), 63.

Fox, M. (1993). Politics and literature: Chasing the "isms" from children's books. *Reading Teacher, 46*(8), 654–658.

Franklin, J. H. (1989). The dilemma of the American Negro scholar. In J. H. Franklin (Ed.), *Race and history: Selected essays 1938–1988* (pp. 295–308). Baton Rouge, LA: Louisiana State University Press.

Freire, P., & Macedo, D. (1987). *Literacy: Reading the word and the world.* South Hadley, MA: Bergin & Garvey.

Herrnstein, R., & Murray, C. (1994). *The bell curve: Intelligence and class structure in American life.* New York: Free Press.

Howard, G. (1999). *We can't teach what we don't know: White teachers, multiracial schools.* New York: Teachers College Press.

Johnson-Feelings, D. (Ed.). (1996). *The best of the brownies' book.* New York: Oxford Press.

McGillis, R. (1996). *The nimble reader: Literary theory and children's literature.* New York: Twayne Publishers.

McNair, J. (2000). Want Dav Pilkey to show you how to draw dumb bunnies?: Using the Internet to acquaint children with authors and illustrators of children's literature. *The Dragon Lode, 19*(1), 11–14.

Morrow, L. M. (2001). *Literacy development in the early years: Helping children read and write.* Boston, MA: Allyn & Bacon.

Nodelman, P. (1996). *The pleasures of children's literature.* New York: Longman.

Patterson-Stewart, K. E., Ritchie, M. H., & Sanders, E. T. (1997). Interpersonal dynamics of African American persistence in doctoral programs at predominately white universities. *Journal of College Student Development, 38*(5), 489–497.

Poussaint, A. (1974). Building a strong self-image in black children. *Ebony Magazine, 29*(10), 138–43.

Sims, R. (1982). *Shadow and substance: Afro-American experience in contemporary children's fiction.* Urbana, IL: National Council of Teachers of English.

Sleeter, C. (1996). *Multicultural education as social activism.* New York: State University of New York Press.

Williams, R. (1977). *Marxism and literature.* New York: Oxford University Press.

Woods, M. (2001). Invisible women: The experiences of black female doctoral students at the University of Michigan. In R. O. Mabokela, & A. L. Green (Eds.), *Sisters of the academy: Emergent black women scholars in higher education* (pp. 105–115). Sterling, Virginia: Stylus.

Children's Books Cited

Bannerman, H. (1899, 1923). *The story of little black Sambo*. New York: Harper & Row.

Clifton, L. (1970). *Some of the days of Everett Anderson*. New York: Henry Holt & Company.

Clifton, L. (1974). *Everett Anderson's Year*. New York: Henry Holt & Company.

Curtis, C. P. (1995). *The Watsons Go to Birmingham—1963*. New York: Delacorte Press.

Herron, C. (1997). *Nappy hair*. New York: Alfred Knopf.

hooks, b. (1999). *Happy to be nappy*. New York: Hyperion Books.

Tarpley, N. (1998). *I love my hair*. Boston, MA: Little, Brown & Company.

Woodson, J. (1995). *From the notebooks of Melanin Sun*. New York: Blue Sky Press.

PART III
SURVIVING THE ACADEMY

Courtney Johnson, Ph.D.

Hometown: Shaker Heights, Ohio
Current Institution: University of Florida
Department: Curriculum and Instruction
Personal Philosophy: The smallest deeds are better than the greatest intentions.

11

THE MASK

A SURVIVAL TOOL

Introduction

Ruth Forman's (1997) poem "Graduate School" speaks vividly of the tribulations associated with Black students and graduate school. Black intellectuals rarely find themselves in the pages of their discipline's literature. Their perspectives, often ignored and overlooked, bear no meaning to the acknowledged leaders in the field. But the need to insert their views arises, frequently with resistance—both self-imposed and external. Forman (1997) insists that with fortitude, this new voice will emerge. The academy seems to be encouraging African Americans to "be seen and not heard" or at least, not heard very loudly. As more brothers and sisters make it to the academy, their voices become more thunderous, both collectively and individually. To join this melodious choir and be heard far and wide, the struggles of the doctoral program must be overcome.

African American students living on largely White campuses bear a burden of trying to fit in. Some White faculty and students fail to realize the magnitude and effect of blatant and implicit expressions of racism on campus. Several African American students arrive on campus expecting more respect than they encounter (Tatum, 1997). Blacks in doctoral programs who feel they should be received favorably soon realize the negative impact of underlying prejudices. Seemingly good intentions frequently mask the stereotyped views held by some White people. Cornel West describes a situation in which liberal White people believe Black people should be assimilated into their society and culture, while conservatives insist on "well-behaved" and acceptable Blacks. This suggests that African American intellectuals foster a relationship with white notions of knowledge and value, rather than nurturing their own. Without a space for an exchange of ideas, African American intellectuals will continue to mount structural and psychological hills during the process of upward mobility (Higginbotham & Weber, 2001).

This chapter shares my reflections as a doctoral student in a Predominately White Institution (PWI). Using several examples, I discuss the experiences and implications of trying to survive in the classroom, within my department, and in personal situations with my White peers and faculty. I describe how I found comfort in various resources in the university community, and conclude with a discussion of how most African American doctoral students endure programs at PWIs.

Survival

Narrative

Nobody said it would be easy. From the moment I considered entering the doctoral program, I expected to encounter obstacles. But it was not until I reached the final phases of the program that I truly appreciated the depth of my experiences. Being an African American woman enrolled in a Predominately White Institution in the South carries its own set of issues and contentions. The insensitive comments and behaviors permeated every aspect of my life as a doctoral student. There was no escape because I was deeply embedded. My task was to survive and transcend.

Survival Mode in the Classroom

Survival mode began as I sat in my first class as a doctoral student. Forced smiles glittered while eyes scanned and perceptions formed. Everybody hankered to relive the high school superlative contest—most intelligent, friendliest, and most likely to succeed. Superficial conversations cracked the ice, but still, it was not broken. Finally, class began with the professor asking each student to introduce himself. The awkward silence following the session revealed each individual's struggle to negotiate his preconceptions with the newfound biographical information. For me, however, there was no silence for I heard the questions brimming in my classmates' minds. She is a doctoral student, but is she Black? She did graduate from an HBCU, so does that make her Black? How old could she be? How qualified is she really? She does not seem to be volatile, so is she Black? She arrived early, her English is articulate, and she is appropriately dressed. No, she cannot be Black, can she? "Yes!" I wordlessly exclaimed to my peers. "I am black. I am African American. And I am a doctoral student, just like you!" I was in survival mode.

In the field of education, conversations about race and class inequities should not be taboo. Unfortunately, a quick glance at a list of readings for any given course seemed to indicate otherwise. I hungered for a prolonged, informed discussion about the improprieties of education, but my appetite was hardly whetted. My efforts to engage in this dialogue throughout each semester were disregarded until permission was granted by the syllabi. The brief chat about multiculturalism or diversity usually resulted in me being the object of the attention. As the sole American person of color in the room, I was deemed the expert representative to some. For them, my every word embodied all African Americans across the nation regardless of the reminder that I speak only for myself. Others viewed me differently than "regular" Black people because I challenged their stereotypes. They doubted my utterances about my "Black experience." But what was I to do? Silence would result in a limited dialogue, as most of my peers were reluctant to talk about "Black issues." My failure to share personal anecdotes would relegate the discussion to the "informed knowledge" of White professors. I could not let them theorize about African Americans and say nothing. I did not let their beliefs go unchallenged.

I was not always the only African American in a class. Though we shared the burden, it was not less heavy. Nobody winced or even looked twice when all of the Turkish students sat and worked collectively. The same could not be said for my peers and me. When we banded together, others were hesitant to join us. In fact, nobody joined us. I realized the dual nature of our exclusivity. On the one hand, we were separated from our classmates, who seemed to prefer us individually rather than as a group. Inside information, to which others often were privy, never traveled to our sector. Few trusted enough to ask us for our opinions or advice. We were seen and treated as an isolated group. On the other hand, it is important for African Americans to find a comfort zone, especially in a situation that does not favor us. Working together provided that, at the perceived expense of our Caucasian counterparts.

Were we wrong for working together? Were we wrong for joining other groups? Which is the best situation for us individually and communally? I was not willing to sacrifice my own relief for theirs, so I found the middle ground.

Survival Mode in the Department

". . . And one more piece of advice. Make sure they see you working in your office." That pearl of wisdom, offered to me by a senior Black graduate student in my department, stuck with me since the day I heard it. As I thought more about it, I realized the importance of her words. After all, I was well aware of the perceptions associated with me and people like me. We are, according to popular misconception, shiftless, lazy, and always looking for a handout. Seeing me in the office—self-motivated and diligently working—would illustrate the depth of my commitment to my scholarship. This is what I believed and this is what compelled me regularly to work in my departmental office. I was visible. I was often the first person in the wing and sometimes the last to leave. I was even spotted on rare weekends. I tailored the office to suit my campus needs and worried little about being disrupted by my officemates. They did not frequent the space, but they did not have to. I was the only African American student in the area. My constant visibility gave way to conversations with professors and peers who grew comfortable enough to approach me. Invitations to serve on committees and panels increased, as did my personal contacts within the department. I am not so naïve to believe that opportunities to serve in my department were solely because of the scholarly perception I established. The need to create diverse panels and committees provided a greater impetus, especially in the wake of turbulent times at the university. Nonetheless, my department and I reaped the benefits of our relationship. I tasted the inner workings of the institution and accumulated entries for my curriculum vitae. The department gained credit for its heterogeneity and the inclusion of graduate students in the decision-making process. I pruned the grapevine and it bore its fruit.

Teaching at the university proved to be an interesting phenomenon. Due to the size and scope of the institution, my undergraduate students were quite accustomed to being taught by a graduate student. The hands-on nature of the course provided my pupils with a sense of autonomy that did not exist in traditional courses. Hence, I did not encounter the power struggles that some of my peers in other departments described. Supervising master's level preservice teachers, on the other hand, was fraught with battles. These students struggled to perceive me as someone in a position of influence. As I visited their classrooms, I noted areas of both strength and concern in their teaching. Sometimes these concerns were founded in racial and gender bias. But how does a young, African American woman respond to an older, White male when he expresses fear toward his Black female high school students? How do I constructively criticize a White female's pedagogy when all she hears is the rambling of a Black girl exerting unearned authority? What do I say when I get an e-mail from a young, White preservice teacher telling me I *must* write him a letter of recommendation, *or else?* While my undergraduates were more agreeable, my master's students forced me to position myself tactfully to deal with their resistance.

Survival Mode on the Road

You never really know a person until you travel together. This adage proved itself on road trips to meetings and conferences. In campus and local informal settings, everybody behaved in a composed and professional manner. Conversations were guarded and limited to external topics. Though friendly to my peers and faculty, I was not comfortable sharing my innermost thoughts and personal issues. Conversely, my colleagues seemed to proceed with caution when addressing me. When day trips to meetings confined us to a car for several hours, however, the level of comfort increased. As my company opened discussions about various topics, their biases and preconceptions surfaced. Some of these topics included education, personal interest, and departmental gossip. My White counterparts talked to me and around me, as though I had no investment in the dialogue. Reminiscent of conversations shared by White slave owners who spoke openly in the presence of Black slaves, they seemed to overlook or forget my Blackness. Though an occasional flushed look indicated a linguistic slip, they appeared at ease while sharing their racial views. Their liberal notions regarding education were often countered by their more conservative ideas regarding personal choice. I noticed an interesting paradox when talk-ing with my White colleagues. Day trips revealed only a portion, but overnight trips were a different matter.

Spending several nights with my White peers gave a more realistic picture of their habits. For them, drinking alcohol was the cornerstone of any evening. They equated liquor with fun, and strove to consume as much of both as possible. After a "wild" weekend with my peers, I would face greater scrutiny on Monday morning. I did not have their freedom to behave unprofessionally. I limited my participation to a level that was comfortable for me, and I thoroughly enjoyed myself. For my colleagues, the drinks caused some of them to loosen to the point of exploitation. Even if I wanted to partake of some of the fun, their views of me would become tainted as I strayed further from my conservative composure. The power of the alcohol took effect when my peers began asking me questions about Black male sexual prowess and the size of their sexual organs. But do I disregard their queries due to the influence of alcohol? Will my failure to answer reinforce their beliefs? How can I fairly respond when their questions represent gen-eralized stereotypes? I learned to reply to and discredit their inebriated conversations simultaneously.

Survival Mode in Conversations

My research interest focused on issues of African Americans in science education. My program specialization was science education, and most of the courses in which I enrolled were science and/or education related. Conversations with my White counterparts, however, revealed that they often regard me only as an African American, and rarely as a science educator. Matters related to our field were addressed objec-tively and as though I had little input. When the topic of Blacks arose, their attention to me changed, as though the discussion was an oppor-tunity for me to share my knowledge. They seemed to believe I was not qualified to discuss topics other than those associated with African Americans. Furthermore, they were under the impression that I took more interest in African American issues than in issues related to sci-ence education in general. For example, large conferences offered a wide variety of sessions. The assumption that I planned to attend only the "Black sessions" was prevalent in the questions they asked about my conference experiences.

My revelation about the narrow perception with which others saw me forced me to assert myself as a science educator. I delicately balanced my specific research interests with my general interest in the field. Regardless of how I positioned myself as a science educator—through my evolution as an instructor of preservice elementary science teachers, my insight of advances in my discipline, and related experiences outside of the university—my colleagues still maintained their views that I am an African American who is only interested in that "Black stuff." Any flyer or e-mail that so much as mentioned diversity, multiculturalism, or underrepresented groups was directed to me, regardless of the nature of the entire message. I felt as though I was being encouraged to tout myself as an African American. I was treated as though I became a doctoral student because I am African American, rather than because of my achievements in science and education. I was offended. I had spent years as a student, a scientist, and as a teacher. The opportunities with which I had been blessed made me more marketable as a science educator. For my colleagues to consider me solely on the basis of my race was an insult to my years of education and experience. How was I to negotiate my desire to be recognized as a science educator who happens to be African American with my reality of being noticed as an African American who happens to be a science educator? What should I do about the guilt I sometimes felt toward wanting to push my race out of the limelight? Where was the middle ground?

Surviving and Transcending

I was motivated not to be discouraged by the daily challenges of being one of few African Americans in my department, and the only one in my program. I did not want the memories of my years as a doctoral student to be painful. I desperately needed an outlet, and I found solace in my relationships. Soon after I arrived at the university, I was introduced to the Black Graduate Student Organization (BGSO). My peers, most of whom I had never seen before, were united by three simple commonalities: our Blackness, our status as graduate students, and our desire to know each other. We needed each other. For many of us, our biweekly meetings were our most consistent opportunities to see other Black graduate students. The collective relief we sighed during our meetings was phenomenal. We smiled, we laughed, we vented, we encouraged, we motivated, and we worked on campus and in the community. BGSO was a support group, not a pity party. Even though our disciplines were widespread, our undergraduate institutions were often athletic rivals, we came from various geographic regions, and we represented a range of experiences; we shared a bond. Each of us encountered various forms of racism and discouragement at this Predominately White Institution. BGSO became a channel for me. It allowed me to escape the rigor and stress of being a doctoral student without forgetting the reality of my situation. It was honest therapy. I was a Black student at a White school whether I was in BGSO or not. The organization reminded me while consoling me.

During the early semesters of my program, a new Black faculty member was hired in my department. As a Black female professor at a research extensive university, she had to fight to be accepted as a Black female scholar and researcher. Her confrontation with issues of publication, teaching versus research, and general acceptance in our department positioned her as a wonderful mentor. We instantly connected. Because she had only recently graduated from her doctoral program, also at a Predominately White Institution, she offered a sympathetic ear. She became someone I talked to often, and her advice was both timely and beneficial. Furthermore, her newness in the professoriate inspired me. I witnessed her relentless navigation through stumbling blocks, and she shared with me a number of experiences. She was determined not to lose herself and her interests in the process, which motivated me to do the same during my matriculation. I enjoyed the uniqueness of my position as an African American doctoral student and as an onlooker to this new Black professor. And it was through this position that I truly realized the magnitude of issues that African Americans in the academy must endure. Our experiences, though different, were quite similar. We encountered many of the same people, perceptions, and attitudes, but in distinguishable ways. Our roles were separate, but not separated. Our mentor/mentee relationship stood out as a beacon of light in a sea of doctoral darkness, and helped me transcend the confusion.

With the exception of my mentor, none in my department seemed to be genuinely concerned with my research interest. In fact, they seemed rather indifferent. They offered distant support, yet sometimes encouraged me to join their bandwagon. I resisted and sought opportunities to satisfy myself. I had heard horror stories of doctoral students whose research proposals were rejected by their committee and were ultimately forced to write about their advisors' whims. I was determined to avoid that scenario. So I found ways to become immersed in the issues about which I was passionate. My part-time jobs, community connections, and constant reading fostered my growth in my field. After all, by the end of my doctoral program, I was expected to be "an expert in my area." I chose to gain expertise through relevant hands-on experiences and staying current with the literature. Furthermore, focusing on my own interest served as an outlet for me. During my semesters of coursework, I often became disenchanted. I was tired of reading what other people deemed important. The readings were fascinating, but I was ready for options. I wanted to read about important issues for me. I wanted to have discussions about topics I considered worthy. My jobs, my own readings, and my thoughts revolutionized my outlook. As I became more familiar with my own interest, I felt free and relieved. Finally, I had found a space in my discipline in which I was comfortable. I learned, I taught, and I was part of the research. Finding my own voice helped me survive and transcend.

Conclusion

African American doctoral students at Predominately White Institutions must wear "the mask." We tussle with stereotypes, discrimination, and prejudiced perceptions, but we refuse to be worn down by these experiences. We recognize our responsibility to provide a new voice to academic dialogue, and we learn to survive amidst the current, louder voices. Many of us are viewed as "good Blacks," and our peers fail to realize the personal impact of their statements and actions. We use the mask as a tool. It grants and maintains access into a community from which we traditionally have been excluded. The many faces of the mask cannot be overlooked—happy, conforming, grateful, unaffected, at peace, satisfied, and the list goes on ad infinitum. We wear the mask that hides the sting of society's oppression. The mask is inevitable. The mask is survival. We seek relief not in the mask, but in our personal lives.

A crucial fact remains: We must never forget that we wear the mask. Once we lose sight of the reality of our situation as African American doctoral students at PWIs, our mask becomes our face. When this occurs our voices blend in and we add nothing new to the conversation. We neglect our responsibility to encourage other African American students to pursue their doctoral degrees. We do not conduct research that benefits our communities. We do nothing to stimulate systemic change and personal perceptions. When we forget the mask is only a mask, we are unable to transcend oppression. Our task, to reap the benefits without becoming "caught up" in the mask, may prove to be a difficult endeavor for some.

Recognition of our individual and collective modes of survival and transcendence is an important part of the doctoral process. The academy remains an elite group of people in American society. Entrance into this group comes by way of criteria prescribed by the dominant culture. Our failure to meet these criteria will maintain the homogeneity of the academy. Our goal to influence the academy can be accomplished first by becoming a part of the academy. Those who have survived and transcended offer practical advice to us. We ought to tap those resources. Additionally, a support group of African American doctoral students provides comfort during critical times at all phases of the program. When we realize our personal resources for inner peace, we become equipped to support others. We must learn to survive without compromising the essence of our character. African American doctoral students at Predominately White Institutions carry a heavy load. Nobody said it would be easy because it is not easy. But it is not impossible. The mask, mentors, support groups, family, close friends, and spiritual relationships each offer a means to survive. It is through survival that transcendence is achieved.

References

Forman, R. (1997). *Renaissance*. Boston: Beacon Press.

Higginbotham, E., & Weber, L. (2001). Moving up with kin and community: Upward social mobility for black and white women. In M. L. Anderson, &

P. H. Collins (Eds.), *Race, class, and gender* (pp. 156–167). Belmont, CA: Wadsworth/Thomson Learning.

Tatum, B. D. (1997). *Why are all the black kids sitting together in the cafeteria? And other conversations about race.* New York: Basic Books.

West, C. (1993). *Race Matters.* Boston: Beacon Press.

Lisa Watts

Hometown: Friars Point, Mississippi
Current Institution: University of Wisconsin at Milwaukee
Department: Curriculum and Instruction
Personal Philosophy: My hand is on the plough, my faltering hand, and all that is before me is untilled land. With many tears the plough gets wet. And yet, my God . . . my God . . . keeps me from turning back.
                    —Anonymous

12

A PERSONAL JOURNEY TOWARD AUTHENTICITY

RECOGNIZING AND RECLAIMING ORIGINS

Introduction

The Sankofa Bird of Ghana, traditionally depicted with its head turned backward, is symbolic of the individual need to recapture the riches of their past. The depiction of the Sankofa bird is quite fitting in telling my story. The journey toward the doctoral program has demanded that I look back over my life and that I gather strength from my past. This journey has demanded that I find out who Lisa is. It has demanded that I confront the conflicts, lies, and untruths as told to me through formal and informal socializations. It has also demanded that I embrace parts of my past that I had considered faulty or unworthy to be a part of my story. It is through the embracing of my past that I am able to preserve the challenges and rigor of a doctoral program.

This chapter focuses on my personal experiences toward the doctoral program. It juxtaposes my home upbringing and my formal educational experiences, two opposite situations that contributed to the uneasy journey toward the doctoral program. It is my hope to highlight those experiences and relate them to the literature that not only speaks of my journey but that sheds light on the experiences of others like myself. This supports the notion that many African American students have and are presently receiving an education that ignores their home and community upbringing versus building on those experiences. This traditional education also devalues what students bring to the classroom by implying that students leave at the door what they have learned from their parents, their grandmothers, their big mamas, and their preachers and teachers in the community. By sharing my personal experiences, I can add additional evidence to the literature, which highlights the need for educational reform.

Reform of education in terms of present and future African American students receiving a different or a more comparable form of education—one that builds on the home and community upbringing—and the accompanying socialization is greatly needed. This reformed education will strengthen the academic foundation of students and more importantly, strengthen their foundation as members of the human race.

As an African American student who attended the Milwaukee Public Schools System (MPS) and subsequently pursued postsecondary education at Predominately White Universities, I have begun a search for self-discovery. Tyson (1998) suggests a similar frame of consciousness as the Sankofa bird when one is pursuing a journey of self-discovery. Tyson (1998), states, "A necessary part of progression is regression." With this in mind, I am forced to look at my past and the circumstances and orientations that have framed my past in order to adequately deal with it and to be able to move forward in a progressive manner. This mental exercise of regression demands that I confront destructive educational and socialization orientations that I internalized through the process of formal schooling. For the purpose of this chapter I will address three of the orientations that permeated throughout my education: (1) competitive individualism, (2) self-denial/hatred, and (3) complacency. These orientations have made my journey toward the doctoral program uncertain versus certain, dark versus bright. These orientations entailed messages that contradicted the messages I received from home and from my community. Because of the divisive and damaging nature of these orientations coupled with their ingrainedness, they are orientations I must battle against daily in order to do my ancestors and myself justice.

Background

My home and community upbringing were explicitly telling me one thing and my school environment, although maybe not as explicit or as open and honest as my home upbringing, was definitely implying something different. For example, at home my mother cooked large meals at dinnertime. She believed that at any given time a stranger may show up at her doorstep hungry and in need of food. Or she may have known of a neighbor in need. She wanted to be prepared to aid this person or this family's need. However, at school this collective communalism my mother was fostering (an academic term which she is unaware of) and that I grew up witnessing and participating in was offset by staunch individualistic competition.

Although we were not explicitly told not to share, as students, we understood what was meant by everybody do your "own" work. On the surface this has merit and a case can be made that in order to assess what a student knows he or she has to do his or her "own" work. As an African American, I was constantly bombarded with themes such as do well in school, and education is the key; coupled with the amount of time spent in traditional K–12 schools, the orientations that I internalized were the ones I received in school versus the ones from my parents (home) and community. I and other students quickly identified the experiences and orientations that were absent from the curriculum or relegated to the margins of society and the educational process and which ones were insignificant and should likewise be demeaned, ignored, or patronized (Gay, 1995). Therefore, I did my "own" work, with little to no thought given to how my peers sitting next to me were doing academically. This orientation directly conflicted with what my parents were attempting to teach me in a less formal and seemingly unconscious manner.

My African American heritage and upbringing—what was natural to me—was not valued at school. However, as one professor told me, I and other students like myself possess internal traits such as collective communalism that are lying dormant inside of us and waiting to be tapped into. It is like a light bulb that is waiting to shine from the inside of us, but it is dusty with the dust of individualism and other eurocentric traits that prevents its shinning and radiation from the inside to the outside.

The message from the Sankofa bird provides me with an opportunity to look at the significance of the lessons my parents were attempting to teach me. As the Sankofa bird looks rearward to recapture the richness of its past, I now see clearly how my parents' lives and their actions painted a different landscape from the landscape of competitive individualism, self-denial/hatred, and complacency. For example, when my mother prepared meals for her family, her neighbors, and strangers, she was demonstrating a profound love for others, which stems first from love of self. However, her humble beginnings did not keep her

184 JOURNEY TO THE Ph.D.

from doing what she had to do. By sharing what little she did have, my mother fostered social justice and collective communalism, thereby defying the first educational orientation that I speak of, competitive individualism.

Competitive Individualism

When I think of women such as Mary McLeod Bethune and Mary Church Terrell, I can seemingly picture their disappointment when I speak of the first orientation that's forwarded in schools—starch and fierce competitiveness. At times, I think I neglected the African American cultural knowledge that says "each one teach one." As Black people there is an unwritten rule we are bound by; it's an obligation to help and assist the next Black person in their area of weakness, an area in which we may be strong. hooks (2000) speaks to this sense of solidarity and the interruption of such solidarity. "After years of collective struggle, by the end of the sixties, liberal individualism had become more the norm for black folks, particularly the black bourgeoisie, more so than the previous politics of communalism which emphasized racial uplift and sharing of resources" (p. 92). It is my stance that the sharing of resources must extend to the sharing of academic knowledge in terms of resources/skills.

During the years of working with African American college students, I have observed students similar to myself who have internalized individualistic competitiveness. While observing students seeking assistance from these highly competitive individuals, I've witnessed shocking responses. What is extremely shocking is the unconsciousness of the response. It was not necessarily an outright refusal, but it was a resistance that informed the seeker that she was not going to receive assistance. Not only am I surprised at the responses from these students, but I am also surprised at my own responses when this fierce competitive nature rises in me. It is as if we have forgotten that "as we climb we must lift." The idea of climbing and lifting simultaneously is a key concept in the African American community that has served to sustain and progress us as a people. The very thought of climbing and lifting leaves no time or room for divisive and destructive competition.

This Eurocentric philosophy of survival of the fittest is devastating and disastrous to the African American community. We cannot afford to lose, hamper, or have stifled any brainpower. The premise is that by encouraging a community of learners, and helping students work against the norm of competitive individualism toward social justice, we are teaching students to care, not only about their own achievement, but also their classmates' achievements. hooks (2000), concurs with this notion when she asserts, "while we need not return to the notion of the talented tenth, we do need to draw on the legacy of constant radical commitment to social justice for all, which undergirds the dream of liberatory black self-determination that was at the heart of Du Bois' vision" (p. 100).

Self-Denial/Hatred

I live in a society where new advancements are made daily. We are in a day and time where we are technologically sophisticated. As a nation, and for many middle- and upper-middle-class Black people, we are in a time of economic boom. However, the question remains, particularly for African Americans, how do you not lose what you have in the name of advancement? I am particularly speaking to segregation, desegregation, and integration.

When I think of people such as Thurgood Marshall and the other lawyers who successfully won *Brown vs. Board of Education,* I know in my heart that what they were attempting to garner was good. Integration on the surface has done much to expand opportunities for African Americans. Unfortunately, my generation and others after me seemingly missed a lot, due to integration. We did not receive the impact of African American legacies, cultural norms, practices, and the village concept that sustained generations of Black people through difficult times. For instance, my generation did not experience standing in the midst of devastating events such as cross burnings and lynchings. Such trials gave our ancestors resilience, strength of character, and passion for advancing a race of Black people that would stand up and fight against such injustices. I am not suggesting that I and others of my generation need to experience all of the tragedies that our foreparents experienced. On the contrary, I am grateful for what they did, so that I would not have to experience such injustices. I am suggesting that we need their legacy of resilience, strength of character, and passion in order to fight our present-day battles.

Instead of a marriage of integration and Black struggle, the ideas of pride, love, and culture were seemingly left behind. Advancement through integration has come at a high cost to my generation. We are more advanced economically and technologically than our foreparents who lived, suffered, struggled, and defied the odds of the 1960s movement and the pre-1960s movement. However, a case can be made that we are also a generation that is socially and culturally lacking, if not deprived.

There is a saying that goes, "if it is white, it is right; if it is black, get back." In no way, shape, form, or fashion does the humorous notion of this saying have any happy endings for African Americans. As a generation that did not experience the blatant and brutal manifestations of slavery, jim crow, segregation, and the subsequent 1960s movement of civil rights and Black pride, I am left with remnants of that time period. I have seen on television and heard of those time periods, but neither of those do justice to actually living through the periods. And because the legacies of those periods were not meaningfully brought forth and transcended—through all sectors—from previous generations I and others like myself are left with notions of advancement, but from where?

I am a product of institutions such as the Black church, which provided me an avenue to study African American "greatness." However, this study was not forwarded or carried forth meaningfully in school. Schools could have fostered the idea that I come from people such as Ida B. Wells, Mary McLeod Bethune, and Fannie Lou Hammer, among others. They could have reinforced that inside of me exist the steadfastness of Ida B. Wells, the resilience and determination of Fannie Lou Hammer, and the tenacity, perseverance, and fortitude of Mary McLeod Bethune.

Instead I would say that school led me down the journey toward self-denial/hatred. It is an orientation where I refer to myself and students like myself as the "white is right student." This orientation comes in many different forms. The orientation can be anything from an outright denial of self to a remaking of self. Personally, this remaking of self involved for me denying the intricacies of my beginnings, my circumstances, and my life in general. The attempt was to become as close as possible to what society deemed valuable. Those valuable societal traits were that my beginnings be easy as opposed to a struggle, my circumstances be effortless as opposed to difficult, and my life in general be straightforward and trouble-free as opposed to my having a story of hard and painful obstacles overcome. Valenzuela (1999) notes marginality evolves when children are socialized away from their communities and families of origin.

One way this type of student emerges is through subtractive forces at school. Valenzuela (1999) remarks on how the capacity of individuals to manipulate their ethnic identity in educational settings is largely mediated by a schooling process aimed at divesting youth of their Mexicanidad. I contend that the same process divests from African American students their Blackness. For thirteen years in a K–12 program, I and other African American students most likely went to schools with predominately Black students who had predominately White teachers and administrators as the authority figures. Gay (1995) notes that in schools powerful messages are conveyed to students about the value and significance attached to them as members of different ethnic, cultural, and social groups through who is included in curriculum content and what kinds of images are portrayed. Students need to see images of themselves and their cultural heritage in positions of importance and influence in school programs.

Self-denial/hatred emerges when we neglect to highlight and emphasize to students the history and the significance of African American people and their contributions in meaningful ways—ways that give attention to African American contributions of historical and scholarly significance instead of to ethnic individuals and events that are trivial, superficial, isolated, and exotic (Gay, 1995).

When students are allowed to witness the greatness of their history, they become personally empowered. This empowerment leads to a personal transformation out of silence and submission into the development of an authentic voice . . . and a social process of self-assertion into one's own world (Kriesberg, 1992). This empowerment is based on a community of shared struggle and support in which individuals and groups come to develop mastery of their lives, control of valued resources, and skills to engage in collective sociopolitical action for mutual problem solving. Banks (1992) adds, "when students are empowered they have . . . knowledge of their social, political, and economic worlds, the skills to influence their environments, and humane values that will motivate them to participate in social change to help create a more just society and world" (p. 154).

Students must be given the opportunity to have their "Blackness" forwarded, thus leaving no room for the damaging nature of self-denial/hatred. When students' "Blackness" is forwarded they come into what Gay (1995) terms as "voice." When students "come into voice," they also engage critically and analytically with all forms of cultural texts and confront ways in which historical legacies, power, and politics can be understood and used to expedite the struggle to democratize social, political, and economic life (Gay, 1995). Through their own personal empowerment students are now equipped to critically look at society and through shared struggle work to correct injustices.

Complacency

The mottos of Historically Black Colleges and Universities (HBCUs) lay a foundation of how we as African Americans are to view our role as agents of change in society. For instance, the motto of Wilberforce University is "Suo Marte," translated from its Latin roots it means "By one's own toil, effort and courage." This motto and others, which are consistent throughout HBCUs literature, all point to the fact that complacency has no place in the African American community. We are a community that has always had to struggle for change and in some cases for shear survival. African Americans have a legacy of having to push the political will of this country toward a more just and moral society. The struggle, as depicted by Wilberforce University, is through one's own toil, effort, and courage. As seen through their mottos, HBCUs have a tradition of promoting to their students the political will to make a difference in society through personal empowerment.

In order for the mottos of HBCUs to be internalized, students must receive an appropriate education. This education could be similar to that espoused at Black colleges and universities. Therefore, I concur with the suggestions of Gay (1995) whose stance is that education must first empower students personally, in order for them to be agents of change throughout society. Gay (1995) notes that an education that empowers students to resist and transform racist practices uncovers the deeply ingrained ideological, historical, economic, cultural, and political factors in society, which generate, embody, and perpetuate racism. Once these factors are uncovered they are underscored by an ethnical outrage and moral indignation at the way the democratic imperative is routinely distorted to justify Eurocentric cultural hegemony and political dominance (Gay, 1995).

Students must understand that in their attempts to change and transform racist practices they are merely exercising the basics for effective citizenship in a culturally pluralistic, democratic society. To not participate and become complacent negates their civic and moral responsibility to continue the struggle for justice and true democracy. This realization is contingent upon students having social consciousness (personally and culturally), moral courage, and political competence (Gay, 1995). We as students must truly believe that we can make a difference in the society we inherited and inhabit.

Unfortunately, students do not always receive the necessary personal empowerment for becoming agents of change in society. Valenzuela (1999) speaks to the subtractive nature of schools and how they "remind students of their lack of power" (p. 108). She further notes students' sense of powerlessness at school by commenting, "they have good arguments, but they have absolutely no argument skills" (p. 108). Unable to articulate their frustration and alienation effectively and inexperienced with even the idea of collective action, most students settle for individual resistance or silence.

Gay (1995) notes that the processes of empowerment and transformation begin in the classroom with students practicing how to acquire, use, and share power. Classroom instructors must forego the tendency to act as if school is neutral and apolitical. Teachers must engage students in action-oriented instructional strategies such as participating in cooperative, heterogeneous, and interracial learning groups; conducting case studies of actual events and experiences to discern contradictions between social ideals and realities; planning and implementing school and community action projects to combat different forms of oppression and inequities; and organizing education campaigns to inform students, parents, and community groups about equity issues in schools and society.

Schools did not suggest to me that actively resisting social and political injustices and struggling for what I believed and valued were merely fundamental parts of my birthright as a citizen in a society that espouses democratic beliefs. Quite the contrary was fostered. The notion of being a good citizen was framed around ideas of paying my taxes and obeying the laws of the land. I am not suggesting that these are not noble deeds; however, struggling for the advancement of freedom and justice for those who are deprived of such are also noble ideas that were ignored in my formal schooling experience. I concur that the ultimate purpose of schooling should encompass a strong focus toward the empowerment of students to transform schools and society for greater freedom, equality, and justice within the contextual realities of cultural pluralism (Gay, 1995).

Conclusion

As I conclude this discussion, I am reminded of the level of intelligence that African American students bring with them to class. Ladson-Billings (1994) makes the case that there are identified cultural strengths that African American children bring with them to the classroom that are rarely capitalized on by teachers. In order to enhance academic and social achievement, teachers must begin to recognize and utilize effectively the specific cultural strengths of African American students. By continuing to allow Black students to be subjected to a technocratic curriculum that ignores their background, experiences, and history we buy into the traditional American pedagogical values and practices that prevent African American students from fully understanding their world (Darder, 1991).

I have recently begun to understand that as an African American growing up in a society where previously set limitations had been established for me, recognizing shortcomings as not only self-limitations or parental limitations but limits that society places on people of color, especially low socioeconomic people of color, are valuable. The stance here is to shift from blaming the victim to recognizing a power block that intentionally predetermines places in life for persons. Darder (1991) states "critical educators perceive their primary function as emancipatory and their primary purpose as commitment to creating the conditions for students to learn skills, knowledge and modes of inquiry that will allow them to examine critically the role that society has played in their self-formation" (p. xvii).

This predetermined self-formation does not occur through overt forces or any other obvious means but through the hidden systematic socialization—which occurs in schools—that in the end controls, contains, and confines individuals to their appointed place in life. This socialization that African American children receive is a hierarchical structure that is informed by values that benefit the dominant culture (Darder, 1991). As such, schools and other institutions produce and interpret knowledge that serves as a silencing agent, in that it relegates greater legitimacy to the abstract reality developed by this knowledge than the actual daily experiences that shape students' lives (Darder, 1991). When the American public education system instills more value to technocratic, sterile, and detached curriculums—rather than a curriculum that is meaningful to students' experiences—we as a Black community can expect our children to fail rather than flourish.

What is needed is a sociocultural orientation. I define a sociocultural orientation as the development of self-worth and dignity through knowledge of a group's history and culture and through images provided by parents, community members, leaders, and teachers. It is also the schooling of Black children that sees value and promise in them, thus pushing them to achieve beyond limits set by society and possibly themselves. Further, a sociocultural orientation is a direct response to the challenges—racism, poverty, crime, and so forth—that Black students face in and out of school (Edwards, 1993; Siddle-Walker, 2000; Steele, 1992). A sociocultural orientation takes into account what the African American community has identified as having its children's best interests at heart. Ladson-Billings (1994) describes the teaching that informs, supports, and forwards a sociocultural orientation as culturally relevant teaching.

This form of teaching uses a student's culture in order to maintain it and to transcend the negative effects of the dominant culture. Culturally relevant teaching is also the development of a "relevant Black personality" that allows African American students to choose academic excellence yet still identify with African and African American culture. Specifically, culturally relevant teaching is a pedagogy that empowers students intellectually, socially, emotionally, and politically by using cultural referents to impart knowledge, skills, and attitudes (Ladson-Billings, 1994).

In regards to education, my personal and previous thoughts surrounding a sociocultural orientation are built upon the work of Ladson-Billings. Specifically, my thoughts on a sociocultural orientation and the work of Ladson-Billings regarding culturally relevant teaching intersect at the point of students being socially and culturally prepared/educated. This education empowers students to think and question critically where they are in life, what roads they themselves have taken to be in that place, and of equal importance what role society has played in their placement. In addition, through an education predicated on emancipatory and liberatory ideas, students should be equipped with the necessary agency to effect personal and societal changes if and when needed.

Schools are needed as additive agents in the lives of students if they are to overcome limitations (Valenzuela, 1999). By additive, I mean schools should assist in building on cultural strengths that students bring to the classroom, as opposed to regulating them to an environment that is foreign and in some cases hostile. A K–12 program that lacks opportunity and role models for Black students to see and experience how knowledge can be used in ways to liberate, empower, and transform their lives, disregards the school's obligation to be an additive agent for students. By the transformation of their lives, they (the students) will gain insight and opportunity to assist in empowering the next generation of Black students toward the same transformation.

Segregated school environments epitomized this type of transformation. This transformation was aided by the fact that teachers identified explicitly with students because they themselves were usually products of southern segregated schools (Siddle-Walker, 2000). Irvine and Irvine (1983) make a similar point.

> In this manner, the teachers both implicitly identified with the students' needs and aspirations and, simultaneously, understood how to negotiate the world beyond the local community. Having lived the benefit of education, the teachers could also tell students how to move beyond the limited life possibilities of a segregated [racist] world and how to use education to achieve a middle-class life. In espousing the philosophies they held, they both re-created themselves in their students and made possible the continued advancement of a people with whom they clearly identified.

It is crucial that we give students the opportunity to move out of one life and its predicaments—if they choose—to a life and place in society that gives them a voice, power, and self-determination. In order for this to happen formal schooling must begin to recognize and internalize historical African American traits. This means turning from fierce individualistic competition to a stance toward social justice and collective communalism. Additionally, students must be equipped with the capacity and the will to make a difference in the world. They must turn from silence to voicing their opinions, from complacency to effective action. This restructuring of the educational process is vital, because, when I look critically at my past I see how the messages from my home and community are sustaining me in the doctoral program. This is not to say that the Language Arts, Math, Social Studies and many other classes that formed my K–12 and postsecondary education were not vital, but I am saying that messages from home are sustaining. Until such a time occurs in our educational systems where there is building on the significance of community and home messages, we as African Americans must do as the Sankofa bird of Ghana, that is look to our past to recapture the richness of who we are.

References

Banks, J. A. (1992). A curriculum for empowerment, action, and change. In K. A. Moodley (Ed.), *Beyond multicultural education: International perspectives,* (pp. 154–170). Calgary, Alberta: Detseling Enterprises.

Darder, Antonia (1991). *Culture and power in the classroom.* Connecticut: Bergin and Garvey.

Edwards, Patricia, A. (1993). Before and after school desegregation: African American parents' involvement in school. *Educational Policy, 7*(3), 341–367.

Gay, G. (1995). Mirror images on common issues: Parallels between multicultural education and critical pedagogy. In C. E. Sleeter & P. L. McLaren (Eds.), *Multicultural education, critical pedagogy, and the politics of difference* (pp. 155–189). Albany, NY: State University of New York Press.

Hooks, Bell. (2000). *Where we stand: Class matters.* New York: Routledge.

Irvine, R. W., & Irvine, J. J. (1983). The impact of the desegregation process on the education of Black students: Key variables. *Journal of Negro Education, 52*(4), 410–422.

Kriesberg, S. (1992). Transforming power: Domination, empowerment, and education. In C. E. Sleeter & P. L. McLaren (Eds.), *Multicultural education, critical pedagogy, and the politics of difference.* Albany, NY: State University of New York Press.

Ladson-Billings. (1994). *The dreamkeepers*. San Francisco: Jossey-Bass.

Siddle-Walker. (2000). Valued segregated schools for African American children in the South, 1935–1969: A review of common themes and characteristics. *Review of Educational Research, 70*(3), 253–285.

Steele, C. (1992). Race and the schooling of Black Americans. *The Atlantic Monthly*.

Tyson, C. A. (1998). A response to "Coloring epistemologies: Are our qualitative research epistemologies racially biased?" *Educational Researcher Journal, 27*(9), 21–22.

Valenzuela. (1999). *Subtractive schooling, U.S.-Mexican youth and the politics of caring*. Albany, NY: State University of New York Press.

April Peters

Hometown: Somerset, New Jersey

Current Institution: The Ohio State University

Department: Educational Policy and Leadership

Personal Philosophy: Yet in all these things, we are more than conquerors through Him who loved us.

—Romans 8:37

13

MAKING THE ACADEMY A HOME FOR THE BRAVE

To be black and female in the academy has its own particular frustration because it was never intended for us to be here. We are in spaces that have been appropriated for us.

—*Nellie McKay*

Introduction

The role and status of African Americans and particularly African American women in the American educational system has been one of struggle and oppression. Historically, African Americans have been denied access to education. During the early part of the history of the nation, slave owners forbade slaves from obtaining an education, fearing that education would lead to uprising and rebellion. In addition, in the slave-owning South, formal laws were passed that made the education of slaves a crime (Shakeshaft, 1999). Of the Blacks that did receive an education, free men were most likely to be taught to read and write. However, as with other data about Blacks in education, very little data about the literacy rates of slaves is available. We do know that prior to the Civil War, despite the threat of punishment and death, some Black women slaves learned to read and write, becoming teachers and passing these skills on to others (Shakeshaft, 1999, p. 27).

Thus it is against this backdrop that the legacy of the educational oppression of African Americans exists. American education is still not free of racism and sexism. Although access and opportunities in higher education are more abundant for students of color, there still exists many challenges that must be overcome. "Over one hundred years later, a large number of blacks are attending traditionally white universities because of curricula opportunities and university prestige; however, the numbers are not indicative of students' attitudes toward their universities" (Aubert, 1996, p. 141). African American students enrolled at traditionally White universities experience feelings of isolation, prejudice, and discrimination (Allen, 1985; Aubert, 1996; Gloria, Robinson Kurpius, Hamilton, & Willson, 1999; Lewis, Chesler, & Forman, 2000).

Several factors contribute to the feelings of alienation and isolation that many Black students experience at traditionally White universities. The ways that students experience interactions with faculty (many of whom are White males) contribute to these feelings. Black students' interactions with White faculty members have been rigid, distant, or lacking warmth (Allen & Niss, 1990; Aubert, 1996). Black students attending Predominately White Institutions may also feel excluded from administrative decisions and marginalized relative to their environment in terms of the curriculum and the advising that they receive (Aubert, 1996; Gloria et al., 1999; Johnson, 1996).

Given that education occurs within the larger context of a racist and sexist society, African American female students face particular challenges. Although African American women have earned degrees at the graduate and undergraduate levels, little research has been done on this population. The research that has been conducted has focused on the barriers and challenges rather than the stories of successful students (Louque, 1999). While it is important to be aware of the roadblocks to success that African American women may face in pursuing degrees, particularly at the doctoral level, it is equally important to note the stories of those who have accomplished their goals. The experiences of these women are salient given the impact of race and gender for African American women. Black women who earned doctoral degrees represented 2.1 percent of all doctoral degrees conferred in 1995 (Louque, 1999). Louque (1999) states "studies show that because Black women are discriminated against regarding both race and gender, the academic experiences of these women are particularly characterized by alienation and exclusion" (p. 102).

In spite of the challenges Black students face at Predominately White Institutions, certain supports may be of assistance in helping to navigate through this system. It is important to identify and harness these supports in order to provide African American students with the cultural, professional, and psychological assistance they need to be successful (Johnson, 1996).

Personal Experience

This chapter examines the experiences that have impacted my life and inspired my research decisions as an African American female doctoral student in the academy. This is done by first foregrounding the historical disenfranchisement of African Americans from the mainstream American educational system. These experiences will be examined with consideration to the impact that race and gender have had in shaping my experiences as a graduate student at a Predominately White Institution (PWI). Attention will be given to necessary supports that have been put in place to be of assistance. These supports include the Providing Research Opportunities for Scholars (PROFS) program and other informal support and mentoring networks. The support received through involvement with student organizations and committees is explicated as well.

I came to The Ohio State University (OSU) with a unique set of academic experiences. I am a third-generation college graduate. My maternal grandmother earned a Master's in Finance. My mother holds a bachelor's degree and is currently pursuing an M.Ed. and a J.D. I grew up in an integrated community and attended the neighborhood schools. I attended two private, elite Predominately White Institutions of higher learning for my bachelor's degree and master's degrees. I earned a Bachelor of Science degree from Northwestern University and Master of Science in Social Work from Columbia University. During this time I experienced race as more salient than my gender. I believe this was because of the academic and social context. I attended universities where African American students were a very small percentage of the population. For this reason there was a good deal of solidarity among Black students. We found strength in our unity. We understood one another and we understood the struggles and challenges of African American students in a White university. Together we answered questions about why all the Black students sit together in the cafeteria (Tatum, 1997), and why it is that all the White kids sit together in the cafeteria. We stood together to confront arguments against the validity of students of color being there.

I spent a total of four years teaching in two different inner-city schools upon completion of my degrees. At the conclusion of my fourth year of teaching, I decided to return to school to pursue a doctorate. I felt that this degree would provide me with the necessary foundation to be successful in attaining my occupational goals. Although every student has varied factors that he or she takes into consideration when selecting an institution in which to embark upon academic studies, the decision for me was painstaking.

I conducted research to determine which programs and institutions were considered among the top in the field. I utilized this methodology to a lesser degree when selecting my undergraduate and graduate institutions. However, for the doctorate, I was extremely conscious of the reputation of each of the schools to which I applied. I made the decision to attend The Ohio State University after having been accepted at Vanderbilt University in Nashville, Tennessee, and The University of Pennsylvania in Philadelphia. I felt that Ohio State would be the best fit for me because of its national ranking in my program (OSU is ranked third in educational administration) and the fact that of the three programs where I was accepted, OSU has the highest ranking in my specialization. Financial considerations also went into my decision, as Ohio State offered me the best financial package. Aubert (1996) states, "most black students who attend traditionally white institutions do so because those institutions best meet their academic needs" (p. 145). In spite of the reputation of a school, there are many factors that are put into play to determine the quality of one's experience.

I found myself to be one of two African American students in my cohort. Although accustomed to being in the category of "one of" or "only Black" in my classes for much of my academic career, this experience was still daunting at times. I can recall an experience in a doctoral class in which we were discussing an article that had been assigned and the instructor asked the other African American student and me, "What is the Black perspective on this?" I was completely taken aback, as I hadn't been expecting to speak for Black folks on this or any other issue. It was particularly disconcerting to have a faculty member pose such a question in that environment. Aubert (1996) posits administration and faculty set the tone for race relations at Predominately White Institutions. Lewis, Chesler, and Forman (2000) further trouble this by arguing that institutions (including faculty, curriculum, etc.) provide a context that may at times be particularly alienating and uncomfortable for students of color. Therefore, students of color may experience discomfort as faculty consciously or unconsciously perpetuate this context of discomfort. Lewis, Chesler, and Forman (2000) suggest "their (faculty) actions and non-actions with regard to these phenomena often permit the reproduction of stereotypic, assimilative, exclusionary, awkward, and resentment-filled experiences for students of color" (p. 85).

Cultural (Ir)relevance

Initially, my research interests were centered on how children learn and the impact of the community on this learning. However, these interests changed very rapidly as I struggled to find footing within the academy. I struggled to find people who looked like me and I struggled to hear their "voice." My professional goals (to become a faculty member and a school administrator) were not reflected in the research or my interpersonal interactions. Lewis, Chesler, and Forman (2000) state, "for many students of color, this absence is another form of exclusion that not only minimizes their intellectual opportunities but also frustrates their desires to gain understanding from and appreciation by others" (p. 84).

That is to say, when I looked around for someone to talk to, to help me make sense of this experience, I found no one immediately available to talk to who shared my subject position. When I went to seek out scholarly work in the field of educational administration, where African Americans were the subjects, I rarely found the stories of my sisters. I had little relevant coursework that reflected my issues and concerns as an African American female interested in engaging in culturally relevant research. Scheurich and Young (1996) suggest that research and scholarship paradigms that exclude epistemologies that are culturally relevant to diverse groups of peoples are epistemologically racist. They define epistemological racism in the following manner:

> Epistemological racism means our current range of research epistemologies—positivism to postmodernisms/poststructuralisms—arise out of social history and culture of the dominant race, that these

202 JOURNEY TO THE Ph.D.

epistemologies logically reflect and reinforce that social history and that racial group (while excluding the epistemologies of other races/cultures), and that this has negative results for people of color in general and scholars of color in particular. (p. 8)

I decided that I needed a different epistemological paradigm than the mainstream paradigms I had been offered. I wanted to ask (and answer) of myself questions eloquently posited by Dillard (2000), "For African American women leaders/researchers living within our highly racist, sexist, and class-conscious society, how do we use experiences of racism, sexism, and other oppressions to inform our research as well as our leadership?" (p. 671).

The words in the title of the Black feminist anthology, *All the Women Are White, All the Blacks Are Men, But Some of Us Are Brave,* have particular power as I consider my position in the academy (Hull, Scott, & Smith, 1982). I desire to carve a niche for myself, to make a home, a scholarly abode, an intellectual residency. I desire this amidst the barriers and politics of race, class, gender, and so forth. It occurs to me that I have no place, being neither White nor male, a status that potentially (and strategically) renders me, the invisible, visible. To successfully carve this niche therefore requires courage, strength, and bravery.

The void in the research to me was a deafening silence. It propelled me to change my entire perspective. I needed to assure myself that I, as an African American female, could contribute to a body of scholarly work about African American females. Our experiences are valid, our voices should be heard. It has been this experience that has made gender more salient for me and demonstrated the ways in which race and gender are inextricable.

It is disheartening to feel alone in the sometimes-cruel world of the academy. It is particularly disconcerting to know that neither one's race nor gender has currency. Further, it is frustrating to try to make others understand that as a Black woman, I don't exist in nice, neat fragments. These components of my identity are multiplicative (King, 1995) and are impacted by one another to construct my identity.

Black women are in a unique position in society at large and within the academy in particular. In many ways these experiences have been exorcised from one another, and essentialized with that of others. For example, the experiences of women are often uniquely depicted as uniform and distinct only from men, with experiences of White women being those that are set aside as the example of the norm. In the same manner, the experiences of Blacks are often depicted via the knowledge and positionality of Black men. The identity marker of race tends to homogenize the group, not allowing for the differences that gender engenders.

In coming to voice and attempting to reconcile these challenges, I have looked to some of the premises and tenets of Black feminism. Many Black feminist scholars have offered insights that have helped me frame the issues that I have attempted to grapple with in the course of this journey. In her article, "Black Women, Shaping Feminist Theory," bell hooks (2001) notes that feminism in the United States did not emerge from the women most victimized by sexual oppression. It instead emerged from the concerns of leisure class White women. These concerns were not representative of the vast masses of women. Modern feminism asserts "all women are oppressed." hooks (2001) states, "sexism as a system of domination is institutionalized, but it has never determined in an absolute way the fate of all women in this society" (p. 134). She goes on to state that oppression is connected to the absence of choices. Although women in this society have been oppressed, the limitation of choices is not universal. Some women have more choices available to them than do others.

I find this to be particularly true in my research on African American women in positions of school leadership, particularly the principalship and the superintendency. While the numbers of women in such positions are few, the research that exposes this remains conspicuously silent about African American women and other women of color.

Tyack and Hansot (cited in Shakeshaft, 1999) have labeled this a "Conspiracy of Silence." This conspiracy of silence allows for African American women and other women of color to be essentially left out of discussions centering on women in school leadership. This omission from the discussion gives a tacit implication that African American women are not effective leaders and are perhaps not even interested in this kind of leadership.

In terms of women in educational leadership, no words could ring truer. The concerns of women in leadership do not traditionally reflect women of color. When such is the case, they are nothing more than a footnote or a book chapter rather than the focal point. And even when the absences of African American women in school leadership is noted, it is rarely questioned. Their plight is only illustrated to strengthen the argument for women in leadership, rather than to examine the nuances and intricacies of a Black woman's leadership style. Dillard (1995) illustrates this point in her article, "Leading with Her Life: An African American Feminist (Re)interpretation of Leadership for an Urban High School Principal":

> In other words, groups that have traditionally been excluded or marginalized within the system of public schooling (and within the leadership in those schools) are assumed not only to engage and interact in the work of schools in the same ways as those whose perspectives have traditionally dominated schools, but also desire the same values, ethics, and morals as well. (p. 542)

A tenet of Black feminist thought is that Black women have a self-defined perspective on their oppression. This standpoint is reinforced by two components: The political and economic status of African American women provides them with a different reality than the dominant group and that reality is interpreted differently from the dominant group.

Black feminist thought is significant because it encourages a "collective identity" by providing Black women with a different view of themselves than that offered by the dominant view. In this view, value is placed on the subjective knowledge base that African American women share. Collins (1990) posits that when the knowledge validation process is controlled by white male powers-that-be, Black feminist thought is often suppressed. Collins (1990) argues,

> The experiences of African American women scholars illustrate how individuals who wish to rearticulate a black women's standpoint through black feminist thought can be suppressed by a white man controlled knowledge-validation process. Exclusion from basic literacy, quality educational experiences, and faculty and administrative positions has limited black women's access to influential academic positions. Thus, while black women can produce knowledge claims that contest those advanced by the white male community, this community does not grant that black women scholars have competing knowledge claims based in another knowledge validation process. (p. 188)

This argument resonates with my experiences as a doctoral student. I have observed how African American applicants were not considered strong candidates particularly when their work wasn't perceived to be scholarly enough. When a viable candidate (an African American female, coincidentally) has emerged from the applicant pool, she has still been overlooked in favor of another candidate. What is especially noteworthy in this situation is that African American females largely responsible for the fate of the candidate in question seemed to operate in a manner in which they used "their authority to help legitimate a system that devalues and excludes the majority of black women" (p. 188). Collins (1990) describes it in this manner:

> One way of excluding the majority of black women from the knowledge validation process is to permit a few black women to acquire positions of authority in institutions that legitimate knowledge and to encourage them to work within the taken-for-granted assumptions of black female inferiority shared by the scholarly community and the culture at large. (p. 188)

Collins (1990) further asserts that Black women in the academy who rearticulate a Black woman's standpoint may find that their work is challenged based on epistemology. She argues that Black female scholars "may know that something is true but be unwilling or unable to legitimate their claims using Eurocentric masculinist criteria for consistency with substantiated knowledge and Eurocentric masculinist criteria methodological accuracy" (p. 188). It is this argument that has been the impetus for my own dissertation research.

Supports

Program Support

In the process of struggling to find a voice and validation of my research interests and professional goals within the academy, I have had the blessing of being a PROFS Fellow. PROFS is a program within the college of education that seeks to provide research opportunities to scholars of color. This program provides nurturing and supports doctoral students academically, personally, and financially. The program is fairly new, and I am in the second cohort of fellows.

I was offered an opportunity to become a PROFS Fellow at the beginning of my second year of doctoral study. Although I knew a few students who were PROFS Fellows, I knew very little about the program. Through this program, I have had an opportunity to come to know other doctoral students of color both in my program and in other programs within the College of Education. We have interacted both in informal and formal settings. They have shared insights regarding navigating the academy. I have had the benefit of their experiences in helping me to navigate through a large and daunting place like Ohio State University.

PROFS has provided support for my research choices. As I struggled to understand myself and come to terms with how I would approach my research, I received significant support from the PROFS students and faculty directors. It has been refreshing to be able to discuss my progress with others who have been through my struggle and have insights on how best to navigate through this system. It is easy to feel isolated and alone. I was one of two African American students in my cohort. Interacting with PROFS Fellows gave me an occasion to see other students who look like me on a regular basis.

Interacting with PROFS Fellows has provided support and validation for my research interests. It has been exciting and interesting to watch other African American doctoral students who have chosen to pursue culturally relevant research interests. It has made me confident and comfortable in pursuing research interests that are related to my own professional goals.

Typically, in our program students connect with advisors whose research they participate in as well. There are no faculty whose research is concerned with women in educational leadership or with women of color in particular. There are no female faculty members of color in my department. Discussing my research interests with the other PROFS Fellows has provided me a forum in which to discuss my interests and also a support network of others interested in doing varied kinds of research, including that which is culturally relevant.

Informal Mentoring

I have been able to receive support and mentoring from other female faculty of color in addition to the PROFS program. Often, they were the individuals with whom I felt most comfortable discussing the frustrations and challenges of the doctoral program. Although their research interests have often been different from my own, they are very personal to them in the same manner that my interests are to me. In addition to having a passion for their research born of their personal and professional experiences, they share with me knowledge about the challenges of being an African American female in a doctoral program. They seem to understand my feelings of isolation and frustration. These women interact with me in ways that let me know that they have an interest in me as a person. We've maintained e-mail contact and they've invited me to their homes and shared their personal contact information with me. The intensity of their desire to see me do well has provided me with a sense of fortitude and strength. I feel as though I'm standing on the shoulders of my predecessors. I'm able to conquer this mountain because, along with many others before them, they've paved the way. Although difficult and challenging, their presence in the academy makes my journey easier.

These persons have functioned as role models, advisors, mentors, and friends. They come to the table with a firsthand understanding of the challenges of being a female student of color in the academy. Gloria, Robinson Kurpius, Hamilton, & Willson (1999) suggest that having mentors and role models who have been successful in their academic pursuits "may create a sense of vicarious self-efficacy" (p. 58). Establishing support networks of peers and mentors helps to decrease African American students' feelings of unease and discomfort at traditionally White universities (Gloria et al., 1999).

Student Organizations/Committees

I have also been able to find support by becoming actively involved with a student organization. The Black Graduate and Professional Student Caucus at The Ohio State University has served as a support network consisting of African American graduate and professional students. This organization provides academic and social support for graduate students and also works to provide mentoring and support to encourage African American undergraduates to consider graduate and professional school. Gloria et al. (1999) emphasize, "a support group of peers effectively handling similar challenges can model coping and persistence behaviors" (p. 58). Being involved with this organization allows me the opportunity to interact with other students who are experiencing similar trials.

In addition to the abovementioned supports, I have had the opportunity to understand some of the intricacies of the university and the college of education in particular by sitting on several committees. These opportunities have provided me with insider information. I better understand the inner workings of the college as well as the politics and policies. While the research suggests that African American students attending traditionally White institutions often feel marginalized (Allen, 1985; Aubert, 1996; Gloria et al., 1999; Lewis, Chesler, & Forman, 2000), the opportunity to participate on committees has provided academic and professional support that I may otherwise not have received (Johnson, 1996).

Conclusion

There is little scholarly work written specifically by or about African American women in K–12 educational leadership. Although there are some (Alston, 1999; Jackson, 1999), there are few African American female professors (or any others for that matter) engaged in this kind of research (even at The Ohio State University).

African American women aspiring to positions of leadership often find that their "multiple jeopardies" impact opportunities to occupy such positions. Unlike their Black male and White female counterparts, Black women do not have the dual role of oppressor and oppressed. I seek to understand the ways in which racism, sexism, classism, and so on, impact and uniquely shape the experiences of Black women in school leadership.

The various kinds of support I have received definitely strengthens my voice. It gives me the wherewithal to continue along my chosen path. It fuels my desire to illuminate voices of those who have been conspicuously silent. It has been these experiences that have led me to understand my responsibility in helping to make the academy a "home of the brave."

References

Allen, W. (1985). Black student, White campus: Structural, interpersonal and psychologic correlates of success. *Journal of Negro Education, 54*(2), 134–147.

Allen, W., & Niss, J. (1990). Chill in the college classroom? *Phi Delta Kappan, 71*(8), 607–609.

Alston, J. (1999). Climbing hills and mountains: Black females making it to the superintendency. In C. Cryss Brunner (Ed.), *Sacred dreams: Women in the superintendency* (pp. 79–90). Albany, NY: SUNY.

Aubert, S. E. (1996). Black students on White campuses: Overcoming the isolation. In K. Lomotey (Ed.), *Sailing against the wind* (pp. 141–146). Albany, NY: SUNY.

Collins, P. (1990). *Black feminist thought: Knowledge, consciousness, and the politics of empowerment.* Harper Collins.

Dillard, C. (1995). Leading with her life: An African American feminist (re)interpretation of leadership for an urban high school principal. *Educational Administration Quarterly, 31*(4), 539–563.

Dillard, C. (2000). The substance of things hoped for, the evidence of things not seen: Examining an endarkened feminist epistemology in educational research and leadership. *International Journal of Qualitative Studies in Education, 13*(6), 661–681.

Gloria, A., Robinson, K. S., Hamilton, K., & Willson, M. (1999). African American students' persistence at a Predominantly White University: Influences of social support, university comfort, and self-beliefs. *Journal of College Student Development, 40*(3), 257–268.

hooks, b. (2001). Black women, shaping feminist theory. In J. James, & T. D. Sharpley–Whiting (Ed.). *The black feminist reader.* Malden: Blackwell Publishers.

Hull, G., Bell, S. P., & Smith, B. (1982). *All the women are white, all the blacks are men, but some of us are brave: Black women's studies.* New York: The Feminist Press.

Jackson, B. (1999). Getting inside history—against all odds: African-American women school superintendents. In C. Cryss Brunner (Ed.), *Sacred dreams: Women and the superintendency* (pp. 141–159). Albany, NY: SUNY.

Johnson, S. (1996). Ethnic/cultural centers on predominantly White campuses: Are they necessary? In K. Lomotey (Ed.), *Sailing against the wind* (pp. 155–162). Albany, NY: SUNY.

King, D. (1995). Multiple jeopardy, multiple consciousness: The context of a black feminist ideology. In B. Guy-Sheftall (Ed.), *Words of fire: An anthology of African American feminist thought* (pp. 291–317). New York: The New Press.

Lewis, A., Chesler, M., & Forman, T. (2000). The impact of "colorblind" ideologies on students of color: Intergroup relations at a Predominantly White University. *Journal of Negro Education, 69*(1/2), 74–91.

Louque, A. (1999). Factors influencing academic attainment for African-American women Ph.D. recipients: An ethnographic study of their persistence. *The Negro Educational Review, 3–4,* July–October, 101–108.

Scheurich, J. J., & Young, M. D. (1996). Coloring epistemologies: Are our research epistemologies racially biased? *Educational Researcher, 26*(4), 4–16.

Shakeshaft, C. (1999). The struggle to create a more gender-inclusive profession. In J. Murphy & K. Seashore-Louis (Eds.), *Handbook of research on educational administration: A project of the American Educational Research Association.* San Francisco: Jossey-Bass Publishers.

Tatum, B. (1997). *Why do all the black kids sit together in the cafeteria? And other conversations about race.* New York: BasicBooks.

Tamara Duckworth-Warner

Hometown: Charleston, West Virginia
Current Institution: University of Florida
Department: Clinical and Health Psychology
Personal Philosophy: If you can talk, you can sing. If you can walk, you can dance.
—Yoruba proverb

14

CHOOSING A MENTOR AND OTHER LESSONS OF THE HIDDEN CURRICULUM OF GRADUATE SCHOOL

Introduction

Earning a graduate degree can be an extremely rewarding but difficult process. The journey through graduate school can be somewhat less daunting if you understand from the beginning that there is a "hidden curriculum" beyond the department's written curriculum and policies. The hidden curriculum refers to the unstated and unwritten academic and social norms and expectations that coexist with the formal curriculum in an educational institution. Snyder (1970) argued that the hidden curriculum was, in part, responsible for the student unrest of the 1960s as students challenged these norms in the quest for independent self-identification. For most African Americans, who are the first in their families to pursue higher education, the lessons of the hidden curriculum can become concealed barriers to successful matriculation through the academy. A number of researchers in curriculum studies have argued that educators have an obligation to make the hidden curriculum more explicit (Portelli, 1993; Sullivan, 1991). This chapter is designed to uncover some of the lessons of the hidden curriculum, particularly in graduate programs in the humanities and social sciences at predominately European American institutions. By delineating strategies to effectively negotiate the hidden curriculum based on the literature and my experience in two different graduate programs at two different universities, my hope is that others can thrive in, and not just survive, graduate school.

It should be stated at the outset that some aspects of graduate school will disappoint you or anger you or both, depending on your disposition. Based on interviews with twenty-six women of color enrolled in Ph.D. programs in sociology, Margolis and Romero (1998) found that many were surprised that: (1) there were few (if any) course offerings or required readings about issues salient to communities of color; (2) there was little, if any, research on communities of color using perspectives, theories, or methodologies derived from communities of color; (3) that, as students of color, they were frequently assumed to be the spokesperson or representative for people of color; (4) that, as students of color, they were assigned or encouraged to teach courses related to race, ethnicity, and gender; and (5) that the allocation of department resources, graduate student recruitment, and hiring and promotion practices tended to favor those with more privilege rather than less privilege. During my first year in graduate school, I was outraged to see that chapters from *The Bell Curve* were assigned as required readings on the intellectual assessment of African American children. In other words, graduate programs in majority institutions mirror the hierarchies and inequalities found in every other institution in American society. To expect otherwise is simply naïve.

Many of the lessons of the hidden curriculum deal with the process of being socialized or "professionalized" into one's discipline. Margolis and Romero (1998) argue that there is both a "weak" form of the hidden curriculum designed to cultivate a professional identity among graduate students and a "strong" form with socialization processes that serve to reproduce inequality. Weak forms of the hidden curriculum include requirements such as developing an "objective" and detached attitude toward one's subject of study, using discipline-specific jargon and abstract theories; developing an assertive self-confidence that disguises overt anxiety; and developing a loyalty and allegiance to colleagues— even to the detriment of one's allegiance to one's community of origin. In addition, the weak form of the hidden curriculum specifies that the acquisition of these qualities and skills take place in an environment of competition and isolation, in which graduate students are expected to engage in aggressive networking and to develop independent work habits (Margolis & Romero, 1998). The strong form of the hidden curriculum involves eight elements: stigmatization, blaming the victim, cooling out, stereotyping, absence, silence, exclusion, and tracking (Margolis & Romero, 1998). The eight processes of the strong hidden curriculum often overlap with and serve to reinforce aspects of the weak hidden curriculum. This essay offers advice to manage some parts of both the weak and strong forms of the hidden curriculum and thereby give graduate students of color the knowledge and skills needed to negotiate the graduate school socialization process more effectively.

Lesson 1: Choosing a Primary Mentor

The first lesson to master in the graduate school hidden curriculum is choosing a primary mentor. The term *mentor* comes from Greek mythology and refers to the friend of Odysseus who became a wise and trusted advisor to Odysseus' son Telemachus. In graduate school, a mentor not only advises but provides access to important resources and identifies opportunities to develop a student's career. The importance of the mentor lesson cannot be overemphasized. If this lesson is not thoroughly understood and executed, all of the other lessons of the hidden curriculum will become virtually irrelevant. To highlight how critical a lesson choosing a mentor can be, let me relate a fable that I first encountered via electronic mail.

> One beautiful fine day in the forest, a rabbit was seen sitting outside her burrow typing away on her laptop. Along comes a fox. The fox asks, "What are you working on?"
> The rabbit answers, "My dissertation."
> Fox: "Hmmm. What is it about?"
> Rabbit (nonchalantly): "The superiority of rabbits over foxes."
> Fox (incredulous pause): "That's ridiculous! Any fool knows that foxes are bigger, stronger, and smarter than rabbits."
> Rabbit: "Come with me, and I'll show you."
> They both disappear into the rabbit's burrow. After a few minutes, the rabbit comes out and calmly returns to her laptop.
> Soon a wolf comes along and stops to watch the hard-working rabbit.
> Wolf: "What's that you're writing?"
> Rabbit: "I'm doing a thesis on the superiority of rabbits over wolves."
> Wolf (guffaws loudly): "You don't expect to get such garbage published, do you?"
> Rabbit: "No problem. Do you want to see why?"
> The rabbit and wolf go into the burrow, and again the rabbit returns by herself. She goes back to her typing.

Finally a bear comes along.

Bear: "What are you doing?"

Rabbit: "I'm doing a thesis on the superiority of rabbits over bears."

Bear: "Well, that's absurd!"

Rabbit: "Come into my burrow, and I'll show you."

Inside the rabbit's burrow, in one corner there is a pile of fox bones. In another corner is a pile of wolf bones. On the other side of the room a huge lion is smiling and picking his teeth.

The moral of the story: It doesn't matter *what* you choose for your dissertation topic. What matters is *who* you choose for a dissertation advisor.

While my outlook is not quite as cynical as this fable, my experience has taught me the truth it contains. Mentors guide and shape your career by *providing access* to usually scarce resources, including research and teaching assistantships, publication opportunities, grant funding, postdoctoral fellowships, and jobs. Choosing the person who will help you navigate the sometimes murky waters of the academy is not always an easy process. Here are a few suggestions for selecting the "lion" who will help determine whether your graduate school ship deviates off course, runs aground, or sails successfully to anchor at the Ph.D. dock.

1. Know yourself and what you need in a mentor. Before you can choose a primary mentor, you must know your own personality and work habits well enough to choose a good match. Are you a person who needs lots of structure, including firm deadlines and regular meetings, or do you work better when given more independence? As a somewhat older graduate student who worked for several years as a professional before returning to the academy, I was not looking for a mentor who would necessarily hold my hand. On the other hand, a classmate of mine who was 21 when she entered graduate school and had never been in the world of work felt more comfortable with a mentor who regularly checked on her progress. Most of us will not have the luxury of choosing a mentor who perfectly matches our personality. Knowing how you work can aid you, however, in identifying and capitalizing on areas of fit, on the one hand, and working around areas where the fit is poor on the other.

2. Be aware that mentors come in all shapes, sizes, and colors. Do not assume that the faculty member of color (if there are any in your department) will be the best mentor for you if you are a graduate student of color. The same goes for gender and age. As an undergraduate, my most inspiring academic role model was an older European American male historian. In my first graduate program, I assumed incorrectly that the younger male African American faculty member, who was an incredibly productive scholar, would be my best guide through the graduate school wilderness. Our personalities and interests differed significantly, so I planned to turn to my "backup" mentor, a younger female African American faculty member, only to learn that she had fallen seriously ill. Too intimidated to approach more senior faculty members, I resigned myself to leaving the university with a master's degree.

3. Know that different mentors can serve different roles. There are at least three different types of mentors. First is the "VIP" (Very Important Person) mentor who can provide access to important resources including funding, research, publications, or other opportunities to develop your career. The VIP mentor is generally a senior, tenured faculty member who is well established both at the university and in the field. The VIP mentor can invite you to co-author a book chapter or serve as a guest reviewer for a journal for which he or she is an editor. While there are always exceptions, most junior faculty members are often so occupied with activities related to establishing their own careers and climbing the tenure ladder that they cannot properly mentor graduate students.

    The second type of mentor is the "How-To" mentor. The How-To mentor provides hands-on instruction, such as the nuts and bolts of writing a research grant. This faculty member is also usually a "What-To" mentor, providing direction for specific tasks during different stages of your graduate career. For example, a "What-To" mentor will advise you about which professional organizations to join, which conferences to submit abstracts to, and which journals to submit your manuscripts to. The third type of mentor is what I call the "Warm-Fuzzy" mentor. This is the faculty member who provides personal and emotional support and encouragement, alternately cheering and comforting you during the inevitable highs and lows of graduate school. In my department, this mentor and his family host an informal monthly gathering for African American students at his home, where we play cards and board games.

4. Get as many mentors as you can but not too many. It is unrealistic to expect any one faculty member to fulfill all three roles of a mentor as just described. In fact, because faculty members are human and have lives and careers of their own, it would be wise to spread these roles among different individuals. You do not want to become too dependent on that one faculty member who falls ill, goes on sabbatical, or gets a tenure offer from a different university.

   Be aware that not all of your mentors have to be on your dissertation committee or even in your department or at your university. Some mentor relationships can be more informal, and because of the more intimate nature of the relationship with a Warm-Fuzzy mentor, it may be prudent not to have that person on the committee that judges your academic progress.

5. Choose your primary mentor based on facts not reputation. Every graduate program has its share of rumors and urban legends. Do not rely on student lore when choosing a mentor. For each potential mentor, find out how many of their students have successfully completed the program and how many are currently ABD (all but dissertation) and, if possible, why. Also, research the average time-to-degree, funding support, and productivity for students of different mentors. Use several different sources of information, if possible, including interviews with current and former students.

   The best fit for you will, of course, depend on your future goals. For example, if you are planning to pursue a career in academia, then you might be better off choosing Professor A, whose students typically take seven years to complete their degrees but have five publications and several postdoctoral fellowship offers over Professor B, whose students typically get their doctorate in five years but graduate with only one publication and are less competitive for postdoctoral fellowships or faculty positions. The bottom line is to select a mentor with a demonstrated track record of graduating productive, well-supported students in a reasonable amount of time.

6. Choose a mentor as early in your graduate career as possible. Ideally, you should begin shopping around for a mentor during the process of applying to graduate school. More specifically, you should identify at least two or three faculty members who you would like to work with at each graduate program to which you apply. Begin by identifying faculty who share similar academic interests through their publications. Begin a dialogue with potential mentors through e-mail and approach them at professional conferences. After you have been accepted to various programs, select the one in which you will matriculate based on conversations with potential mentors and their current graduate students. After starting graduate school, you should identify a mentor by the end of your first semester.

Lesson 2: The Hidden Curriculum "Do's"

After tackling the first major task of choosing a mentor, there are several other unspoken rules of graduate school's hidden curriculum to which one must be attentive. The following is my list of top ten "Do's" and "Don'ts" for negotiating the hidden curriculum within your graduate program:

1. Select a "balanced" committee. When putting together your dissertation committee, strive for a committee with a balance of personalities. Find out which faculty members work well together and which do not. You do not want your dissertation proposal to be held up, for example, by a heated methodological debate between two committee members. This is more likely to occur between two VIP mentors with large egos. Again, based on the fable, it is probably safest to have a senior, tenured VIP mentor as your dissertation chair although you could have a more junior chair if the VIP mentor on your committee does not have a large ego.

2. Put in "face time." Socialization into a discipline is one of the primary functions of the hidden curriculum, and this takes place in both formal and informal settings. Be visible in your department. In addition to attending and being on time for seminars and meetings, visit faculty during their office hours. You will be expected to participate in activities and social events sponsored by your department. These can range from "optional" research meetings to Friday evening "happy hours" at a local bar to an annual Christmas dinner hosted by the department chair. You do not have to enjoy all of these gatherings, but you do need to make an appearance. Do not fool yourself into thinking that you will not be missed if you do not show your face on a regular basis.

3. Take care of yourself. Graduate school can be an alienating place, so self-care must be a priority. Maintain some balance through adequate amounts of sleep, nutrition, and exercise. Develop leisure activities to reduce stress. Have some fun because no matter how hard you work, you will never fully overcome the "imposter syndrome." Stay grounded culturally by volunteering in the community with children or elders and going home when you can, if home is a place of comfort for you. Stay grounded spiritually by going to church, temple, or synagogue.

   Two of my self-care activities, which were also acts of resistance, have been delivering clinical services to lower-income African Americans in the local community and mentoring undergraduates of color at my university and other graduate students of color in my program. To unwind, I have also taken beginning tennis and golf lessons and make beaded jewelry. My favorite self-care activity, however, was having a potluck Sunday dinner with two female friends and colleagues from my department. We initially got together to study statistics but enjoyed our "soul food brunches" so much that we started a tradition that lasted three years. By doing it potluck style, we could rotate who was responsible for the main dish and indulge in wine and decadent desserts once every week.

4. Develop a strong support system (in addition to your various mentors). Family and community members are usually an

important part of the social support network, but often our parents, aunties, and spouses do not have advanced degrees and cannot fully understand the demands of graduate school. Cast a wide net when constructing a support system, including folks both inside and outside of your department. Classmates and more advanced colleagues can be helpful sources of advice, unless the environment in your department is very competitive. Join the graduate student association, teaching assistants' union, or an organization for graduate students of color. Build an alliance with the dean or director of the administrative office on campus dedicated to supporting minority graduate students (found at most majority institutions). During the dissertation writing stage, you may want to join or form a support group.

Additional sources of support can be found off-campus through religious and community organizations including churches, political groups, book clubs, and sports teams. Friends and associates who are not involved in the university or departmental culture and politics can be important links in one's social support network because they provide a much-needed diversion from your academic work and can help you maintain perspective on the relative importance of your life in the ivory tower.

5. Seek help when you need it, not when it is too late. Health crises, financial troubles, and family problems can and do occur during graduate school. You may need to ask for an extension on a paper, take an incomplete in a class, or request a leave of absence for a semester. You may need to reduce your research or teaching load or seek counseling. Whatever is required, intervene sooner rather than later. Graduate programs generally make significant investments in their students and would rather see a lower return than an outright loss.

6. Keep your eyes on the prize. You do not get tenure as a graduate student. The purpose of qualifying or comprehensive examinations is to demonstrate competence not mastery. Your dissertation will not be your magnum opus: In fact, most of your mentors would probably tell you that their dissertation is their worst piece of work. If you plan to pursue a career in the academy, the dissertation represents the beginning, not the end, of

your research career. Choose a "practical" dissertation topic, one that can be completed with a reasonable amount of effort in a reasonable amount of time. As my "How-To" mentor advised me when I was putting together my dissertation proposal, "Be a branch on the tree. Don't plant a new tree." In other words, build on what others have done and try to make a small contribution to the literature by adding another single layer to the structure of knowledge. Remember why you are in graduate school: to get a doctoral degree, not win the Nobel prize.

Lesson 3: The Hidden Curriculum "Don'ts"

1. Don't spread yourself too thin. Develop a planned program of study in which you outline, semester by semester, your coursework, research objectives, and other requirements. This outline should include specific application dates for grants and submission deadlines for conference abstracts to keep you on track. Select a balanced schedule of courses each semester. Attend *some,* but not all, professional conferences and meetings. Judiciously choose leadership and volunteer activities, especially extra-departmental activities.

2. Don't be a "lone wolf." Do not isolate yourself from others, particularly during stressful periods. I believe the paradigm that prized the independence and individualism of the isolated scholar is gradually being replaced by one that values collaborative, interdisciplinary research. Work on joint research projects with faculty and peers. My first publication was one I co-authored with a fellow graduate student.

3. Don't let money interfere. Do not allow part-time or full-time work to hamper your academic progress. Buy your own books and supplies—do not borrow them—and buy the publication manual for your field. It is difficult to build a successful graduate school career if you do not have the basic tools to do the job. Budget your money wisely—stick to a plan and plan ahead. Not being able to buy books at the beginning of the semester while you wait for a student loan check to come through is a very uncomfortable position to be in.

4. Don't win the battle but lose the war. As noted at the beginning of this essay, certain aspects of the graduate school culture will likely annoy if not outright offend you. As Margolis and Romero (1998) point out, while originality may be one measure of intellect, going too far outside the dominant paradigms of one's field is likely to be labeled as "bizarre" rather than creative. Being too passionate or politically involved, particularly with respect to matters of race, ethnicity, class, or gender, might be seen as incompatible with the development of the proper distance from a subject. Don't engage in heated arguments with faculty. It is a battle that is rarely won, and you will be much more effective in fighting that battle *after* you have earned your degree.

This is not to suggest that you "sell out" in order to get your degree. I purposefully chose the terms *negotiate* and *manage* to refer to the relationship that graduate students of color must develop in relation to the lessons of graduate school's hidden curriculum because I believe that finding ways to resist the culturally alienating aspects of graduate school is an important strategy for surviving the doctoral socialization process. When *The Bell Curve* was assigned as required reading, I launched a frontal assault by preparing a two-page summary of critiques of the book written by well-known scholars to distribute to my classmates and the professor teaching the course. Mentoring other students of color has not only been a self-care activity, as noted earlier, but also a way of undermining some of the oppressive aspects of the hidden curriculum. Presenting the lessons I have earned at two national conferences and preparing this manuscript are further attempts to combat the reproduction of the status quo that is a result of the hidden curriculum. For other ideas about other strategies for resisting the hidden curriculum, the reader is referred to Gainen and Boice (1993), Margolis (2001), and Morley and Walsh (1995).

Conclusion

There are likely to be many more lessons of the hidden curriculum that vary based on the culture at the institution and in the specific department. I have highlighted only a few based on my experience and reading of the literature and offered strategies that have worked for me. By being savvy about the unwritten and unspoken rules of the hidden curriculum, you will be well on your way to joining the precious few in our community who hold doctoral degrees.

References

Gainen, J., & Boice, R. (Eds.). (1993). *Building a diverse faculty.* San Francisco: Jossey-Bass.

Herrnstein, R., & Murray, C. (1994). *The bell curve: Intelligence and class structure in American Life.* New York: Free Press.

Margolis, E. (Ed.). (2001). *The hidden curriculum in higher education.* New York: Routledge.

Margolis, E., & Romero, M. (1998). "The department is very male, very white, very old, and very conservative": The functioning of the hidden curriculum in graduate sociology departments. *Harvard Educational Review, 68*(1), 1–32.

Morley, L., & Walsh, V. (Eds.). (1995). *Feminist academics: Creative agents for change.* Bristol, PA: Taylor & Francis.

Portelli, J. P. (1993). Exposing the hidden curriculum. *Journal of Curriculum Studies, 25*(4), 343–358.

Snyder, B. R. (1970). *The hidden curriculum.* New York: Knopf.

Sullivan, T. A. (1991). Making the graduate curriculum explicit. *Teaching Sociology, 19,* 408–413.

Tarcha Rentz

Hometown: Gainesville, Florida
Current Institution: University of Florida
Department: Special Education
Personal Philosophy: To whom much is given, much is required.

15

THE ROLE OF MENTORSHIP IN DEVELOPING AFRICAN AMERICAN STUDENTS AND PROFESSIONALS WITHIN THE ACADEMY

Over a year ago Barry became my friend and the closest thing to what I can call a mentor. He has been instrumental in helping me through the transition of public school teacher to a full-time doctoral student. Even though Barry is a year ahead of me, he is concerned with my academic and social well-being through the doctoral process. Currently, he and I are the only full-time African American doctoral students in the department of special education at a Predominately White Institution in the South. Like so many other African American doctoral students, we welcome the opportunity to be mentored by caring and supportive faculty members who would take a personal interest in us.

A Raisin in a Bowl of Milk

Imagine that you have been invited to join a campus organization which you've been told will look good on your vitae. Remembering what your mama taught you about first impressions, you've dressed conservatively and businesslike. As you enter the room people are enjoying the snacks, talking and laughing with each other. Having walked around the room, you realize no one is familiar to you, so being the confident person you are you decide to sit at a table where there are organization members. While enjoying your refreshments you realize no one in this grouping of Caucasian students has greeted you. You decide to make the first move. Turning to those sitting at your table you smile and say, "Hello." In response you receive a look of "Are you speaking to me?" The meeting starts and you're introduced by the sponsor of the group as a new doctoral student. Your neighbor turns and says, "So you're Tarcha."

There are many benefits in having a college degree. College graduates are less likely to commit a crime and approximately 30 percent less likely to be unemployed compared to someone with only a high school diploma (Caberra, Nora, & Terenzini, 1999). Perna (2000) reveals that even though there is an increase in the number of minorities entering higher education, there exists underrepresentation between the undergraduates and those having received bachelor's degrees when compared to their traditional college population. The issue of more African Americans enrolling in college than graduating from college, in addition to the decrease in the numbers of African Americans entering graduate and professional schools, continues to be a critical matter (Green, 2001). Numerous researchers suggest that mentoring is an essential ingredient to the retention and attrition issues of African American students and African American faculty in the academy (Branch, 2001; Gregory, 1999; Lee, 1999; Weidman, Twale, & Stein, 2001).

What Is a Mentor?

The word *mentor* is defined as "a wise and trusted counselor or teacher." It is derived from Greek mythology wherein Odysseus the King of Ithaca went off to fight the Trojan War leaving behind his son, Telemachus, with a dear friend by the name of Mentor. Odysseus would not leave the heir to the throne with just anyone; Mentor was his trusted and wise friend. Mentor would prepare the young Telemachus to one day take the throne, becoming the next King of Ithaca. Lee (1999) conveys a "mentor as a relationship between a senior (the mentor) who is knowledgeable of the culture and a junior (mentee/protégé) who wants to become a member of the culture" (p. 27). During a lifetime, a person can have several mentors with each relationship being unique.

The mentoring relationship is generally formal or informal. Formal mentoring relationships are usually arranged by outside forces such as institutions or political mandates (Johnson, 1996). The mentee/protégé is involuntarily assigned to a volunteered mentor. This mentoring relationship is intentional, structured, and planned. Most mentoring relationships are informal. According to Lois Zachary (2000), in informal mentoring relationships the relationship occurs by chance or circumstance. For example, the mentor and mentee/protégé may be the only African Americans in the department sharing similar interests. The mentee/protégé may initiate a relationship that evolves into one of mentorship.

Many faculty and students understand mentoring to "be counseling or advisement, which it is in part, but mentoring goes beyond advisement" (Johnson, 1996, p. 64). True mentoring is a partnership between the mentor and mentee/protégé. Watkins (1998) cites Jearol Holland's 1993 study on the Relationships Between African American Doctoral Students and Their Major Advisor in describing a "true mentor" as having "actively socialized and networked the protégé into his field of study laying a detailed roadmap for the protégé to become personally knowledgeable of the professionals in the field; thus enhancing his ability to communicate with scholars directly without feelings of inhibition" (p. 11). Some attempt to equate a mentor with a role model; however, "the model could be completely unaware that someone is modeling his or her behavior" (Lee, 1999, p. 32). A mentor can be a role model, but being a role model alone requires no necessary contact or personal investment. Watkins (1998) conveys a role model must be an active participant to be a true mentor. For a mentoring relationship to endure over time, trust and communication must become a foundational part of the relationship. By using today's various technologies such as e-mail, online chats, video conferencing, and telephones, successful long-distance mentoring is made possible (Zachary, 2000).

Phases of the Mentoring Relationship

Lois Zachary (2000) provides four terms similar to Kram's (1985) terms—initiation, cultivation, separation, and redefinition—for describing the possible phases of successful mentoring. Zachary's (2000) terms—preparing, negotiating, enabling, and closure—are useful to the mentor and the mentee/protégé. Preparing is the process by which the mentor examines his or her motivations for wanting to be a mentor. This process requires self-examination and reflection. "Discovering core motivation is a little like peeling back the layers on an onion and finding even more layers underneath. What you find will depend on how truly candid and self-reflective you can be" (Zachary, 2000, pp. 68–69).

During this phase, external and internal motivations are questioned such as, Do I want to give back to the community? Does it mean more prestige for me? Am I mentoring because everyone is expecting me to do it? Mentoring relationships require time. Zachary (2000) reveals the quality of the time spent between the mentor and mentee/protégé is more important than the quantity of time. Conversations between the mentor and the mentee/protégé take place to assess the viability of a mentoring relationship.

In the negotiating phase, the mentor and the mentee/protégé come together to discuss the terms of the mentoring relationship. Before the work phase of the mentoring relationship can begin, well-defined goals and objectives must be clearly and candidly discussed. Zachary (2000) suggests "when mentees/protégé do not have well-defined goals, goal setting becomes a first priority, and the mentor's immediate task is to assist the mentee/protégé in clarifying and defining goals" (p. 96). The mentor and mentee/protégé return to these goals and objectives throughout the mentoring relationship, using them as benchmarks for success. Throughout the negotiating process developing shared understanding, expectations, and details is important. Oftentimes assumptions are made about the meanings of words and behaviors (Zachary, 2000). For example, when a mentee/protégé says he wants confidentiality with his mentor, does that mean continuously or for the duration of the mentoring relationship? Sensitive topics such as boundaries and limits in the mentoring relationship are addressed openly. If the mentor or mentee/protégé wants to have scheduled meeting times or unlimited access the wants and needs must be directly addressed.

Most of the contact between the mentor and mentee/protégé occurs during the enabling phase. In this phase the mentee/protégé is provided with conditions that will facilitate his or her growth and development: support, challenge, and vision (Zachary, 2000). The mentor's task is to manage the process, maintain the momentum, and encourage the movement of the mentee/protégé. For example, a doctoral student (mentee/protégé shares what she has experienced in her research and the mentor provides regular feedback (managing the process). The mentor coaches the student about how to test her hypothesis using various t-tests and ANOVAS (maintaining momentum). When the student has moments of doubt about the validity of her findings, the mentor encourages her to refer to what she knows about t-tests and ANOVAS (encouraging movement). Bullough (1996) describes his enabling phase with mentor Paul Klohr:

> He posed questions pointed in the direction of possible answers, and nudged us to engage issues that might otherwise have gone unnoticed. He listened a lot more than he talked which proved frustrating at times for those socialized, as were we, to expect answers. (p. 259)

The closure phase can be filled with various emotions: "discomfort, anxiety, fear, disappointment, relief, grief, fear of separation, joy, or excitement" (Zachary, 2000, p. 146). Doctoral students who have had true mentors may have feelings of joy and excitement mixed with relief and some anxiety. In a healthy mentoring relationship the mentor uses the established goals and objectives to evaluate the mentee/protégé and acknowledges the mentee/protégé's successes. During this phase the mentor celebrates the successes of his or her mentee/protégé while allowing the mentoring relationship to evolve into one of colleague/ friend (Zachary, 2000). For someone who has trouble saying goodbye this can be a sad moment in the midst of great celebration. Bullough (1996) beautifully writes, "After graduation we came to realize that just as we had chosen Klohr as mentor, he had chosen us and in the process we had changed" (p. 263).

Cross Cultural Mentoring

> Hi Dr. _____. I'm Tarcha _____. Dr._____ recommended that I should come and talk with you about my future plans in the doctoral program. She thought our interest might be the same. Have a seat. How can I help you? I heard you're interested in minority children in _____. You know Tarcha I'm not sure our philosophies match. I suggest you read _____.

With more African American students than available African American faculty within Predominately White Institutions (PWIs), some African American students are turning to Caucasian faculty for mentoring. "Research consistently shows African Americans attending PWIs experience more stress, racism, and isolation and are less likely to persist than their counterparts" (Jones, 2001, p. 9). Zachary (2000) conveys four competencies for establishing a cross-cultural mentoring relation-ship: become culturally self-aware, develop a working knowledge of and appreciation for other cultures, improve communication skills, and become culturally attuned to other cultures.

Becoming culturally aware requires self-knowledge and self reflec-tion. The mentor and the mentee/protégé must examine his or her atti-tudes and beliefs about their own cultures as well about the cultures of others. For example, the mentor and mentee/protégé may realize that they've developed stereotypes about certain cultures being smarter, more talented, or lazy. "Those who become conscious of their own val-ues and assumptions and critically examine them will be rewarded with a deeper understanding of their own behavior" (Zachary, 2000, p. 41). Jones (2001) reveals that "a lack of familiarity with the background and expectations of African American students account for infrequent socialization among students" on college campuses (p. 10). Developing a working knowledge and appreciation for other cultures is important in supporting the social and academic goals and objectives of African American students. African Americans are not a monoculture where we all have rhythm, play basketball, and eat watermelon. "Mentors, who are in the best position to facilitate learning, are willing to learn about the basic functional elements of their mentee's culture" (Zachary, 2000, p. 41). Strategies that could be utilized include seeking to under-stand the history of African Americans in Africa as well as in the United States, cultural achievements of African Americans, the family and social structure, economics and industry, dominant religious beliefs and practices, educational systems, and entertainment (Zachary, 2000). The competency of improving communication skills involves the listening and speaking component of the mentoring relationship. Mentor and mentee/protégé should ask open-ended questions and not be afraid of silences. Zachary (2000) suggests checking "for understanding by asking what specific words, phrases or expressions mean" (p. 42). Becoming culturally attuned to other cultures "means being able to "read the culture" of the mentee/protégé and understanding what is happening and what is expected through the context and nonverbal behaviors" (Zachary, 2000, p. 42). This competency is gained through interactions and communication with the mentee/protégé and his or her culture.

Wanted: A True Mentor

There are various reasons for having mentors for African American students and professionals within the academy. One, many African American students and professionals are unprepared for the college and university culture. African Americans have many similarities within the culture, but there are also many differences. Like African Americans, colleges and universities have a culture. Oftentimes the African American culture and university culture conflict with each other. The success of the university is dependent on the individual successes of the faculty and the students. Importantly, being aware of the values, practices, and attitudes of one's discipline and the university transforms the student into the colleague (Johnson & Ottens, 1996). Second, most of the African American undergraduate, graduate, and professionals within the academy are first generation college students (Jones, 2001; Lee, 1999). These students are oftentimes unprepared for the social, academic, and financial expectations within the academy. Being the one, first, or the few can be stressful for African American students and professionals (Johnson, 1996; Lee, 1999).

Third, African American students and professionals need mentors who inspire. When an African American student or professional meets another African American who is successful within the academy, he or she is inspired to think, "You made it, I can too" (Gregory, 1999; Weidman, Twale, & Stein, 2001). Fourth, African American students and professionals need protection and sponsorship. Without a mentor, African American doctoral students are not afforded the opportunities to publish or make presentations that are requirements for future tenure (Watkins, 1998). Weidman et al. (2001) purports in a Midwestern study comparing graduate women's experiences, White women were more likely to have mentors and to have co-authored and presented scholarly works than Black women. Commonalities in research and scholarship can be built between mentors and mentee/protégé.

Mentor Benefits

There are several benefits to having mentoring relationships in the academy. African American students and professionals are provided role models, which inspire them to maintain momentum. This African

American conveys the sentiment well,

> I would love to have a person that I could talk to about my field! It would be great to talk to someone who has already been there . . . I would like to see success . . . It'll let me hang on to the idea that I can do it too. (Lee, 1999, p. 36)

Believing that they will be respected and have their needs fulfilled, African American graduate students desire strong bonds with African American faculty. Another benefit is that African American students and African American faculty are able to build commonalities while encouraging each other. Branch (2001) suggests professors benefit from interactions with their African American graduate assistants who have similar interests and want to enhance their communities. Faculty mentors are able to pass their ideas and vision on to the next generation. For White faculty members, a benefit could be culture sharing opportunities. For African American students and professionals at PWIs, finding African American mentors is difficult. For African American students at PWIs such as North Carolina State University (NCSU) where there is one African American faculty for every twenty-seven African American students, it may be more important to have a mentor in the same field than to have an African American faculty member (Lee, 1999). In a true mentoring relationship an African American student or professional can enhance and broaden the worldview of White faculty. The mentoring relationship can be fruitful for both the mentor and the mentee/protégé.

African American students develop a higher commitment to graduation (Lee, 1999) and effective retention of African American students occurs (Jones, 2001) through a positive mentoring relationship. In contrast to African American students at PWIs, according to Davis (1994) African American students at historically Black institutions have higher grade point averages. This may be attributed to more contact and encouragement by faculty (Moore III, 2001). Gloria, Kurpius, Hamilton, and Wilson (1999) convey social support, university comfort, and positive self-beliefs as being the major factors in the academic and social persistence of African American students at PWIs. Because of this mentoring relationship, the university environment is made more hospitable. Many African American students are in need of academic and social support on college campuses, especially at PWIs. In a group interview of African American students and their parents Feagin, Vera, and Imani (1996) reveal recruitment of Black graduate students and faculty members is a critical part of the corrective action that would be necessary to make the PWI's environment much more hospitable. The presence of African American graduate students, doctoral students, and professionals is evidence to African American undergraduates that they can graduate and be successful in the academy (DeFour and Hirsch, 1990). Finally, the retention of African American faculty will be enhanced. Branch (2001) reveals the "paltry number of African American graduate students also contributes to an institution's inability to retain African American faculty members" (p. 180). African American faculty like to see African American students on their university campuses. There is a great likelihood that an African American student on campus has similar interest in the African American faculty's pursuits.

So Many Hats

When you are the one, first, or the few in the academy, having true mentor relationships can be difficult. Because you're the only or the few the college obligations are many (Aguirre, 2000; Gregory, 1999; Watkins, 1998). Aguirre (2000) purports because they are the "only or the few" their representation is in great demand. Consequently, minority faculty members serve on more committees. Kridel, Bullough, and Shaker (1996) describe common practice that is taking precedence over teaching and mentoring at many universities of young faculty scrambling to publish in order to meet publication quotas for promotions and tenure. At PWIs African American faculty are generally expected to mentor the African American students (Aguirre, 2000; Watkins, 1998) as well as provide service to the university and teach. There are generally more African American students at PWIs than there are African American faculty, such as the case at NCSU, leaving many African American students without an African American mentor and African American faculty burned out. Added to the frustration of being overstretched, mentoring is not valued when faculty seeks tenure (Weidman et al., 2001). Kridel et al. (1996) retain "the money changers are in charge, entrepreneurialism has swept across higher education and threatens the quality of the teaching and learning relationship that underpins educational excellence" (p. 7). Perhaps one or a few faculty members will kick over a table or two to be a true mentor to an African American trying to make it in the academy.

Opening the Doors

Mentoring opens up opportunities that would otherwise be closed to African American students and professionals in the academy. Weidman et al. (2001) suggest that because of personality characteristics or more accurate anticipatory socialization, some students adapt to the institutional culture of colleges and universities. The effective retention of minority students involves the establishment of mentoring programs where minority students are connected to faculty who can support and guide them toward social and academic success (Jones, 2001). Through the mentoring relationship African American students and professionals are provided with a sense of hope and vision for the future. "The best young scholars and teachers are the ones most likely to acknowledge the influence of senior colleagues and teachers in their work. The most satisfied seniors are those who see their own influence in the work of the younger generation" (as cited in Kridel et al., 1996, p. 6).

> Recently Barry and I attended a conference for African American doctoral students and African American researchers in the field of education. Initially unable to put a name with a face, I met the many African American researchers whose work I had read and had not read. They greeted me with smiles and welcoming arms, knowing what obstacles I might face. While encouraging, they were also attentively listening to OUR stories and OUR interests. As I left for my Predominantly White Institution, I began to understand even more clearly that the work, the isolation, and misunderstandings within the academy are not in vain for we are opening the doors even wider for those coming behind us.

References

Aguirre, A. (2000). Women and minority faculty in the academic workplace: Recruitment, retention, and academic culture. *ASHE-ERIC Higher Education Reports, 27*(6), 1–110.

Branch, A. (2001). How to retain African American faculty during times of challenge for higher education. In L. Jones (Ed.), *Retaining African-Americans in higher education: Challenging paradigms for retaining students, faculty & administrators* (pp. 175–191). Sterling, VA: Stylus.

Bullough, Jr., R. (1996). Professorial dreams and mentoring: A personal view. In C. Kridel, R. Bullough, Jr., & P. Shaker (Eds.), *Teachers and mentors: Profiles of distinguished twentieth-century professors of education* (pp. 257–267). New York: Garland Publishing, Inc.

Caberra, A., Nora, A., & Terenzini, P. (1999). Campus racial climate and the adjustment of students to college: A comparison between white students and African American students. *The Journal of Higher Education, 70*(2), 134–160.

Davis, J. (1994). College in black and white: Campus environment and academic achievement of African American males. *Journal of Negro Education, 63*(4), 620–633.

DeFour, D., & Hirsch, B. (1990). The adaptation of black graduate students: A social network approach. *American Journal of Community Psychology, 18,* 487–503.

Feagin, J., Vera, H., & Imani, N. (1996). *The agony of education: Black students at white colleges and universities.* New York: Routledge.

Gloria, A., Kurpius, S., Hamilton, K., & Wilson, M. (1999). African American students' persistence at a Predominately White University: Influence of social support, university comfort, self-beliefs. *Journal of College Student Development, 40*(3), 257–268.

Green, P. (2001). The policies and politics of retention and access of African American students in public white insititutions. In L. Jones (Ed.), *Retaining African-Americans in higher education: Challenging paradigms for retaining students, faculty and administrators* (pp. 45–57). Sterling, VA: Stylus.

Gregory, S. (1999). *Black women in the academy: The secrets to success and achievement.* Lanham, MD: University Press of America.

Johnson, I. (1996). Access and retention: Support programs for graduate and professional students. In I. Johnson & A. Ottens (Eds.), *Leveling the playing field: Promoting academic success for students of color* (pp. 53–67). Ann Arbor, MI: Jossey-Bass Inc.

Jones, L. (2001). Creating an affirming culture to retain African American students during the post-affirmative action era in higher education. In L. Jones (Ed.), *Retaining African-Americans in higher education: Challenging paradigms for retaining students, faculty and administrators* (pp. 3–20). Sterling, VA: Stylus Publishing.

Kram, K. (1985). *Mentoring at work: Developmental relationships in organizational life.* Glenview, IL: Scott, Foresman & Company.

Kridel, C., Bullough, Jr., R., & Shaker, P. (Eds.). (1996). *Teachers and mentors: Profiles of distinguished twentieth-century professors of education.* New York: Garland Publishing, Inc.

Lee, W. (1999). Striving toward effective retention: The effect of race on mentoring African American students. *Peabody Journal of Education, 74*(2), 27–43.

Moore III, J. (2001). Developing academic warriors: Things that parents, administrators and faculty should know. In L. Jones (Ed.), *Retaining African-Americans in higher education: Challenging paradigms for retaining students, faculty and administrators* (pp. 77–90). Sterling, VA: Stylus Publishing.

Perna, L. (2000). Differences in the decision to attend college among African-Americans, Hispanics, and Whites. *The Journal of Higher Education, 71*(2), 117–141.

Watkins, G. (1998). *Satisfaction and mentoring: An African American perspective.* California, U.S. (ERIC Document Reproduction Service No. 427596).

Weidman, J., Twale, D., & Stein, E. (2001). Socialization of graduate and professional students in higher education: A perilous passage? *ASHE-ERIC Higher Education Reports, 28*(3), 1–112.

Zachary, L. (2000). *The mentor's guide: Facilitating effective learning relationships.* San Francisco, CA: Jossey-Bass Inc.

James Minor, Ph.D.

Hometown: Detroit, Michigan
Current Institution: University of Southern California
Department: Education
Personal Philosophy: Education is one of the most valuable commodities in the country and the world. Those who are able to obtain it will have an abundance of opportunities to enrich their lives in the way they see fit.

16

FOR BETTER OR FOR WORSE

IMPROVING ADVISING RELATIONSHIPS BETWEEN FACULTY AND GRADUATE STUDENTS

Introduction

It is a little known fact that the dropout rate among all doctoral students is roughly 55 percent (Bowen & Rudenstine, 1992; Golde, 2000). Between 1977 and 1994 the total number of doctoral degrees awarded increased by 30 percent. The increase among African Americans was only 7.3 percent during the same time frame. More disturbing is the fact that of the total number of degrees granted, those granted to African Americans dropped slightly from 3.8 percent in 1977 to 3.1 percent in 1994 (Nettles & Perna, 1997). Given such daunting numbers combined with low rates of attrition, the reason for these statistics must be questioned. As early as the 1960s Heiss (1967) states that, "the quality and character of the relationship between the doctoral student and major advisor is unequivocally the most sensitive and crucial element in the doctoral experience. It not only influences the graduate student's scholarly development, but also has far-reaching aftereffects" (p. 48). This chapter focuses on graduate student advising as a potential source of the problem as well as an avenue for improving the success rate of African American graduate students.

Although faculty advising is often linked to graduate student attrition, there is little scholarship on the affect that faculty advising has on graduate students in general, or African American graduate students in particular. Over the past decade student advising for undergraduates has become more of a profession. The addition of advising centers and the acquisition of additional human resources aimed at providing better advising has improved undergraduate advising significantly (Higgins & Penn, 1984). Arguably, graduate schools have not responded with the same fervor to improve advising for graduate students. As a result, many graduate students endure what has become a common culture of long suffering due to poor advising relationships during their graduate experience.

I titled this chapter "For Better or For Worse" mainly because I liken the relationship between graduate students and faculty advisors to marriages that could either be extremely rewarding, or dreadfully awful. Like common marriages, there are usually symptoms that indicate problems, there are steps one can take to prevent them, and there are consequences for divorce. The purpose of this chapter is to bring to light challenges of faculty advising for graduate students. In doing so, I use my own experience (as a graduate student and now advisor) as a basis for understanding the dynamics and overcoming the challenges. Hopefully the results will enhance understanding of the relationship between graduate students and their advisors in a way that improves the chances of student success.

The Perils

Unfortunately, it is commonplace to hear graduate students complain about a wide range of issues related to advising. To be clear, I am not suggesting that there are not graduate students who enjoy the benefits of good relationships with their advisors. Instead, I am suggesting that there are a significant proportion of students whose graduate school experience is stymied or frustrated due to poor advising relationships. Allow me to use myself as just one example. As a master's student, I made plans for my out-of-town family and friends to attend the May commencement ceremony of which I was to be a part. Two days before my April defense I learned that the chair of my committee (my advisor) opted to go to a conference instead of attending my defense. As a result, I was left to reschedule the defense according to the other committee members' schedules, which happened to be well after commencement. More than that, on the day of the rescheduled defense my advisor did not show leaving me to fend for myself, and leaving the chair of the department to sign off on my thesis. Not only did I suffer emotional distress from not defending and graduating on time, my family incurred financial losses from botched travel plans.

While this may seem to be an isolated event, there have been other critical events that have called attention to the nature of graduate student advising in recent years. Most notable is the suicide of Harvard student Jason Altom. Altom, a graduate student in chemistry, left behind a letter linking his advisor to his death (Schneider, 1998). This tragedy and other incidents, including shootings and a number of related lawsuits, symbolize problems in graduate student advising that are grossly ignored.

As a way of addressing the challenges, I identify the problems of poor graduate student advising as related to three issues: (1) lack of scholarship, (2) inattention to the contextual dynamics that impact advising relationships, and (3) the lopsidedness of graduate student/ faculty relationships. In what follows I address each of these issues and offer some pathways to overcoming the challenges of graduate student advising.

Lack of Scholarship

Given the evidence of poor practice, graduate student advising remains desolate as an area of scholarly inquiry. As early as the 1960s scholars identified problems in the faculty/graduate student relationship (Wolf, 1969). The dearth of research that exists on graduate students leaves the higher education community with little insight other than the fact that graduate student advising should be improved. One psychologist sarcastically suggests that the trauma associated with the pursuit of the Ph.D. might have discouraged many scholars from returning to such a painful subject (Bowen & Rudenstine, 1992).

The amount of research devoted to undergraduate advising greatly outweighs that given to graduate students. Scholars have concerned themselves with a wide range of issues related to undergraduate advising, such as the use of technology in advising and the affects of peer advising among students (Althen, 1995; Billo & Bidanda, 1994; Higgins & Penn, 1984; Kramer, 1986; Treuer & Belote, 1997). Although undergraduate advising is important, the relationship between faculty members and their graduate advisee(s) is arguably more meaningful and contingent for student success. Unlike undergraduates, graduate students rely on their advisors for much more than course planning and information on degree requirements. Literature addressing graduate student advising does exist but is far more limited both in quantity and substance.

According to a survey conducted by The Council of Graduate Schools, Mooney (1991) reports that graduate advising is in poor shape. In a survey to evaluate graduate programs across the country, the Council concluded that there is a great need for better faculty advising. During a recent conference of the National Association of Graduate and Professional Students, participants called for reforms to improve the quality of graduate advising. Using data from an online survey completed by over 6,000 graduate students, mainly in science and engineering, Sanford (1999) reports that 21 percent of respondents feel that their advisors see them as a source of cheap labor to advance their research. As far as a life outside of school, 22 percent say that their advisors expect them to work so many hours that the workload is difficult for them to maintain.

Research conducted on graduate student success supports the idea that faculty advisors are important for success (Golde, 2000). Frequent quality contact with faculty has also been associated with increased retention and positive progress among university students (Hawkins, 1992). Additionally, Lange (1988), in a study of psychology graduate students found that advisors are seen as a key factor in career development and as critical figures in the socialization of graduate students into their professions.

Still, few studies delineate best practices for advising or how advising directly impacts graduate student attrition or dropout. For example, Selke and Wong (1993) introduce a mentoring-empowered model for advising graduate students based on a psychosocial and human development theory but offer no assessment of whether such an approach is effective. Likewise, Berg and Ferber (1983) discuss differences among men and women with respect to success in graduate school. While they mention the fact that women in their sample are more likely to have better relationships with their faculty members in a female-dominated discipline, the consequences of such are not considered for men or women.

The lack of research devoted to graduate student advising leaves many critical questions unanswered. Those interested in improving advising have little research to inform their practice or the development of new policy. Pursuit of the following questions can provide substantial understanding to those concerned with improving the quality of graduate student advising in higher education.

- How do the advising needs of graduate students differ according to academic disciplines?
- How do racial and gender dynamics impact advising relationships?
- What attributes define quality advising relationships versus poor relationships?
- What role does advising play in the decision of students who drop out versus those who successfully attain degrees?

The lack of research makes it difficult to do more than speculate about the reasons for poor advising in graduate programs. As a result, graduate schools, faculty, and students concerned with advising are left to speculate about how to make improvements. Still, the lack of scholarship is but one reason for the challenges related to graduate student advising. I argue that some of the current challenges associated with graduate student advising can be avoided by having a better understanding of the contextual dynamics of academe, and the lopsidedness of advising relationships. Doing so allows students the opportunity to independently improve their advising relationships in the absence of systemic or institutional changes.

Contextual Dynamics

In search of answers, both graduate students and faculty often pay too little attention to the contextual dynamics that can affect advising relationships. Departmental constraints, faculty reward structures, and time are just a few contextual issues that can impact the nature of an advising relationship.

Departmental constraints refer to an academic department's structural or cultural characteristics, which might impede quality advising. Graduate programs are among the most autonomous units in colleges and universities. The structural and cultural elements of graduate programs, even those in the same discipline, can vary significantly. For example, some programs serve specific student populations, some exist to serve a function in their respective state, and some have healthy enrollments of full-time students while others may offer courses online. As a result of such differences, the quality of advising that students receive can depend on a number of departmental factors. Think about programs that serve mainly full-time students versus those that serve mainly non-traditional students who attend class at night and hold full-time jobs. It is likely that the advising of students who attend class at night and work during the day will be different from those who attend school full-time and work as research or teaching assistants. Yet, quality advising is likely equally valuable to both.

Another contextual factor has to do with the reward structure for faculty. With the dominant criteria for faculty evaluation being research in most departments with graduate programs, teaching and service usually run a distant second and third respectively. It may be safe to say that advising is, at best, a low priority in relation to the reward structure for faculty at doctoral universities. In many departments it is even less of a priority depending on the political climate and other dynamics a faculty member must negotiate. For example, when a faculty member is facing a stressful tenure decision or has a negative impression of the department, that could impact advising because rewards are not given based on the quality of advising. The autonomy of faculty members allows them to place advising where they wish on their personal list of importance. With that autonomy, faculty have the ability to choose which advisee(s) they will devote their time and attention to based on a number of personal or academic reasons.

The student to faculty ratio in a particular department can also impact the quality of advising. It is not reasonable to think that a faculty member who is responsible for advising fifteen students will be able to provide the same quality as someone of equal stature advising only five. Additionally, some programs will have faculty who only visit campus twice a week. Cultural elements such as history, tradition, or professional values also factor into the advising equation.

In almost every study or conversation I have observed about graduate advising, time is a concern. It is common to hear academicians lament about the workload in relation to the limited time one has to accomplish tasks. Likewise, graduate students also face the pressures of time given their academic workload. In an environment where the culture of "being busy" is so prevalent, when does quality advising take place? Is it reasonable to think that an assistant professor in a research intensive institution will have the same amount of time to commit to students as a tenured faculty member? These questions are based on the assumption that in order to provide quality advising, there must be time to do so. While I agree with such a notion, I do so from a different conceptual perspective on time as that of a contextual factor that impacts advising.

There are a number of alternative ways by which advising takes place that can ease the strains of time. For example, faculty research projects provide opportunities for intellectual exchange, collaboration, and professional socialization. The use of technology can also offer opportunities. I have a colleague who posts "rules of the road" on his personal website as a way to offer advice to students on common issues. Included are recommended course sequences, essential articles and books that are a "must read" for the profession, course syllabi, and advice for progressing through the program. Some faculty members engage in social activities with their students, such as dinner or a play, which can provide an opportunity to advise a student on a number of issues. The acceptance of such a notion depends on one's definition of advising, but the idea is to think of advising taking place in a more integrated fashion rather than in static blocks of time.

In recent years some advising trends have emerged in an attempt to make more efficient use of time. Some faculty now advise students in small groups or research teams that meet regularly as a way to increase efficiency and quality. Some graduate programs have initiated "group dissertations" where one faculty member advises small groups of students with closely related topics. The problem is that there is virtually no empirical evidence that delineates the effectiveness of these methods.

Viewing time in the traditional sense creates challenges given the nature of faculty and graduate student work. Certainly the issue of time can be viewed as a structural obstacle. However, thinking of time and advising more broadly can, to some degree, reduce the associated structural challenges.

The point is that these contextual elements are often overlooked when discussing graduate student advising. Both structural and cultural elements can constrain or enable quality interaction between students and faculty. Taking this notion into account then calls for consciousness of the impact that certain contextual factors have on advising across different disciplines and what they mean for students. An examination of graduate programs from a contextual standpoint is warranted to determine which factors most critically impact advising. Departmental characteristics, faculty and student makeup, faculty autonomy, faculty reward structure, departmental culture, and time represent only a handful of contextual dynamics that can influence student advising in graduate programs.

The Lopsided Marriage

At the beginning of this chapter I likened the relationship between faculty advisors and graduate students to a marriage. Now, I would like to make one caveat while, at the same time, explaining the use of such a term. In the event that an advising relationship is less than desirable, the negative consequences usually rest with the student, causing lopsidedness in the relationship. There are two paths to improvement when considering the challenges associated with graduate student advising: improving the quality of scholarship and developing a better understanding of the contextual dynamics. Considering the lopsidedness of advising relationships and the consequences is the third issue I consider to be of significant importance.

Faculty members at doctoral institutions are evaluated on research productivity and to a lesser degree, teaching and service. Notice the fact that advising was not included. One would be hard pressed to find a case where a faculty member was disciplined or not awarded promotion or tenure on the grounds that they were a poor advisor. My point here is that poor advising relationships with graduate students have little to no negative affect on the work and career of faculty members. On the contrary, poor relationships with faculty members can place graduate students at a grave disadvantage.

During the time I was finishing my dissertation and searching for a job, I had the fortune of talking to a now colleague who had a position open at her university. Our conversation helped cement my thinking on the relationship between faculty advisors and graduate students. When I asked her about my chances for landing the position she lamented: "Well I have to be honest with you, there are some others in the pool who have more publications and presentations than you coming out of graduate school." While discussing the consequences of such, one key observation was made. The difference between two candidates finishing graduate school, with respect to readiness for the job market, does not always have so much to do with one's ability as much as it does the nature of their advising relationship. In other words, the relationship a graduate has with an advisor is critically important for development during graduate school and the transition into the workplace. To make my point, advising relationships have little bearing on the career trajectory of faculty.

The introduction into the profession is a good example to illustrate the dependence graduate students have on faculty advisors. Something as simple as a letter of recommendation from your major advisor can make a significant difference in job placement. Once a fellow graduate student complained that his advisor refused to write him a letter of recommendation due to discord in their relationship. That decision of his advisor made the inherently difficult transition into the profession ever more daunting. Again such an outcome only will have negative consequences for graduate students. Other dependencies of graduate students include the timely completion of the dissertation, mentorship, and a much needed faculty advocate for financial support in departments where resources are limited.

Taking into account larger educational, institutional, and career expectations placed on faculty, I do not charge them with being oppressors of graduate students. Neither do I see graduate students so much as victims. Yet graduate students can easily be placed in situations where they are susceptible to poor advising that can cause graduate school to be a depressing experience. The silver lining is that many graduate students have managed to successfully attain the Ph.D. I argue that a better understanding of what factors may impede progress is helpful. Lack of scholarship, contextual dynamics, and the lopsidedness of the advising relationship are factors that can negatively impact relationships. Yet, in spite of these factors I believe that graduate students by their own diligence can capitalize on the benefits of having a rewarding relationship with a faculty advisor.

Plausible Pathways

Advising is one area that can be improved by the personal choices of students along with an increased understanding of the dynamics that surround the relationship. What follows are recommendations that, if considered, can help students make better choices about advising, and to some extent, graduate school in general. Looking back at my own graduate experience and considering the experience of others, I offer the following to help trek the path to the Ph.D.

Accurate Expectations

Often students have immediate problems in graduate programs because they are nothing like they expected them to be. After being shocked into reality, there is a recovery period when students pull themselves back together and are then more equipped to deal with the realisms of graduate school. As it relates to advising, students should understand that the term *advising* carries multiple meanings for different departments and different people. Certainly advising will mean something different in the chemistry department than it will in an English department. Keeping in mind that graduate programs are highly autonomous, even within a particular discipline, there can be significant differences with respect to how students and faculty approach advising.

Students should develop accurate expectations about particular faculty advisors. While having an initial talk with my doctoral advisor I learned that he did not like "needy" students. This insight afforded me the perfect opportunity to assess whether we could work together. If in fact I was a "needy" student then it would be unfair to expect my advisor to meet with me twice a week, read every manuscript I wrote, and give me frequent pep talks. It is important to recognize that faculty also conceptualize advising differently. Some faculty are more able to give than others, depending on rank, current advising loads, teaching responsibility, or personal preference. Certainly faculty take different approaches to advising just as they do with their research and teaching. When considering faculty advisors students should be careful to develop realistic expectations based on an understanding of what advising means for their department and particular faculty advisors. The consequences of such an action can deter negative or unproductive interaction between students and faculty members. Students in graduate programs should quickly develop accurate expectations about the kind of advising they are likely to receive. Failure to do so can open the door for discord in advising relationships.

Be open

While in my doctoral program, never did I think that I could establish such a meaningful friendship with my advisor, a middle-aged White man. To my surprise, the relationship with my advisor turned out to be one that extended far past the academy. Many times students, particularly African Americans, fall into the trap of thinking that the best person to work with is the lone faculty member in the department who shares the same ethnic background. I take exception to such thinking based on the fact that advising relationships are multidimensional. The faculty member who might best suit the needs of a student as a writer, researcher, and future professional can look and think very differently than the student. While a master's student, I suffered an extremely poor advising relationship with a Black faculty member and it had very little to do with race. In fact, that may have been the only thing we had in common. While faculty members of the same ethnic background may offer certain comforts, it does not guarantee success in graduate school. The faculty member in that department who was most helpful to my academic development was White, female, and lesbian.

In being open, I also charge students with broadening the concept of advising. I frequently advise new graduate students to work with more advanced students in their program. Students who have successfully matriculated through a program can, in many ways, serve as an advisor to a newer student. For example, advance students can assist newer students with navigating tough courses, preparing for comprehensive exams, securing financial support, and even reading and editing work.

By being open, students are able to identify others (closely or loosely) associated with their graduate program who can fill many functions of an advisor. Because there are no rules, students are at liberty to consult or seek help from as many different people as possible. By doing so, one may discover a network of people who are, at various times and according to various situations, able to informally serve as an advisor. In my case, my faculty advisor was good mainly for intellectual matters. The department coordinator who knew the course selections, program requirements, and the graduate school requirements almost verbatim was most helpful with the technical aspects of the program. A network of other graduate students were helpful with conceptualizing ideas, providing feedback on early drafts of my work, and providing social support. Advising can come from a variety of people and in a variety of ways. The more open students are to such an idea the better off they are likely to be.

Take and Give

The term *relationship* denotes interaction between two parties. Advising relationships are greatly enhanced when graduate students see themselves as having an impact on the relationship and assume responsibility for the outcome. Faculty members are people who have dispositions, bad days, personal problems, anxieties, fears, social dependencies, and personal preferences just like everyone else. Faculty members are sometimes more able to give if there is reciprocity. Graduate students must see themselves as being able to improve advising relationships by bringing what they have to offer. In other words, students should consider providing something that makes the relationship worthwhile and meaningful for faculty members. In some cases this will mean providing excellent research support, being an intellectual stimulant, being an editor, being a friend, or simply representing a bright future for the profession. The point here is that advising relationships can be enhanced significantly if faculty see them as productive and meaningful.

The overwhelming majority of graduate students I have talked to see themselves rightfully on the receiving end of the relationship. Given the context that allows faculty to determine their level of devotion to a student, it is not likely that one would invest quality time and energy to a student they get nothing from. Keeping in mind the thin line between students being of value to an advisor and being a burden, the advising relationship should be viewed as an exchange. Although the percentage of take and give will vary, I emphasize a shift in the way advising relationships are traditionally conceived.

Conclusion

Due to the current lack of coordination among graduate programs it is not likely that advising will be systematically overhauled. Consequently, it is critically important for students to take it upon themselves to be informed about the consequences of their selection and how to enhance their advising relationships with faculty. To be clear, my point is not to scare those who desire pursing the Ph.D. with stories of fatal advising relationships. As I stated earlier, there are a good number of students who enjoy the benefit of a quality, or at least, adequate faculty advisor. My aim is to emphasize the importance of having such a relationship and the consequences of having the opposite.

Among all of the external factors that increase the chances of student success, advising is among the most critical. I have often thought that pursuing the Ph.D. is one of the most difficult tasks an individual will ever undertake even with having a "good" advisor. I know firsthand how much more difficult the task can be having to work with a dissonant faculty member. My parallel between marriage and graduate student advising comes from hearing married couples acknowledge the fact that sustaining a happy marriage is hard work.

For many years students of color have been underrepresented at every level of the academy, with the exception of athletics. For this reason it is important to understand the hurdles that are between the start and finish line. The Ph.D. continues to be seen as the crown jewel of higher education. Attainment for students of color has economic, social, and educational consequences that extend far beyond personal achievement. During a time when higher education is suffering an affirmative action backlash and budget cuts, it is critically important that scholars of color remain in the pipeline. Even more important is that they successfully move through.

I see establishing a productive and rewarding relationship with a faculty advisor as key to student success. I charge graduate students with taking it upon themselves to ensure that advising relationships are productive and rewarding. If they are not, the consequences will be negative for students only. However, as with a marriage, each individual must recognize the permanency and commitment needed to complete the journey.

References

Althen, G. (1995). *The handbook of foreign student advising.* Yarmouth, ME: Intercultural Press.

Berg, H., & Ferber, M. (1983). Men and women graduate students: Who succeeds and why? *Journal of Higher Education, 54*(6).

Billo, R., & Bidanda, B. (1994). A student advising system for undergraduate engineering curricular scheduling. *Computer and Education, 22*(April).

Bowen, W., & Rudenstine, N. (1992). *In pursuit of the Ph.D.* Princeton, NJ: Princeton University Press.

Golde, C. (2000). Should I stay or should I go?: Student descriptions of the doctoral process. *The Review of Higher Education, 23*(2).

Hawkins, K. (1992, October). Communication apprehension and academic advising: Advising the communicatively apprehensive student. Paper presented at the annual meeting of the Speech Communication Association, Chicago, IL.

Heiss, A. (1967). Berkeley doctoral students appraise their academic perspective. *Educational Record, 48.*

Higgins, J., & Penn, R. (1984). Students advising: An institutional and student perspective. *Community College Review, 11*(Winter).

Kramer, H. (1986). Faculty advising: Help for student athletes? *NACADA Journal, 6*(1).

Lange, S. (1988). Critical incidents aren't accidents. *Journal of Counseling and Development, 76*(2).

Mooney, C. (1991). Crowded classes, student-advising systems are targets of report on liberal learning. *The Chronicle of Higher Education, 37*(Jan.)

Nettles, M., & Perna, L. (1997). *The African-American data book: Higher and adult education, Volume I.* The Frederick D. Patterson Research Institute of the College Fund/UNCF.

Sanford, S. (1999). Adapt or die: The grad school survey. HMS Beagle. *The BioMedNet Magazine, 68*(Dec.).

Schneider, A. (1998). Harvard faces the aftermath of a graduate student suicide. *The Chronicle of Higher Education, 45*(9).

Selke, M., & Wong, T. (1993). The mentoring-empowered model: Professional role functions in graduate student advisement. *NACADA Journal, 13*(2).

Treuer, P. I., & Belote, L. (1997). Current and emerging applications of technology to promote student involvement and learning. *New Directions for Student Services, 78*(Summer).

Wolf, R. P. *The ideal of the university.* New Brunswick, NJ: Transaction Publishers.

Carolyn Hopp, Ph.D.

Hometown: Durham, North Carolina
Current Institution: University of Central
Florida
Department: Director of Urban Teaching
Residency Partnership
Personal Philosophy: Integrity has no need of
rules.
—Albert Camus

Vincent Mumford, Ph.D.

Hometown: Frankford, Delaware
Current Institution: University of Central
Florida
Department: Sports Administration and
Leadership
Personal Philosophy: It's not over until you
WIN!

Franklyn Williams

Hometown: Nassau, Bahamas
Current Institution: University of Central
Florida
Department: Education
Personal Philosophy: My life's creed has
become: pass it on. When others invest in
our lives—no matter the type or how
great or small the investment—it is incumbent upon us to then also in like manner
invest in other's lives.

17

THE ROLE OF MENTORING FOR FUTURE ACADEMICIANS

The Role of Mentoring for Upcoming Academicians

Mentor is a word that profits from the rich shades of meaning in the English language. Traditionally, a mentor has been defined as "a wise and knowledgeable person who undertakes a special commitment to counsel, teach, and advise a younger and less experienced person" (Hughey, 1997, p. 101). In the glow of the mentor's wisdom, the novice grows in knowledge and experience. Remembrances of mentors create portraits of a teacher, or of someone who has cared for, nurtured, or helped to raise the level of potential in the individual. There is also the intrinsic element of caring in the mentoring relationship.

An historic definition of mentoring comes from the story, *The Odyssey*, by the Greek poet, Homer (Palmer, 1998). Homer profiled the wise teacher, Mentor, whom Odysseus entrusted to nurture, protect, and teach the King's son in the absence of his father. Mentor took charge of Telemachus' education, helping him to mature, to learn courage, prudence, honesty, and a commitment to serving others. The relationship between Mentor and Telemachus went beyond that of teacher–student. Mentor's responsibility was to care for, nurture, inspire, encourage, and to shape a vision of excellence in life and living that Telemachus would never forget.

In the African American community, all who cross the path of a child teach life's lessons. In our days as students, we experience mentoring before we can intellectualize the concept. There are remembrances of family members who always chided children about the "right thing to do," and "knowing better." Through all of life's experiences, there are strong memories of individuals who "held our feet to the fire," kept us in school, and kept our behavior "in check." There was never a question about aspiring to bigger and better things in life. There was never a question about being cared for. But the most important expectation was to achieve excellence. There was always the potential to be better. No matter what our aspirations, success was always an expectation. It mattered not what obstacles we encountered.

The Academy

And so, here we are, mentors and protégé—for one mentor, many years later, for another mentor and protégé, only a few. Our aspirations have led to membership in the American Education Academy. For some, the journey was not always easy, but the gentle push to stay on the path was sometimes all that was needed to keep an eye on the prize. For others, the journey was riddled with difficulty and the path strewn with obstacles that seemed insurmountable. Perseverance was the motivator, the need to succeed was what helped to endure, and achieving the goal was the prize.

African American membership in the academy has a rich tradition. Since the late nineteenth century, the few who reached the pinnacle and earned doctorates in their field paved the way for scholars to follow. One can only imagine the difficulty of those experiences, but perseverance, endurance, and courage were indeed the foundation of their success. More importantly, there were shoulders to stand on in their families and in their communities. Their mentors believed in the potential of these scholars to succeed, and thrived on the hope of that success.

Reasons to Aspire and Not Get Weary on the Journey

The narrative tapestries related in the stories that follow are from the perspectives of a protégé and two mentors from different backgrounds and cultures. Franklyn, a doctoral student, tells of an educational journey from the Bahamas to the United States; Carolyn recalls experiences being raised on the campus of an historically Black college, and the impact of "seeing" mentoring happen among Black scholars; and Vincent weaves his story through recollections of experiences with individuals who embodied the essential qualities of mentors, and who virtually changed his life. Vincent's anecdotes contain elements of all of our experiences. In a final conversation, mentors and protégé share reflections about what it all means and how they expect the process to continue.

Though as scholars, we came to the academy with different experiences and traveled different pathways, there was a common goal: ultimate success within the academy. The pursuit of the doctorate was no small notion. Once the journey began, there was no turning back. But that journey began with a determination to succeed, and as aspiring scholars, we looked to those within the academy to support, nurture, inspire, and eventually applaud success. For the African American scholar pursuing the doctorate, support, nurturing, and inspiration are essential to their success, but are difficult to find in many instances, and sometimes altogether missing.

Kept from Fallin'—Franklyn's Perspective

My mentoring experience has led me to some of my own conclusions about its nature. I believe that some of these conclusions apply specifically to students of color, while others apply to all students regardless of racial or ethnic background. Based on that experience, I have concluded that:

- The person being mentored must welcome and desire a mentoring relationship.

- For students of color, it is helpful to have a mentor from one's own race.

- In a mentoring relationship, there must be a sense of mutual respect between the mentor and the person being mentored.

- Mentoring relationships across academic disciplines are beneficial to the person being mentored.

- Institutional commitment to and support for mentoring is essential.

- Students of color benefit significantly from mentoring.

Each of these conclusions is discussed in greater depth in the following pages. Together, they infer several implications for other students of color who engage in a mentoring relationship. For the purpose of illumination, each conclusion is discussed within the context of my own personal experience. Both mentor and protégé must welcome and want to engage in a mentoring relationship. This allows a personally fulfilling exchange for the person being mentored. Information about my early years is helpful in understanding what I mean by "desire."

I was born and raised in the Bahamas—a country that is predominately Black. Approximately 85 percent of the population is of African descent, and most of the remaining 15 percent is of European ancestry. For the first seventeen years of my life, I lived in a society where there were many more Blacks than Caucasians. In fact, most of the Caucasians that I saw in my early years tended to be either expatriate teachers and bankers, or tourists from North America. More importantly, I lived in a society where Blacks were prominent in positions of leadership and power, and as a result, positive role models from my own race surrounded me in all facets of the community. It was not uncommon for me to know Black doctors, lawyers, bank managers, and entrepreneurs.

As I began my journey to membership in the American academy, it occurred to me that something was missing from the experience. This realization was almost immediately apparent. My first place of study in America was in Springfield, Missouri, a small Midwestern city that is almost entirely White. When I arrived there, I looked around me and realized there were very few people who looked like me. It was immediately evident that there were no positive Black role models, to which I was accustomed in my experience at home. Consequently, I developed an earnest desire for a mentor and role model, someone like me to whom I could feel connected, and who would guide and accompany me on my academic journey.

The desire for a meaningful connection was not quenched when I arrived in Kearney, Nebraska, five years later as a graduate student. To be sure, while there, I had a very strong role model in my faculty advisor. I credit this Caucasian woman with doing much to foster my personal and professional development. Yet, the desire for a mentor of color did not subside. I was ready for a mentoring relationship with someone from my own race. I was in the right mental and emotional state for such a relationship.

After the experience at the University of Nebraska, I began my doctoral studies at the University of Central Florida. As a doctoral student, I was invited to become a Holmes scholar. The Holmes scholar program is a support network of minority doctoral students from across the country who are supported and mentored as they study. The goal of the support of the Holmes scholar is the smooth transition to the academy and into tenure-track faculty positions. At the University of Central Florida, there are seven Holmes scholars. There are also two Holmes scholar alumni who serve as mentors and continue to actively contribute to the program. They meet regularly with the newly appointed Holmes scholars for fellowship and to discuss activities and opportunities.

The Holmes alumni, Vincent and Carolyn, became the mentors that I have always desired. In their own ways, they encourage me, advise me, and serve as role models within the academy. Their strong presence reassures me and makes me feel as if I have a world of support in my quest for the Ph.D. I feel as if there is always someone that I can go to just to chat on those days when I am feeling overwhelmed. The fact that they are also scholars of color makes me feel they can identify with my challenges as a person of color in the academy. This is helpful to me in that it keeps me enthusiastic about our mentoring relationship.

According to my understanding of the ideal mentoring relationship, mentors seek out, and are available to, those they mentor. My mentors at the University of Central Florida have been available and have unselfishly offered their time to simply listen as well as to advise about what it takes to be successful and survive as a person of color in a Predominately White Institution. These relationships have developed over time without any formal arrangement, no doubt driven by my mentors' recognizing that there are others who come behind who are in need of support, motivation, and encouragement.

In a powerful way, my mentors have provided me with a sense of affirmation. To me, this is evidenced by strong moral support and their belief that I can and will do well. They have also provided me with validation. I have been made to feel that I have a right to be a member of the academy and to have access to all the privileges and responsibilities that it affords by virtue of my own unique ability and talent.

Concurrently, I admire that they have been through the struggle of graduate school—and survived. I look to them as sources of wisdom and advice on what it takes for me to survive as well.

Interestingly enough, these mentors are not even within my own discipline. Often, the expectation is that one develops a mentoring relationship with someone in the same academic concentration. However, this has not been the case, and it has been very positive. The relationship across disciplines has resulted in an unexpected benefit: whole versus program preparation.

Cross-discipline relationships have allowed me a comprehensive overview of the current, important issues in the field of education in general. They involve me in discussions that consider the viewpoints of other specialties within the field. This has moved me beyond an insular perspective that would have focused primarily on the concerns of my particular area. I believe that this is better preparing me to be more informed as an educator.

It is notable that mentoring of doctoral students of color within the College of Education at the University of Central Florida is encouraged and supported by the institution itself. The Holmes scholar program is a demonstrated commitment to mentoring on the part of the Dean and her administrative staff. This inspires the development of informal bonds, and allows them to flourish in a supportive environment. It serves as reassurance that support is in place to build and sustain mentoring relationships.

I assert that there are important factors about mentoring that make the graduate school experience more fulfilling: desire to mentor, mutual respect, consistent support, validation, affirmation, and the belief in the protégé's ability to succeed. My own experiences lend credence to the notion that students benefit from mentoring—especially students of color. While every aspect of mentoring may not be evident in the experience of every graduate student of color, it is worth ensuring that at least a few are in place in order to enhance these experiences. Only then will the experiences of graduate students of color be deemed worthwhile.

Carolyn's Remembrances of Black Scholars

In Durham, North Carolina, I was raised on the campus of an Historically Black University in the 1950s and 1960s, surrounded by scholars who encouraged each other as well as other young, aspiring scholars. There was indeed the expectation to achieve excellence that transcended the segregated environment in which we lived, worked, and learned. There was never a question that students would be successful. My teachers from kindergarten through high school maintained only the highest expectations, and standards of excellence were understood. We saw—and we "lived"—mentoring before we intellectualized the concept.

Growing up on a college campus meant there was never a question that my brother and I would go on to college, or even pursue advanced degrees. Living with that expectation meant that only the highest quality of work was acceptable. We could never let our guard down. Yes, the pressure was great. One day, in my third-grade class, Miss Foster, a tall, elegant, monumental presence in the classroom, made a statement to all of us that forever impacted me: "It matters not where you come from, who your parents are, or what they do. You all have the potential to be great scholars. And you will be—only with hard work and perseverance. But you cannot *ever* let down. Not for one single moment."

One of the strongest memories I have of growing up in the university environment was the opportunity to observe African American university professors advise doctoral and master's students who were pursuing degrees at various universities both in the local community as well as out of state. However, my recent entrance into the academy has transformed my reflections, which have moved beyond fond remembrances to a quest for understanding. The rate of success of doctoral scholars was very high—and always expected. There was never any talk of failure, nor plans made in case success was not achieved.

The conversations between advisor and student usually began with talk of family and general well-being, and seamlessly moved to talk of the experience of school. Often student and scholar held equal footing in the conversations, but when the scholar began to speak of research and scholarship, the relationship between teacher and student— between mentor and protégée—emerged. These conversations occurred often throughout the pursuit of the doctorate, and only intensified as time passed. In my own reflections, what has been most striking is the consistent tone of encouragement, nurturing, and motivation. More significantly, scholars were always willing to listen and never passed judgment. It was as though in the process of being mentors, they recalled their own experiences and what they *didn't* have. Their role was to look back and take the hand of the scholars who came after them.

In making my own way professionally, mentoring has been the cornerstone of my work as a teacher, as a scholar, and as a member of the academy. I find inspiration in the story of a man who pursued his doctorate in the late 1950s when there were only a few African American Ph.D's in the country. He completed all of his coursework, and passed the written and oral comprehensive examination with an "exemplary" evaluation, only to be told that in spite of that success, the university would never grant a Ph.D. to a "colored man." A telephone call to an old friend—and mentor—to extol the experience and its devastation resulted in acceptance at the university where his mentor taught, and successful completion of the Ph.D.

I heard this story many times, but I never heard any bitterness in the telling, only that it was a mere bump in the road on the pathway to eventual success. And I do often wonder about the lack of bitterness. But the more I hear the story, I am struck by the man's look of absolute respect and humility when he speaks of his mentor, who became his rock, and who believed in his ability to be successful.

My father's story continues to inspire me. More importantly, it defines the importance of a strong mentoring relationship and its impact on the success of the individual. His story defined for me the importance of my presence in the academy as a role model and a mentor, which is at the core of the work that I do.

Reachin' Landin's . . . Vincent's Story

Mentors have incredible power. John Heisman, the legendary football coach once stated that coaches have the power to change a person's life. According to Heisman (2000), ". . . a winning football coach can do more, either for good or for evil, with the average player of school and college age, than can any other person under the sun" (p. 17). Mentors have that same type of incredible power. They can directly influence the success of students seeking a degree in higher education. Mentors can change lives and they can change generations.

I once heard T. D. Jakes ask, in one of his televised sermons, "What do you do . . . if you don't know what to do?" It was one of those questions that stop you in your tracks. It was such a deep and profound question. It was such a thinking person's question. As he paused and walked across the stage, I tried to come up with an answer. "What do you do . . . ?" He answered the question before I could come up with an answer of my own. His answer was quite simple yet insightful. His answer was, "you do what you were taught."

I believe the experience of "not knowing" is one that frightens many talented students. This fear of the unknown is more responsible for keeping talented young men and women out of the academy than either academic ability or financial capability. It is the unknown aspects, and not knowing how to navigate through the academy, that rob many students of successful futures. It is essential for mentors to create expectations. They should help students understand the possibilities.

The term *statistic* has negative connotations when used to describe the plight of people. Statistics usually do not have a bright future. By many accounts, I should have been a statistic. I grew up in a small, rural farming town with a population of a little over 500 in which the major industries were poultry factory work and farming. My mother was a single mother with two children. My father died when I was a year old. My mother's salary did not meet poverty guidelines, and she worked as a domestic her entire life. My older sister also worked as a domestic. No one in my family graduated from high school.

Our small town was peaceful and quiet. My mother provided everything we needed. She enjoyed her job and was a community humanitarian. We ate a lot of poultry. But, my greatest mentor knew that statistics could say whatever you wanted them to say. She always encouraged me "to be whatever I wanted to be." Early on, she stressed the importance of my education. She set the parameters for grades that were acceptable and grades that were not acceptable. She was both judge and jury on that point. In the 7th grade when I brought home a "D" in one subject for the marking period, she informed me that I could not play sports until I brought the grade up. It was my first and last "D." My education was important to her. She created my expectations.

Although my mother was my greatest mentor, mentors do not have to be family members. A mentor can be anyone who desires to help bring out the potential of others, or who takes a special interest in the success of their students. My mentors have been teachers, coaches, counselors, and supervisors. Mentors see things in you that you may not see in yourself. The mentors that I have had throughout life possessed the wisdom and vision to know that I had the potential to achieve, and that I could, indeed, be successful.

The Light—Mentoring Strategies

Whether at a major research university, a teachers' college, a two-year college, a professional development school, or as part of an association, all members of the academy have tremendous opportunities to help mentor students faced with the challenges and pressures of pursuing a higher education. Mentors have the ability to make the student's experience a positive one and to help shape the student's outlook on graduate school and the academy.

Tenured and tenure-earning professors know the secrets to getting through the educational process. They all have been through it and can identify the obstacles that can hinder as well as the opportunities that facilitate student success.

Mentors might share these secrets in different ways, but the common denominators present in most successful mentor–mentee relationships have lasting effects on students' growth and success. Applying the following five strategies can result in students' experiencing quantum increases in achievement:

Help students dream

If you know a student's goal is to become a professor, share your experience with them. Don't keep it a secret. Share time and ideas with them regularly. Introduce them to as many colleagues as possible. Introduce them to other students who are going through the process. Ask students to engage in the dreaming process and solicit their suggestions of possible schools and areas of study or research. Engage them in the brainstorming process. The essence of mentoring is influence. Sharing their dream with others helps paint the big picture and gives students something to buy into. It also helps communicate what things are important in the academy.

Help students develop a game plan

Students need to know where they are going. Show them where they are headed by helping them develop a vision and strategy. Have expectations of excellence. Tell them what is most important to the success of their career. Identify key goals that they need to accomplish. Have them write out their plans. A clear vision and action plan provide students direction and confidence. A game plan also helps ensure that both mentor and protégé are focused on the same results. Involve the student in a rigorous planning process. Let them research best academic practices. Give them a framework and let them develop strategic objectives and goals. They are more likely to stay motivated if they see exactly how their individual goals relate to the big picture. Planning helps them prioritize what is important.

Push students to get up and go

Once they have fully developed the written game plan, have them do something with it. Don't let them sit idly by. Push them to implement it. Too often plans are developed and then placed on a shelf or in a notebook to collect dust. Find a way to focus the energy and resources of the student on the things that are most important to their success. Give students responsibility. Provide them with interesting and challenging research projects, teaching, writing, presentation, or committee assignments. Have them submit an article for publication. Have them present at a national conference. Let them participate on college committees. Eliminate obstacles to their professional growth. Give them time lines and then get out of their way. Action creates a feeling of energy. Energy creates a feeling of excitement. Taking action helps them do what is important.

Show students how to keep score to win

Keeping score helps them learn and improve. Explain to students how colleges and universities measure performance. Spell out exactly what is expected. To be successful, students must translate their vision into a set of key performance indicators that can be measured. Those key indicators must be designed to assess the student's progress toward achieving their goals and objectives. Use real departmental assessment forms as a constructive tool to measure student performance. Make it fun. Let students conduct self-appraisals evaluated against departmental or school expectations. The key is to use it in a positive fashion to help provide information, measure progress, and improve performance.

This process is a great opportunity to establish goals, enhance skills, and provide regular feedback to students. As the mentor, you must keep your mentee aware of the score at all times. Keeping score helps them monitor their current performance. Keeping score also helps them learn more about the requirements of teaching, research, and service. Keeping score helps them measure what is important.

Encourage students to celebrate to recharge

Students need to be rewarded for achieving goals and surpassing your expectations of excellence. They need to feel appreciated. Celebrating their accomplishments underscores the value that they bring to the table and confirms that expectations have been met. Celebrating also serves as a motivator for future learning opportunities. Work with students to identify meaningful opportunities for celebration. Celebrations do not have to be expensive or excessive. They can be as simple as a pat on the back after completing a project, a congratulatory e-mail after a successful presentation, or as complex as a full-blown party after a defense. Mentors and mentees who celebrate together have better working relationships. Celebrating helps reward what is important.

Mentors do not need to reinvent the wheel to see significant improvement in student performance. They do need to focus on helping students navigate through the educational process. This can be accomplished by sharing their time, knowledge, and energy with students. To help students succeed, mentors simply need to demystify the process, engage in collaboration, and teach them what to do.

Institutionalizing the Process—Turnin' Corners

In order to have the greatest and most far-reaching impact for students of color, the mentoring process should be institutionalized. Too often, the needs of many are sacrificed because of the ability of a few. At many institutions, there are only a few faculty who are either willing or able to mentor students. This small number of mentors is spread so thin that the quality of the mentoring experience is diminished and the process itself is less effective.

To eliminate this practice, institutions must make a commitment to mentoring their students at all levels. This commitment requires the allocation of sufficient resources necessary to design, conduct, support, and maintain mentoring activities and a diverse environment. The Holmes Partnership is a consortium of universities that is committed to providing opportunities for students of color to pursue the doctorate and reach the academy. The Holmes Scholars Model at the University of Central Florida is an example of a commitment by a university to institutionalize mentoring in the academy. The model consists of three main strands:

- *Mentoring* that includes support groups, networking, and collaborative activities
- *Professional growth* that provides opportunities to demonstrate scholarship and to work in areas of interest
- *Expectations of excellence* required of all Holmes scholars, as well as excellence demonstrated in research and publications

Commitment and Practice

Completing the Journey

As mentors to Franklyn, a Holmes Scholar, Carolyn and Vincent participate in the process of the Holmes scholars Model. In a final conversation during collaboration on this chapter, mentors and mentee focused on the meaning of commitment to institutionalizing the mentoring process.

> In this model, there is a connection to personal growth . . . there is a connection to mentoring in general, involvement, support, and leadership development. If you look at the individual elements of the Holmes Scholars Model . . . all of those things we would try to do to support a scholar . . . a student of color . . . are all the things that are going to lead to success throughout their experiences, so that by the time they leave, they are able to achieve more than they ever thought they would. (C. Hopp, personal interview, April 14, 2002)

In this experience, commitment also requires leaders to work diligently to improve mentoring by making diversity a priority, promoting a supportive atmosphere, advocating for supportive policies, and modeling articulated values. An essential and vital element of this commitment is an environment in which the institutional value of diversity is emphasized, promoted, and practiced. At the University of Central Florida, the Holmes scholar network is directly supported by the dean and associate dean in the College of Education, and the university provost.

> . . . institutional support is so important . . . like my thoughts about the absence of a mentor, I shudder to think what it would be like if we didn't have this model . . . if we didn't have that institutional support . . . what would happen. (F. Williams, personal interview, April 14, 2002)

To institutionalize the mentoring process, these facets must come together to make the process an integral and sustainable part of the institution.

> I think it is commitment. We keep coming back to the institutional commitment. I think the most powerful message for anyone who reads this chapter and that will help ensure the success of students coming into the colleges and universities . . . is commitment to that success. And you can't say you are committed to success . . . and not provide *support* for that success. (C. Hopp, personal interview, April 14, 2002)

Still Climbin'

Making Meaning

> I know for me, it makes me feel very blessed to be a part of an organization . . . or an institution that wants to see me succeed . . . that puts me in communication and fellowship with *people* that want me to succeed. That's the power of mentoring. (F. Williams, personal interview, April 14, 2002)

This collaboration brought us full circle. We learned about each other and from each other. Though our experiences were different, we came to be in this place—at the University of Central Florida—together. Our different experiences did, however, have things in common. There were people who cared about us, who provided role models, and on whose shoulders we stood. The mentors in our lives saw things in us that perhaps we just did not see. They kept us on the right pathway—but more importantly, they kept us focused on our goals and we completed the journey.

References

Heisman, J. (2000). *Principles in football*. Athens, GA: Hill Street Press.

Hughey, J. B. (1997). Creating a circle of many: Mentoring and the preservice teacher. In C. Mullen, M. Cox, C. Boettcher, & D. Andoue, (Eds.). *Breaking the circle of one: Redefining mentorship in the lives and writings of educators* (pp. 101–118). New York: Peter Lang Publishing.

Palmer, P. (1998). *The courage to teach: Exploring the inner landscape of a teacher's life*. San Francisco: Jossey-Bass Publishers.

CONCLUSION
THE Ph.D.: A PROCESS NOT A PRODUCT

My Experiences as a Doctoral Student

Many feelings and thoughts were conjured up while working on this book. Both were positive and negative. In reading the chapters and visualizing the words that the authors wrote, it made it inevitable for me not to reflect on my own doctoral experiences. I would like to take some time to relive these experiences as well as provide some lasting impressions of what it means to me to have earned the right to understand the Ph.D. as a process and not a product.

I entered the Ph.D. program in educational psychology at Florida State University in August 1996. Prior to me feeling ready and deserving to walk on the campus, I visited the department on several occasions. I wanted to become familiar with my new home and wanted them to know me. I had many meetings with my advisor, who ultimately became a great mentor and friend. I felt that he had my best interest in mind and wanted to see me succeed almost as much I wanted success for myself. These experiences instilled confidence and assurance that if I continued to be a presence in the face of those around me, even when their faces did not look like mine, then I would matriculate through the program.

Other reassurances came in the manner of support groups and elders who took an interest in me. As an incoming graduate student, you are eligible to apply for a program called the Black Graduate Student Orientation Program (BGSOP). This program was funded by the university and managed by a well-known and respected senior-level professor. BGSOP was a three-week orientation program prior to attendance at the university. Graduate students who were selected, based on a set of criteria, were exposed to the campus, administrators, faculty members, and other graduate students. This was an unforgettable experience because of the amount of advice and guidance that was provided. We were given advice on research, teaching, course selection, community environment (churches, restaurants, hair stylists, etc.), and developing mentoring relationships across the campus. One thing that was told to me during this time is still an important factor in my life, years after the doctorate. The director of BGSOP told us, "Focus on the left toe-nail of the frog, this is how specific you should be in selecting a topic and writing your dissertation. You are not here to save the world with your piece of work; this is to get you out of here and then you can save the world with your degree in hand."

Armed with such an abundance of advice, I was soon to be challenged. I lost my major professor in the second year of the program. He accepted a position at another university and I was left to find a major professor for my dissertation, a mentor for academic guidance, and a friend for advice. I even went so far as to tell him that he could take me with him because I had not started collecting data on my research and had finished all of my course work. So I was *free* to go. Well, of course I did not leave; he advised me to stay and assured me that I would be just fine without him. I found another major professor, mentor, and friend who viewed my research interests as important and wanted to see me graduate from the department. She was well respected in our department, the chairperson to be exact, and I trusted her intent for seeing me do well. Today, I remain in contact with both advisors and still receive advice for my academic career. Many chapters have discussed the benefits of having a great experience with a major professor or advisor who has your best interest in mind and at heart. This exposure can grow into colleague relationships, research collaborations for publications, and tenure promotions.

I have been blessed with opportunities to work with outstanding scholars and unknown mentors who have taken the time to teach me things that no four walls within a classroom could ever do. I say unknown mentors because these are the academic office assistants and managers who know everything about the department and the professors. One individual took me under her wings the first day I arrived. Lucy Kelly-Brown made it a point to introduce me to the department faculty and chairperson. I am still very grateful for her attention and support so early on. Additionally, the associate dean of curriculum and instruction in the College of Education, a young African American male, served as a friend and mentor for me. We came to the college at the same time and our newness drew us together. He is still very much an enormous part of my academic and professional life as well as a trusted friend.

With these types of experiences and exposure to the academy, I quickly learned how to market myself as a scholar, how to conduct research that is important to me and add value to publications, and how to mentor and advice graduate students and college students on the opportunities for pursuing advanced degrees. This is an ongoing process that is nurtured at academic conferences, office meetings, and social events.

By this point in your reading, I am hoping that you start seeing the Ph.D. as a process and not a product. I have learned this along the way and think that it is one of the most necessary lessons that I had to learn. It allows me to keep an open mind to various opportunities that present themselves in and outside of the educational arena. As a graduate student going through the "process," I also learned that you can do as much as you want with a graduate degree. It is not an isolated tool that locks you into education. I am living proof of this. I have experience in educational and business consulting, government contracting and grants, as well as university professorial. It is very exciting to become associated with colleagues who are not in the same career field and a positive challenge to explore other avenues of employment.

Dialoguing with a Purpose

An important point that I want all readers to take away with them is that this book is a "dialogue with a purpose." You have read personal accounts of many graduate students' experiences in preparing for and the pursuit of the Ph.D. This type of dialogue has a purpose because anyone with a sense of perseverance, motivation, determination, and opportunity has a fighting chance of obtaining graduate degrees. The question remains: Do I attend a Historically Black College and University (HBCU) or a Predominately White Institution (PWI) for my graduate degree? Some statistical data are alarming as they reveal the small numbers of HBCU that offer doctoral degrees. The following are

HBCUs that offer doctoral programs, many of them only offering one program of study: Alabama A&M University, Bowie State University, Clark Atlanta University, Fayetteville State University, Florida A&M University, Grambling State University, Hampton University, Howard University, Interdenominational Theological Center, Jackson State University, Meharry Medical College, Morehouse School of Medicine, Morgan State University, North Carolina A&T University, South Carolina State University, Tennessee State University, Texas Southern University, and Tuskegee University (Florida A&M University School of Graduate Studies and Research, 2002). I thought it was noteworthy to list these schools and mention that we have no submissions from a graduate student attending one of these universities. I am uncertain of the reason why this is the case, but will conclude that the lack of graduate programs offered by HBCUs may affect the large number of African American graduate students attending PWIs.

In the ivory tower of academia, graduate students of color do not always feel inclusive, especially African Americans. I say this in regards to the entry process-standardized tests, funding support and academic program offerings, the adapting process-academic and research guidance and assistance, and the survival process-student and faculty mentoring and advising. These issues have been discussed extensively throughout the book. It is our sincere effort to offer graduate students, professors, administrators, and graduate student organizations a tool that is a guide for successful matriculation in graduate school, a recruiter for African American students, and a source for the university community to retain its talented graduate students and future scholars.

Reference

Florida A&M University School of Graduate Studies and Research. (2002). *HBCU graduate programs and degrees offered.*

APPENDIX

Preparing for the Professorate

Dr. Scott and I thought the book would not be complete unless we added an appendix that briefly directs your focus to "life after the Ph.D." To this end, we are offering you information needed to prepare for your chosen careers. Many of you may continue in academia as professors and researchers. Others may be less conventional and pursue careers in local, state, or federal government; private industry; or as entrepreneurs.

We have spoken to many scholars who are currently professors at universities and asked them what they did as doctoral students to prepare for employment in the academy. Responses varied based on prior experiences and personally set goals. Prior employment as high school teachers, accountants in corporate America, and entrepreneurs have influenced many to return to school for the doctoral degree. These individuals bring a different perspective to their Ph.D. programs. They already know that they want to be university professors, they know their research interest, they know their preference for the type of institution they want to be employed by, and they are aware of what is needed to succeed as a doctoral student and a professor. We have used this composite of information to provide you with a brief description of "how to prepare for employment in the academy." It is difficult to place the information in a time line because as doctoral students, the following information is ongoing and should begin as early as possible.

Solicited Advice

- Make the decision as early as possible as to what your goals and reasoning are for obtaining the Ph.D. Many cited that they wanted to give back to the communities that assisted them in their educational pursuits, others realized their passion for working with students, and others decided that having the Ph.D. provided flexibility for families and careers.

- Obtain as much teaching and guest lecturing experience as possible while pursuing the Ph.D. It is important to have student evaluations of your teaching. If you do not have the opportunity to teach, it is imperative that you take education courses that focus on teaching, learning, and the presentation and delivery of information for a career in the academy.

- Involve yourself with professional development classes that assist in developing your teaching methodology, research writing and methodology, and grant writing seminars. All of these are important in preparing for a job in academia.

- As early as possible you should begin developing an academic portfolio that includes short- and long-term goals, personal statement, vitae, resume, biographical sketch, letters of recommendation, published and unpublished research, teaching and research experiences, grant writing samples, and student evaluations.

- Expose yourself to your respective discipline and interdiscipline conferences and annual meetings so that you can network with colleagues and present your research. Developing your research agenda and collaborating on published papers and books are required for a job in academia. You also have the opportunity to set up job interviews at these conferences.

- Have an idea as to what your preference is for the type of institution that you want to be employed in. The academy revolves around teaching, research, and service. The various types of universities and colleges emphasize these in different ways. For example, a Liberal Arts college promotes the scholarship of teaching and service more than research. Knowing if you are interested in academia or the private sector will assist in your efforts for seeking employment while pursuing the Ph.D.

- Networking with your major professor and other advisors creates a vehicle for your entry into the job market. They make referrals for you, assist you in your research publication, and guide you in finding a mutual fit for you and your chosen career path.

- Market yourself as a scholar who is not locked into a specific research area of interest and discipline. Keep an open mind that your degree is versatile and that you have the freedom to be an expert as well as a novice who will try a new academic discipline—for example, an educational psychologist employed in a business school. You must also know the market for employment and what are the current salary ranges. Much of this information is public record and can be obtained at a university or public library.

- Universities will invite you for an interview and may or may not require that you present your research to the faculty and guest lecture in a course.

- DO NOT LEAVE YOUR DOCTORAL PROGRAM FOR A JOB WITHOUT COMPLETING YOUR DEGREE.

About the Editors

Anna L. Green, Ph.D., is a native of Opelousas, Louisiana. In 1992, she received her bachelor of science in psychology from Xavier University in New Orleans, Louisiana. She received her master of science in educational psychology from Clark Atlanta University in 1994. Her doctorate of philosophy is from Florida State University in educational psychology. She currently serves as an assistant professor with the School of Business and Industry at Florida A&M University. She is the co-editor of *Sisters of the Academy: Emergent Black Women Scholars in Higher Education* and also serves as president of the Sisters of the Academy (SOTA) Institute (www.sistersoftheacademy.org). Dr. Green's personal philosophy is "Visualize opportunities, not obstacles."

LeKita V. Scott, Ph.D., is a native of Pine Bluff, Arkansas. She received her bachelor of science in elementary education from the University of Arkansas at Pine Bluff in December 1992. She received her master of education in educational psychology in December 1994 from Texas A&M University at College Station. Her Ph.D. is in educational leadership from Florida State University in Tallahassee, Florida. She currently serves as the science academic coordinator for the Florida–Georgia Louis Stokes Alliance for Minority Participation scholarship program at Florida A&M University. Dr. Scott's personal philosophy is "Work like you're not getting paid; love like you've never been hurt before; dance like nobody's watching."